DHARMA PATHS

DHARMA PATHS

by Ven. Khenpo Karthar Rinpoche

Translated by Ngödup Burkhar and Chöjor Radha
Edited by Laura M. Roth

Snow Lion Publications
Ithaca, New York USA

Snow Lion Publications
P.O. Box 6483
Ithaca, New York 14851
USA

Copyright © 1992 Karma Kagyu Institute (% Karma Triyana
Dharmachakra)

Printed in USA

Frontispiece: Photographer unknown. Photo provided by
Karma Triyana Dharmachakra.

ISBN 1-55939-002-6

Library of Congress Cataloging-in-Publication Data:

Khenpo Karthar Rinpoche, 1924–
    Dharma paths / by Khenpo Karthar Rinpoche ; translated by Ngödup
Burkhar and Chöjor Radha ; edited by Laura M. Roth.
    p.   cm.
    ISBN 1-55939-002-6
    1. Spiritual life—Buddhism. 2. Spiritual life—kar-ma-pa (Sect)
I. Roth, Laura M., 1930–   . II. Title.
BQ7805.K47   1992
294.3'923—dc20   92-28542
                                                              CIP

Contents

ACKNOWLEDGMENTS   7

PREFACE   9

1   INTRODUCTION TO BUDDHISM   15
    The Buddhist Path
    Tibetan Buddhism and the Modern World
    Acquiring a Tranquil Mind

2   THE FIRST TEACHING OF THE BUDDHA   33
    The Life of the Buddha
    The Four Noble Truths

3   REFUGE AND LAY PRECEPTS   53
    Refuge
    Lay Precepts

4   TAMING THE MIND   79
    The Meditation Technique
    Obstacles to Practice
    Results of Practice

5   ENTERING THE PATH
       OF THE BODHISATTVAS   109
         Generating Bodhicitta
         Sending and Receiving
         Benefits of Training in Bodhicitta
         Dedication of Merit

6   THE SIX PERFECTIONS   141
         The Perfection of Generosity
         The Perfection of Discipline
         The Perfection of Patience
         The Perfection of Enthusiastic Effort
         The Perfection of Meditation
         The Perfection of Wisdom

7   STAGES OF THE PATH   207
         The Five Paths
         The Path of Accumulation
         The Path of Unification
         The Path of Seeing
         The Path of Meditation
         The Path of No-Learning

8   THE THREE VEHICLES   237
         Hinayana
         Mahayana
         Vajrayana

NOTES   271

GLOSSARY   275

Acknowledgments

This first presentation in book form of teachings by the Venerable Khenpo Karthar Rinpoche has depended on and benefited from the help of many people. Obviously the book would not have been possible without Ngödup Burkhar and Chöjor Radha, who directly translated the oral teachings. I undertook this project at the request of Willard Roth, the director of Karma Kagyu Institute, which is sponsoring the work. Willard, who is my husband, has given me immeasurable encouragement and shown unending patience. Tenzin Chönyi, the president of Karma Triyana Dharmachakra, helped with the selection of topics to include, in accordance with Rinpoche's wishes. In transcribing the oral teachings I would like to acknowledge the great help of Jeanne Mathewson, and also thank Andrea Roth, John Fudjack, Dirk Hoekstra, and Joanna Kirkpatrick for their participation.

I am indebted to Malinda McCaine, David McCarthy, and Trinley Wangmo for their extensive assistance in editing the manuscript. Jack Labanauskas also helped with editing, Nancy Namdag helped to clarify many crucial points, and John Fudjack read over the final manuscript. I would like to thank KTD Dharma Goods for providing line drawings by Sange Wangchug. I must especially express my appreciation to Michael

Erlewine for designing the cover and providing extensive help with editing, as well as for his constant enthusiasm, support, and criticism, which have been invaluable in bringing this work to completion.

With the help of these people and numerous others, I have tried to convey the meaning of Rinpoche's teachings as accurately as possible, but if any parts are unclear or incorrect, I take full responsibility. Of course, it is nearly impossible for a mere student to articulate the complete sense of his profound teachings. In spite of this, I hope the reader will gain some knowledge and appreciation of Rinpoche's exposition of the Dharma through this book.

Laura M. Roth

Preface

At the present time, when we are aware of so much confusion and suffering in the world, the teachings of the Buddha, the compassionate enlightened one, seem increasingly relevant. The Buddha taught a way to overcome suffering and develop our inherent potential for complete happiness and mental awakening. Westerners are hearing more about Buddhism now, as teachers from various traditions come to our country and establish centers. One such teacher is the Venerable Khenpo Karthar Rinpoche, the gentle, compassionate abbot of a Tibetan Buddhist monastery located on a mountain above Woodstock, New York. Rinpoche's kindness and wisdom have attracted many students to Karma Triyana Dharmachakra and to a number of affiliate centers throughout the country, where he has been teaching seminars on the Dharma since 1976.

The present book of Khenpo Karthar Rinpoche's teachings is designed to be an introduction to Buddhism in the Kagyu tradition of Tibetan Buddhism. The theme of the book is the three paths or "vehicles" within the teachings: hinayana, mahayana, and vajrayana.* This reflects the fact that the Buddha taught people in different ways according to their abil-

---

*For an explanation of Buddhist terms, see the glossary.

ities and interests. In fact the title of the book is a somewhat free rendering of Rinpoche's Tibetan title, which means literally "opening our eyes to the three vehicles." The unique quality of Tibetan Buddhism is that the three paths or levels of the teachings are integrated and seen as a progression.

The hinayana or small vehicle is concerned with noticing the unsatisfactory, suffering aspect of our personal experience, and turning away from the attitudes and actions that bring about this suffering. This path involves becoming more disciplined and less attached to the ego, and also developing tranquility through meditation practice.

The mahayana or great vehicle is concerned with noticing that all other sentient beings are suffering, not only ourselves. This path involves generating unlimited loving-kindness and compassion toward all these suffering beings, and developing the wisdom to see the emptiness and interdependence of all phenomena. The aim at this level is not only to free ourselves from suffering but to liberate all beings from suffering and establish them in complete enlightenment. Actually, developing compassion toward others develops our own qualities and thus leads to our own awakening.

The third vehicle, vajrayana, is concerned with learning profound methods, passed down through a lineage of accomplished masters, for quickly attaining the goal of the path. In Tibetan Buddhism this path is the most important expression of the teachings of the Buddha. It is interesting that the main center where Rinpoche teaches, Karma Triyana Dharmachakra (KTD), has a name that reflects the three Dharma paths. *Triyana* means "three vehicles" in Sanskrit, and *Karma* refers to the Karma Kagyu tradition of Tibetan Buddhism, the lineage of the Karmapas. *Dharma* refers to the teachings of the Buddha, while *chakra* means "center." The affiliate centers are called Karma Thegsum Chöling (KTC), which has the same meaning in Tibetan.

The order of the chapters in the book reflects the concept of the three vehicles. After giving an introduction to the ideas of Buddhism, Rinpoche presents a teaching on the four noble truths, the basic hinayana teaching of the Buddha. The Buddha was born as a prince twenty-five hundred years ago, but renounced the life of luxury, came to enlightenment through meditation and other practices of the path, and then taught the Dharma. The first noble truth is the fact that humans and many other beings undergo suffering. Second, the cause of suffering is not something external, but our own negative emotional patterns, which lead us to experience suffering through the law of karma. Third, if these negative patterns can be overcome, there will be no more suffering, only happiness. The fourth noble truth is the path that leads to the end of suffering. Actually, most of the teachings are about the various methods and levels of the path.

In the next two chapters Rinpoche describes the basic hinayana practices. Going for refuge in the three jewels is the first formal step on the Buddhist path. The three jewels are the Buddha, the Dharma, and the Sangha, or the teacher and example, the teachings, and the spiritual community. We turn to these sources of refuge for the inspiration and guidance needed for the journey. Next Rinpoche describes the lay precepts, the rules of behavior that we can adopt. The moral precepts, such as refraining from killing, are not imposed from the outside but are taken on as a discipline. In "Taming the Mind" Rinpoche gives a description of the practice of shamata or calm abiding meditation, with practical instructions. This practice is beneficial for anyone, Buddhist or not, and is aimed at developing a calm, stable, and tranquil mind. Rinpoche explains how to sit, what to do with the mind, how to deal with the problems and obstacles that may come up, and what signs of progress we can expect.

In the next chapter Rinpoche takes up the basic mahayana idea of bodhicitta, the attitude of generating loving-kindness and compassion toward all beings, and the aspiration to attain enlightenment for their benefit. One who develops these qualities is a bodhisattva. He describes the way of the bodhisattva further in the succeeding chapter on the six perfections, which are practical ways to develop attitudes and actions that benefit ourselves and others. The first is generosity, which is easiest to practice. Then comes discipline, and next patience, which is the heart of the bodhisattva practice: tolerating the abuse others give us, and not taking revenge but having compassion for those who harm us. Under enthusiastic effort Rinpoche gently admonishes us to get up in the morning and not procrastinate. Under meditation he explains the difference between ordinary and spiritual approaches to meditation. Finally the perfection of wisdom concerns the teachings on the important philosophical concept of emptiness.

In "Stages of the Path" Rinpoche gives a comprehensive view of the Buddhist journey to enlightenment. This is described in terms of the "five paths," the paths of accumulation, unification, seeing, meditation, and no-learning. The journey begins with the basic philosophical understanding of egolessness, and continues up to the lofty heights of buddhahood. In the final chapter on the three vehicles, Rinpoche summarizes the views and practices of the hinayana and mahayana, and then goes on to give a brief introduction to the vajrayana, which involves the higher teachings of the Tibetan schools of Buddhism. The methods of the vajrayana are all firmly based on the hinayana and mahayana, but have a special quality that is very inspiring.

The above outline, however, fails to convey the complete character of Rinpoche's teaching and the integration of the three vehicles in Tibetan Buddhism. The problem with identifying certain chapters with hinayana is that Rinpoche really never teaches strictly on the hinayana level. The "hinayana" topics are taken up with mainly a mahayana view, and Rinpoche always emphasizes the need to develop the qualities of loving-kindness, compassion, and altruism. Thus he encourages us to take refuge with the mahayana attitude of wishing to attain enlightenment to benefit all beings. We should take the lay vows with the attitude that disciplining ourselves will enable us better to help others. We should combine meditation practice with acquiring merit through practicing compassion and generosity, in order to develop greater insight.

If we add to this Rinpoche's admonition that the vajrayana

practices are only effective when done with the mahayana attitude, we see that bodhicitta, the compassionate attitude, is the hinge-pin of the entire teaching. As Rinpoche says, "The practice of the Dharma is the practice of bodhicitta." In sum, the integration of the three vehicles is practicing the hinayana disciplines with the altruistic attitude of the bodhisattva, and into that incorporating the profound methods of the vajrayana.

This bodhisattva attitude of kindness and compassion perhaps best characterizes Khenpo Karthar Rinpoche himself, and it is reflected in his exchanges with students as well as in his presentation of the Dharma. He presents the teachings with humor as well as scholarly depth, making the Tibetan Buddhist tradition accessible to everyone.

Khenpo Karthar Rinpoche was born in 1922 in Kham, the eastern part of Tibet, and entered Trangu Monastery at the age of twelve. After many years of training, including long retreats, pilgrimages, and philosophical studies, Rinpoche became an accomplished teacher of the Dharma. When the communists took over Tibet in 1959, Rinpoche escaped to India, where he provided spiritual leadership at the refugee camp at Buxa, and later taught at Rumtek Monastery in Sikkim, which is the main seat of His Holiness the Gyalwa Karmapa, the spiritual leader of the Kagyu lineage. Rinpoche also served as abbot at Tashi Chöling Monastery in Bhutan and then at Tilokpur Nunnery in northern India.

In 1976, His Holiness Karmapa sent Rinpoche to the United States, where he began teaching the Dharma in New York City and Woodstock. Soon a number of affiliate centers became established, over twenty-five in the United States. Rinpoche has also travelled to Taiwan and Venezuela to teach the Dharma, and in recent years he has had the opportunity to return to Tibet to teach at Trangu Monastery, which is beginning to be rebuilt after its destruction by the Chinese armies. Khenpo Karthar's main residence is Karma Triyana Dharmachakra in Woodstock. The presence of this wise and gentle teacher is an auspicious sign that the tradition has survived intact.

Laura M. Roth

Shakyamuni Buddha

1 Introduction to Buddhism

THE BUDDHIST PATH

Buddhism is relatively new to the West and is just beginning to become established in this country. Yet it has a long and ancient history, going back twenty-five hundred years to its beginnings in India. When we encounter the tradition of Buddhism, it is natural to be curious about its fundamental nature and the role it plays in people's lives. To begin with, the founder of Buddhism was Shakyamuni Buddha, the fully awakened, fully enlightened one. The teachings of the Buddha are referred to as the Dharma or the path, and those who follow this particular path are known as the Sangha, or the community of practitioners. The Tibetan word for the teachings of the Buddha is *chö*, which means literally "that which straightens" or "that which cures." The teachings have the quality of straightening out that which is crooked or incorrect, or of curing a kind of sickness we have.

All of us, no matter who we are, share a deep longing to experience happiness, well-being, peace, and harmony, and to experience these continuously. All of us want to eliminate whatever stands in the way of experiencing happiness and peace. Yet only a few people are able to fulfill such aspirations and longings. When we ask what the nature of Buddhism is, and what positive contribution the Dharma can make to our lives, the answer is that Buddhism is a collection of various methods or skillful means. If we understand these methods, apply them, and integrate them into our lives, they can lead us to discover our inherent ability to experience complete happiness and to develop the basic potential of our minds. Those who have the opportunity to encounter as well as to learn and apply these methods will experience the benefit of developing their potential. This is not because these people are in any way unique or special, but because auspicious circumstances have enabled them to encounter and apply the methods.

In Tibetan the term for Buddha is *Sangye. Sang* means free from confusion and negative emotions, and *gye* means fully developed, having fully developed transcendental knowledge and wisdom. *Gye* also means fully ripened: the potential to experience ultimate wisdom has fully ripened. Initially Shakyamuni Buddha was an ordinary person like us. He had the potential to attain a completely sane and awakened state of mind, yet he had habitual neurotic patterns that needed to be removed. However, the Buddha saw the possibility of developing his potential to experience an awakened state of mind and to free himself from habitual patterns. He put this vision and understanding into practice, and he actually gained freedom from confusion and ripened his potential to experience an awakened state of mind. When he experienced complete freedom and ripening through the skillful means of the path, he realized that all people have the same potential, and he began to teach the path by which he attained this state of mind. Thus the Buddhist teachings are based on the Buddha's own experience and insight.

A person who attains the perfect awakened state of mind also develops immeasurable loving-kindness and compassion toward others. This means having a great concern for the well-being and happiness of all beings without exception, and a complete dedication to eliminating their suffering and confusion. Because of this limitless loving-kindness and compassion, an enlightened being such as the Buddha has no hesitation about sharing with others the methods to achieve perfect enlightenment, which are based on first-hand experience. He or she openly reveals to others whatever is necessary, because the means of attaining such an awakened state of mind is not to be hidden or kept secret. In this way the path has been taught and explained with untiring, unceasing commitment and dedication for many centuries.

Such compassion arises from the experience of enlightenment, because an enlightened person sees the confusion and the neuroses that ordinary beings are involved in and becomes aware that they need help. For example, suppose that in a community of blind people there is one person who can see. The blind people have certain purposes and wishes in life, but their blindness may lead to mistakes and confusion. Their sincere desires and wishes may not be fulfilled by their actions, and they may endanger themselves by walking toward cliffs or into fires. If there is a person who can see and who can help them, how could this person resist helping?

The Buddhist teachings are directed toward taming and training the mind. Taming the mind means bringing about mental stability and tranquility through the practice of meditation. After the proper foundation of a stable and tranquil mind is established, the mind is trained to develop greater insight and to begin to remove habitual emotional patterns. This quality of the teachings is often referred to as pacifying and cooling. The chaos and intensity of habitual patterns are gradually pacified through the practice of the teachings. The more such patterns of confusion and restlessness are pacified, the more a state of clarity and joy comes about. It is like a cool breeze coming to soothe someone who is tormented by the heat.

Again using the analogy of the blind people, if these were people whose sight was only temporarily impaired, then giving them a treatment to restore their sight would cause much of their burden to be lifted. They would experience peace, happiness, and ease, because they would not be so vulnerable to dangers and they would have a better sense of direction. In the same way, although all beings have the potential to experience an awakened state of mind, because they are blinded by their confusion, they have not realized this state. Instead they remain trapped in confusion and suffering. The Buddha presented the methods of the Dharma, the true and supreme path, to show beings a sane way of life.

TIBETAN BUDDHISM AND THE MODERN WORLD

Hearing specifically about Tibetan Buddhism, we may think this is a unique religion created by the Tibetans. While the form of Buddhism taught and practiced in Tibet is called Tibetan Buddhism, it is not correct to think of it as something Tibetan. The history of Buddhism goes back many years before it came to Tibet. The teachings that Shakyamuni Buddha introduced twenty-five hundred years ago, based on his personal experience and insight, have been practiced and taught in Tibet for centuries. They now come to the West.

We might question whether such an ancient tradition can be valid in the present Western world. We have gone through many changes, even within the past few decades. How could a philosophy or way of life introduced at such a remote time be practical and valid today? Also, when Buddhism was founded, it was based on the needs of a particular group of people within a particular cultural setting. Since culture and customs differ so much from one country to another, how can something that was relevant to that culture be equally relevant to the society and culture of the West?

Buddhism is valid at the present time because the Buddhist teachings are based on examining our ultimate nature, our inherent potentials, and our habitual patterns. The teachings address such fundamental realities as who we are and what is the nature of our emotions. Whatever their cultural setting, beliefs, or customs, people in the past had negative emotional patterns and, at the same time, certain inherent potentials. It is the same for people living in the modern world. We have emotional upheavals of all kinds, much the same as those experienced by people in the past. We also have the same inherent potentials; therefore the teachings are equally valid for us. As an analogy, the nature of water was fluid in the past, and it continues to be fluid in this modern world. Water quenched people's thirst in the past and serves the same purpose now. It is not as if water burned things in the past, while fire made things wet, whereas now water makes things wet and fire burns.

The teachings of Buddhism concerning a wholesome and sane way of life have continued to exist in an unbroken line since the time of the Buddha. Through the hard work of many people, Buddhism was brought into Tibet, and though there were great differences in the cultures of India and Tibet, Buddhism came to have a very important place in the lives of the Tibetan people. From a material and technological point of view, Tibet was far behind the rest of the world. This was not because the Tibetan people were lacking in ability but because they were isolated and hence not exposed to the world of technological advancement. On the other hand, the Tibetan people did have the opportunity to assimilate fully the teachings of the Buddha. In that small country there came to be hundreds and thousands of enlightened people, people who experienced basic sanity and awakening of the mind.

In the outside world, where such opportunities were not so readily available, people began to have the idea that Tibet was almost not a part of this world, but was somewhere off by itself, completely mysterious. They thought the inhabitants were almost not real human beings, and that happenings in Tibet were very mystical and magical. Such speculations are understandable, because when we are ignorant about something, it is human nature to see it as mysterious and alien. The Dharma relates to the most fundamental things in our lives, but until we understand its nature and purpose, we may think of it as quite foreign.

There is something very significant about the terrible hardships the Tibetan people went through a quarter of a century ago, when many were forced to flee their country. These events took place at a time when Buddhism was blossoming fully in

Tibet. There was widespread knowledge of the words and meaning, as well as the experience, of the teachings. Accomplished masters from an unbroken line since the time of the Buddha could be found among any group of Tibetan people. Therefore, extremely learned and realized masters came out of Tibet, and these masters can now share the living teachings with the whole world. Since this transmission has taken place, many people have begun to develop their inherent qualities of goodness and wholeness. While it was a tragic experience for a great many people, it was in some sense good news for the world that these things happened in Tibet when they did. If Buddhism had completely degenerated in Tibet before this happened, nothing worthwhile could have been brought to the rest of the world. By analogy, if a huge fire is destroyed while it is blazing fiercely, wherever the sparks fly from that destruction, new fires are started.

People from all walks of life can benefit from the study and practice of Buddhism, whether they are rich or poor, no matter what their sex, race or culture. There are no exceptions whatsoever. Just as water quenches the thirst of all people equally, so the Dharma can enable all people equally to experience something genuine, rich, and wholesome about themselves. If there is a difference, it is whether or not we have the opportunity to hear and understand the teachings, because we cannot apply something of which we are ignorant.

Another difference is whether or not we are sincere and diligent. In order to accomplish anything, either worldly or spiritual, we must have a certain amount of commitment and perseverance. Those who are diligent and sincere will make the teachings a practical experience and will benefit from them, while those who are not diligent are unlikely to experience any benefit. The difference here is not caused by what is available but by self-imposed limitations.

Furthermore, the study and practice of Buddhism are not matters of custom. We do not have to sit in a particular way just because it is traditional or because "that is the way it has always been done." We do not have to wear special clothes or appear in a certain way simply because it is customary. Such superficial matters are of no importance. There were vast differences in customs, dress, and appearance between the people of India and Tibet, but that was irrelevant for the transmission of the truth and the meaning of the teachings into Tibet. However, we do need to make a change in our state of mind. We are so distracted and externally oriented that we fail to take even a small glimpse at ourselves. There are certain things we should recognize about ourselves and take responsibility for. We have many kinds of negative emotional patterns: aggression, pride, jealousy, attachment, frustration, fear, and restlessness. These patterns are not very pleasant. When they crowd into our lives, it is like lying on a bed of thorns and being pricked and scratched from all directions—a painful experience. We must recognize that we have such patterns and that we need to work them out. The teachings are concerned with diminishing and eventually uprooting our negative patterns, not changing our superficial appearance. The change must be within us.

The situation is far from hopeless because, in the midst of our negative patterns, we have some element of wholesomeness, richness, and resourcefulness. No matter how aggressive we may be, there is a certain element of gentleness in every one of us. There is compassion, loving-kindness, tenderness, and warmth. We all have a spark of goodness in us, a powerful potential for developing warmth, openness, tenderness, sanity, and an incomparable sense of well-being and richness that cannot be approached by material or physical wealth and comfort. The teachings are aimed toward developing such potentials within us.

Questions

Q: On the basis of your experience of Western culture, what do you think are the problems that we should be working on? Also, what particular gifts should we be receiving from Buddhism?

A: Frankly, if I am not mistaken, the biggest problems in the United States seem to be a lack of moderation and a sense of competition. To some degree these are problems everywhere, but they are especially strong here. There are many admirable things about this country. Most people are very well educated, intelligent, and efficient, and the country is very advanced materially and technologically. However, in the midst of this, there is a sense of competition and a lack of moderation. Everyone seems to want to get ahead of other people in status, material things, and any other way possible, regardless of their talents.

The contribution Buddhism can make is not any one thing in particular. Buddhist methods are simply a very wholesome way of life, which anyone can benefit from following. Whoever applies the methods, in whatever part of the world, will be able to break through the confusion and cares of the mind and experience greater tranquility and stability, which brings with it greater moderation.

Q: What is the viewpoint of soul in the Buddhist teaching, and what is the aim of the teaching?

A: The Buddhist term for "soul" might be *mind* or *consciousness*. It is the thinking mind, this knowing ability that we have as we are living right now. This knowing ability, this consciousness, is not material or substantial. It has no color or dimensions or form of any kind, yet it is always present. When we die, this consciousness or awareness leaves the body, so it may be soul in the same sense you mean.

As to the aim of Buddhism, we can say that the aim is to experience perfect joy and to develop the complete potential of the mind.

Q: Would you clarify for me what are the differences in the technique of meditation between Tibetan Buddhism and, say, Zen Buddhism, which we have heard about from Japan?

A: Since the practices of the different schools of Buddhism are all in accordance with the teachings and experiences of the

Buddha, they are all essentially the same. Both Japanese Buddhists and Tibetan Buddhists uphold the Buddha as the ultimate example and source of inspiration. Yet there are differences in the practices because of the way Buddhism has spread in the world and the way it has been preserved in different countries. For example, the three paths or vehicles of Buddhism—the hinayana, mahayana and vajrayana—are equally practiced, preserved, and emphasized in Tibet, whereas in many Buddhist countries they are only partially practiced. In addition, there are many techniques and practices in Buddhism at all levels, preliminary as well as advanced. Because particular lines of practice have been established, and the practitioners have particular needs, certain techniques are emphasized more by some schools of Buddhism than by others. Finally, there is the cultural aspect: how a gesture is made, what attire is worn, how certain objects are made and arranged, and so forth. In these areas there may be superficial differences. But essentially there is no difference.

Q: Are there women scholars and teachers in Buddhism?

A: Yes, definitely. As I have already mentioned, differences between people are not made by things like the color of their skin, their sex, or their age, but by whether they can generate a noble state of mind.

Q: If the Buddha was the first person to reach enlightenment, more or less on his own, can any individual arrive at the same point of knowledge by listening to her or his own inner voice, even someone who is not aware of Buddhism as such?

A: Actually there are two ways we can look at this. One is that the Buddha appeared as an ordinary human being but he displayed extraordinary commitment, perseverance, and decisiveness. If you read the life of the Buddha, you will see that he had a good sense of his potential. He was not caught up in the life around him but had a sound judgment about what was real. He was born into a royal family, brought up in luxury, and lavishly entertained. This was a life many people long for, yet he renounced that life. He was convinced that he had something more worthwhile to do than be a prince, so he left the palace, which took a great deal of courage. Then he went into solitary meditation for six years, which was something quite unknown among those people. After six years he had a rather good sense of his mind.

In this explanation, the Buddha was not extraordinary, but what he did was extraordinary. He did something unique, and while everyone has the opportunity and the ability to do the same, most lack the courage and commitment to grasp the opportunity. By following his example, we can reach the point of complete wakefulness even in one lifetime. Based on his experience, the Buddha made the teachings available to other people. Countless people since then have experienced an equally enlightened state of mind, or some degree of realization.

The other way to look at this is that the Buddha had studied and practiced the Dharma in former lifetimes. This leads to the subject of rebirth, which we will take up later on. The events in the Buddha's life were almost a matter of demonstrating what it is like to be enlightened and how one becomes enlightened. For example, a beautiful flower may open today, but it did not start growing just today. Some time ago the seed was sown, then the plant grew, and today the flower opened. Today it demonstrated its full potential of being a flower.

Q: Would you describe the state of consciousness of one who has achieved an awakened mind? What is that experience like and how is the world seen differently?

A: Not having achieved an awakened mind myself, I cannot tell you exactly what the experience is like. It is probably somewhat like the difference between clear water and muddy water. Looking through clear water, we can see things distinctly. There is something refreshing about it, something very bright and uplifting. Muddy water has none of these qualities.

ACQUIRING A TRANQUIL MIND

The Tibetan word for Buddhist is *nangpa,* which translates literally as "one who is inner-directed." While attention is given to the various outer fields of knowledge such as philosophy and natural science, much greater emphasis is placed on turning inward and studying the nature of the mind, to find out who we are and what is the most sound and fruitful approach to our lives.

All of us are constantly busy with many kinds of activities. When we ask ourselves why we are so busy, we find that we are trying to bring harmony, joy, and peace into our lives. We always feel the need to have a joyful, harmonious, and sane life, but more often than not we encounter ups and downs. At one moment, things seem to be pleasant and reliable. Then there is a sudden switch, and our lives become filled with discomforts and disturbances that make us feel uncertain and discouraged. No matter who we are, rich or poor, popular or unknown, we frequently go through uncertainty and dissatisfaction. In an effort to make things better for ourselves, we become even busier. To be honest, this usually results in more chaos, disturbance, and uncertainty. Something must be wrong in our approach to achieving greater harmony and well-being for ourselves.

If we look closely at the situation, we will see that each one of us has the ability and the potential to generate harmony and openness. We have neglected to tap these inner resources. Instead, we have been externally directed, and we think that by putting pieces and things together outside we can bring about joy, happiness, and harmony. However, that is clearly impossible, first, because we do not have much control over external things, and second, because external things are unreliable and constantly changing.

We try various ways to gain happiness and well-being. Sometimes we move to a different place. We think we feel troubled because there is something wrong with the place we are living in. If we move to a quieter, more remote place, perhaps things will be better for us. Sometimes we feel the trouble is caused by the people we are involved with. If we break one relationship and try another one, surely things will be better for us and work out more smoothly. But even though we try many different things, the dissatisfaction and disturbance continue. That is because true harmony and openness are qualities of the mind that we can develop, and are not dependent on external circumstances.

We have too much faith and confidence that external things will help us experience a pleasant, joyful, and sane life. For example, a person may be in excruciating pain from some illness. Instead of undergoing treatment to cure the disease, suppose the person gets a more comfortable bed and softer blankets, or changes position, lying first on the left side and then on the right. These alternatives might give some superficial relief, but they would not help much, because the proper treatment has not been given and the disease is still there. However, if the sick person undertakes the necessary course of treatment, the medicine gradually begins to cure the pain and the sickness, and the patient feels more and more comfortable and relieved.

Right now, when we work to make things better for ourselves, we do so in a very confused way. For example, if we are being burned by very intense rays of the sun on a cloudless day, our present approach is like trying to cover all the different places from which the light comes, so the rays will not reach us. If the weather is windy and cold, our response is like trying to cover all the different places from which the wind is blowing, so we will not feel cold. If the ground is rough and stony, it is like covering the ground with carpet so our feet will not be torn. Certainly these are difficult tasks that could never succeed.

However, since we are sensible people, if the sun hurts our heads, we wear a hat. If it is windy and cold, we wear warm clothes. If the rough ground hurts our feet, we wear a good pair of shoes. Removing everything in our way so we will not be hurt or feel pain is quite impossible. In the same way, if we try to bring harmony and contentment into our lives by making external things comfortable and not disturbing to us, we will never succeed. We cannot rely on outer things to run smoothly or work out well. Furthermore, no matter how wonderfully things work out externally, if our minds are irritated and disturbed, we will not experience harmony and contentment.

Buddhism emphasizes working with the mind. If we are able to clear the mind, we will experience a state of stability and tranquility. Then no matter where we are or what happens, there is a sense of harmony and balance in our lives. If we are successful and things are going wonderfully for us, we are not overly carried away by this. If we are going through external difficulties and failures, which can happen to anyone, we are not completely overwhelmed and depressed by them. A stable and tranquil state of mind is a kind of portable wealth, a portable store of richness, harmony, and openness, which is trustworthy in any place or situation.

Although you may agree that a tranquil and undisturbed state of mind is very important and helpful, you may argue that we still need food, wealth, and a comfortable place to live. Certainly it is necessary to have proper accommodations and provisions for physical well-being and comfort. Buddhism does not deny the need for basic sustenance and material things, but the idea that material things by themselves provide a sense of physical comfort and well-being is not completely true. In fact, most of the time it is far from the truth. If we do not have a stable, tranquil, and open state of mind, we do not feel comfortable physically either. There is nothing mysterious or difficult to understand about this. It is a very basic situation in our lives.

Sometimes we are very happy and contented, with a very stable mind. We all have such moments. We may be loaded with work, but we feel fine and have no resentment. It is a little surprising that after all this work we do not feel a need to complain. However, at other times we are filled with resentment and anger, and our minds are disturbed. We might be sitting in a most comfortable place, eating a delicious meal, yet the food does not taste good and we cannot enjoy our pleasant surroundings. Even when lying down in our own very comfortable bed we cannot sleep, but feel awake and restless. We might even reach the point of attempting to harm ourselves. This happens because the sense of comfort and well-being of the physical body is mainly brought about by stability and tranquility in the mind, and the sense of discomfort and disturbance in the body is mainly caused by disturbance and agitation in the mind.

To achieve a tranquil, stable and harmonious state of mind even in the midst of chaos, it is important to practice meditation. Some people think meditation is something strange and mysterious, far out of the context of their lives, which they will never be able to do or understand. However, it is not at all mysterious or strange. The basic meditation practice in Buddhism is described as dwelling in a state of harmony. Simple techniques are taught in which we focus our attention on an object, and whenever we find ourselves distracted, we simply bring the mind back to the object. As we develop concentration, the mind becomes not only calmer but clearer and less distracted. In a sense we become more intelligent when we are not distracted by outside disturbances or absorbed in mental chatter, fantasies, and so forth. When the mind is clear, we can direct our attention with precision toward our daily chores, communication with others, or whatever activities we engage in. Often when things go wrong, it is not because we do not know how to do something, but because we become distracted and make unnecessary mistakes. Of course, becoming annoyed with ourselves does not help. Through meditation practice, we become more efficient and thorough because our minds are calmer and clearer and we are more focused on what we are doing.

As an individual, as a member of a family, and as a member of the community, it is very important to have a tranquil, stable, and open state of mind. We can maintain a tranquil and open state of mind, even in the midst of external chaos and disturbance, if we do the work of taming our minds. Another person may be very disturbed and irritated, while we may be experiencing a stable and open mind. When such a disturbed person's anger is directed toward us, we will be tolerant of the situation because of our open and tranquil state of mind. We will experience patience, rather than becoming overwhelmed by anger and behaving just like the other person. When we are able to remain calm, tranquil, and composed in such a situation, it is very sane and beneficial for us. It also helps the other person, because we have not stimulated further anger and aggression.

We could say that Buddhist meditation practice is a good kind of family therapy. When we are able to maintain a tranquil and open mind, we are not so easily disturbed by the ups and downs that are bound to happen in a family. There is give and take. Some things go well; some things go wrong or do not work out the way everyone in the family would like. Even one individual who has a sense of accommodation and an open, calm, and stable mind can bring about harmony and friendship in the entire family.

When the leader of a community or a country has a very open, stable, and tranquil mind, there is a greater chance for peace and harmony in the lives of the people of the whole community or country. The past few generations have had the awesome and dreadful experience of two world wars. These two world wars did not happen because all the people in the world were angry and disturbed. The wars were provoked by a few disturbed, angry, confused people, perhaps fewer than one hundred. Unfortunately, a few very disturbed people with control over a country can produce tremendous destruction and disaster. On the other hand, a few people with tranquil, open, and sane minds can be a tremendous help in producing harmony and peace in the world. Therefore, a tranquil and open state of mind is not only a benefit to the individual but also an important contribution to the peace of the world. Simply talking about peace in the world has never resulted in peace; peace comes about by example. We must be models of peace by practicing it, and not merely speak eloquently about peace and harmony.

When we practice meditation, we are able to say and do things more precisely and intelligently. We are more calm and collected in pursuing our mundane affairs, and more sure and intelligent when we explore spiritual paths and practices. In summary, Buddhism teaches methods for attaining a saner state of being, a happier life, and ultimately an awakened state of mind. The process begins with taming the mind to develop stability and tranquility through the practice of meditation.

Questions

Q: Can the practice of meditation in the Buddhist tradition be considered a form of prayer?

A: There are prayers in Buddhism, and these are different from meditation practice. As I have mentioned, in the basic meditation practice we work with techniques that involve focusing the mind on an object, in order to develop stability and clarity in the mind and diminish our patterns of anxiety, frustration, and so forth. The mind is very fickle and restless, always slipping away, and often finding itself in very painful situations. The basic meditation practice helps tame this fickle mind.

There are different kinds of prayers in Buddhism. The most important are prayers of aspiration and prayers of supplication. Briefly, a prayer of aspiration might be wishing that certain wholesome and beneficial things will happen for the happiness and well-being of all sentient beings. There are many such prayers directed toward virtuous and altruistic aspirations. A prayer of supplication is remembering the kindness of teachers or the great examples of enlightened beings. From such prayers of supplication we derive inspiration and a sense of promise in our lives.

Q: It is very nice to say that peace comes about by example, but is it not important also to think and talk about peace?

A: Talking alone will not serve the purpose of bringing about greater peace. It is more meaningful to practice what brings about peace and harmony. You may be for peace and harmony. You may appreciate those who practice and talk about peace, encourage others to practice peace and harmony, and talk about the goodness of peace. But it makes more sense if you have also had some experience of peace and harmony within. For example, if you give a beautiful lecture on peace, some people may argue with you and resent what you say because, unfortunately, not everyone likes peace and harmony in the world or in their lives. If the peace you are talking about is only in your head, you may become upset and angry about this, but if you have some experience or taste of peace and harmony, you will be patient with those who react negatively.

Q: I have a Christian background and, through my experiences, I am convinced of my faith. I would like to enrich the way I experience my prayers, my meditation, and my lifestyle, and I feel I need more training in the mind control Buddhism offers. If I decide to take this training, would it convince me to renounce my Christian faith or would it help me enrich my faith?

A: I really cannot say what would happen because I do not know what is happening with you right now. Actually I do not know much about Christianity: what the practice is, what kind of faith is involved, and what kind of insight and experiences are linked with this faith. I can say one thing, if this is of any help. While it is important to relate to external sources of inspiration and guidance, it is also important not to rely solely on external examples. Things will not work out if you try to do that. This has nothing to do with having faith or not having faith; it is just the basic chemistry of the way things happen. Working on the internal development and growth of the mind, together with outer examples of guidance, will bring about true development of the mind. With the help of the rays of the sun and your eyes, you can see things. You cannot see with just your eyes alone if there is no light. If there is light but you do not have eyes, you also cannot see. It is like that.

Q: In the nuclear age in which we live, I wonder if the confusion and anger individuals feel are not worse than in the past. We each have more problems to cope with, because of the fear of nuclear annihilation, because of the fear that the great powers will not control nuclear weapons. Perhaps this makes it more difficult to meditate in today's world.

A: It is pointless to be preoccupied with such fears. We fear that a nuclear holocaust will take place, perhaps in the immediate future, but what can we do about it? Subjecting ourselves to fear, frustration, and anger does not make the situation any better. We think that if a nuclear holocaust or some other external catastrophe does not take place, everything will be calm and tranquil and we will live forever. However, reading and watching television show us that thousands of people in our country die in many different ways every day. We cannot even imagine the ways they have died. What guarantee do we have that we are not going to die at any moment like one of these people?

The very fact that we are born means we will die. Moreover, accidents can happen to us, no matter who we are, whether we are healthy or sick, in one place or another, doing good things or involved in unwholesome activities. Many of us will have been gone a long time before any nuclear holocaust takes place. The moment of death will come, and the prospect is quite bleak right now. What can we do to gain a better insight into what comes next? This should give you greater fear than the possibility of a nuclear holocaust.

The most sensible thing you can do is try your best to work for peace, harmony, and well-being for yourself as well as for others. You can begin by developing some degree of control over your mind. You should not get wound up in speculations about whether a nuclear holocaust is going to happen, what disasters it could bring, when it will come, and so forth. There is nothing beneficial in this for you, for the people around you, or for the world.

2 The First Teaching of the Buddha

The first teaching that Shakyamuni Buddha gave to his earliest disciples was on the four noble truths. In this basic teaching, the Buddha explained how the interdependence of cause and effect applies to the suffering of samsara and the awakened state of nirvana.

THE LIFE OF THE BUDDHA

I will first give a brief biography of the Buddha. During the time the teachings of the third Buddha[1] were declining, Shakyamuni Buddha was a bodhisattva living in the higher realms, where his name was Dampa Dugkarpo. When he saw that the teachings had completely disappeared, he descended to the earth and took birth in the human realm. In order to benefit the greatest number of sentient beings, the Buddha chose to be born into the noble family of a king.

At that time the queen dreamed that a white six-tusked elephant entered her body through the crown of her head and went into her womb. Immediately after the dream, the queen experienced a tremendous bliss and peacefulness in her mind, and she felt a very strong wish to go into retreat. The queen asked the king to send her to an isolated place where she could meditate in solitude. The king granted her request, and thus she went into a deep forest and meditated for nine months and ten days. After completing the retreat, she was walking outside in a grove of trees when she felt some pain. Taking hold of the branch of a tree, she immediately gave birth to the child Buddha from the ribs of her right side.

The Buddha took birth without any obscurations, defilements, or stains. Immediately after birth he took seven steps in each of the four directions, east, south, west, and north. As he took the seven steps, lotus flowers blossomed beneath his feet before they touched the ground. Then he raised his right hand, pointed his finger up to the sky, and said, "In this world and in this era, there is no one who is superior to me."[2] This was a sign that the Buddha had accomplished all the purifications, developed all the qualities, and accumulated all the merit and wisdom of the path. His very unusual birth, his ability to walk and talk, and the blossoming of the flowers on the ground beneath his feet were clear indications of his complete purity. However, from that day onward, he had to develop as an ordinary human being formed of flesh, bones, and blood.

At that time, when a child was born into a royal family, there was a tradition that a wise brahmin would come to foresee the future of the child. If the wise brahmin saw anything negative in the future of the girl or boy, it was the rule that the child would be thrown into the river and allowed to die. Accordingly, Shakyamuni Buddha's parents invited a very wise brahmin to foresee his future, even though they knew he showed very unusual powers at the time of his birth. When the brahmin came to the palace, he looked carefully at the infant, studying his shape and the texture of his skin. He suddenly burst into laughter; then tears came into his eyes and he wept for a while.

When the king and queen saw the wise brahmin crying, they were very frightened and thought there must be some negative thing in the child that would require him to be thrown into the river. They implored the brahmin to tell them the truth, whatever it was. He explained that when this infant was twenty-nine years old, he would either become one of the most powerful kings in the world, or he would become an enlightened being, one of the rarest teachers in all the universe. "I laughed because I saw the qualities and the wisdom of the child," the brahmin said, "and I followed that with tears because I am too old to live long enough to receive teachings from such an authentic, wise teacher. Realizing that I will never hear him teach, I felt tremendous sadness."

When the wise brahmin told the king that the infant would become either one of the most powerful rulers on earth or one of the most enlightened teachers, the father's motivation was very simple. He had no wish to benefit sentient beings. He wanted his son to follow in his footsteps and become a powerful king; therefore, he prevented the child from meeting any spiritual people. The child was always kept in the palace, guarded by the army and entertained by beautiful women. Since the Buddha's mother had died seven days after his birth, he was brought up by his aunt.

As the prince grew older, the time came for him to choose a queen. The family invited one hundred of the most beautiful princesses from every part of the country, and the prince chose one of them as his bride. In addition to having a wife, he was continually entertained with dancing and singing by five hundred beautiful women. The king wanted to ensure that the prince would never become bored and therefore would never think of going out where he might come in contact with spirituality.

Furthermore, in order to prepare for the life of a ruler, the prince was educated in various fields of learning: art, science, metaphysics, medicine, and even sports such as wrestling. He was extremely intelligent. The moment one of his teachers spoke about a topic, the prince would expound on it himself. The student's knowledge seemed to be more profound than that of his teachers.

To gain experience about the people of his country and the conditions they were living in, the prince once left the palace for four days. He rode out in a chariot with one attendant. On the first day, he went to the eastern part of the country, where he encountered women giving birth. On the second day, he went to the south, where he saw many aged people. On the third day, he went to the west, where he saw many sick people lying in the road. Finally, on the fourth day, he went to the northern part of the country, where he saw many people dying in the road. By going out of the palace for only four days, the prince learned about the conditions of human existence: birth, old age, sickness, and death.

When the Buddha saw people experiencing birth, old age, sickness, and death, he realized that as a king he would not be able to free people from such conditions of pain and suffering. Therefore, one night when everyone was asleep, he decided to leave the palace. He confided in only one person, his very loyal attendant. He asked the attendant to take him into a forest where he could meditate and practice for the rest of his life. Accordingly, they rode away from the palace, and as the dawn broke, they came to a stupa. The prince realized that people would recognize him by his royal garments, so he asked a passing beggar to exchange clothes with him. The prince gave his royal garments to the beggar and dressed himself in the beggar's worn-out clothes. In those days, kings had very long hair, so the prince also cut off his hair. After that he made the vow, "Until I become one who can liberate all beings from samsara—the condition of birth, old age, sickness, and death— and bring them to complete nirvana, I will never return to my palace."

The place where the Buddha meditated was beside the Neranjana River. Of course, religious practice was not new at that time. There was a Hindu practice in which people cultivated inner peacefulness. This corresponds to the basic level of meditation known as shamata in the Buddhist tradition. Through this practice people experienced inner peacefulness, which they thought was the highest achievement possible. The rule at that time was that a person who set out to do shamata meditation was expected to do shamata for life. The Buddha practiced in this way for six years and came to realize that shamata alone was not enough to enable him to benefit other sentient beings. Because of his past purification, it was not at all difficult for the Buddha to develop peacefulness of the mind. However, he realized that it was necessary to go on to a further level of meditation, known as vipasyana or profound insight, in order to attain the highest stage of realization and to benefit sentient beings.

After the six years of shamata meditation, the Buddha's body had become extremely weak. One day two farmer's daughters offered him some milk. The Buddha accepted the milk, and after regaining his health, he went into meditation again. This time, wishing to benefit limitless sentient beings, he practiced vipasyana meditation. As he went into the profound meditative state of vipasyana, the Buddha vowed, "From the moment I sit down until I attain complete enlightenment, I will not move my body or legs."

In the highest stage of the Buddha's meditation, hordes of evil beings tried to prevent him from attaining complete enlightenment. They created many distractions, manifesting themselves around the Buddha in different forms, both fearful and attractive. But because he was in profound samadhi, or meditative concentration, nothing could distract his mind. Neither fear nor temptation could distract the mind of the Buddha, and therefore he overcame all the outer, inner, and secret obstacles.

In this way the Buddha became what is known as a stainless being: unstained by faults, unstained by obscurations, unstained by negative karma. Immediately after the Buddha had overcome all the outer, inner, and secret obstacles, a voice came from the sky and said, "We have found the greatest teacher of all, one who will benefit limitless sentient beings in time to come." The sound of the voice was heard by all the beings living at that time. Since they knew the voice was referring to the Buddha, they requested him to reveal the teaching to them. However, the Buddha did not accept their request but went back into the meditative state for forty-nine days, knowing that at that moment his realization of profound wisdom was too complex and difficult for people to understand.

After the Buddha's forty-nine days of profound meditation, all the bodhisattvas on the higher levels of realization, knowing it was the right time for the Buddha to reveal the teaching, manifested in the form of Brahma and other divine beings and requested the Buddha to turn the wheel of Dharma. This time the Buddha accepted the request. However, he said that he must first turn the wheel of Dharma in the right place as well as at the right time. His first teaching took place at Sarnath near Varanasi in a grove called the Deer Park. The teaching he gave was the four noble truths.

It was not possible to hear the teaching of the Buddha without having a past karmic connection with him. Accordingly, when the Buddha gave the teaching on the four noble truths, in the assembly receiving the teachings were five human beings and 80,000 beings of the god realm. If we go back to the previous lives of the Buddha, we can explain the karmic connections these beings had with him. In one of his previous lives, the Buddha was born as the youngest of three princes. When he was only five years old, the three princes were in a forest playing together at hide-and-seek and other games. As they were walking in the forest, they came to a cave where they saw a wounded female tiger with five cubs. The mother tiger was very weak and was unable to provide food for the baby tigers. The Buddha's older brothers went to search for some food, and they asked the young prince to stay near the cave to take care of the mother tiger and the five cubs.

While the Buddha was taking care of the wounded mother tiger and her five cubs, he began to think that it was not proper to kill other beings and give their flesh to the tiger. He found some large thorns and pressed them into his neck, and as the blood came out, he let the cubs and their mother suck the blood. In fact, he gave his whole body to the five cubs and the mother tiger as an act of generosity. As he did this, the Buddha prayed, "Right now I am only able to give temporary help to these starving beings, just removing their hunger. May these tigers who are enjoying my flesh, blood, and bones be reborn in a higher realm, and may I be able to teach them and lead them out of cyclic existence."

The next time the Buddha took birth he was another prince, whose name was Cheu Chubö. One day, while he was walking near a lake, he saw that many fish were dying. The climate was extremely hot and no rain had fallen, so the lake was drying up and the fish were trapped. Since he was a powerful prince, he was able to provide some water carried on an elephant, but because the drought was so severe, he could not keep this up for long. Since he knew the fish would eventually die, he prayed at that time, "May these fish, who will soon experience death, be reborn in a higher realm, and may I be able to teach them and lead them to complete liberation in the future."

As a result of their karmic connection, the five cubs were reborn in the human realm and were thus able to receive the first teaching from Shakyamuni Buddha directly. The 80,000 fish that died took birth in the god realm and were able to descend to the earth to receive the teaching from Shakyamuni Buddha. This explains the karmic connections between the Buddha and his first students. When the Buddha completed his first teaching on the four noble truths, the five men who received the teaching from him attained the level of arhat, while the 80,000 gods attained the first bodhisattva level.

THE FOUR NOBLE TRUTHS

The four noble truths are the truth of suffering, the truth of origin, the truth of cessation, and the truth of the path. The Buddha explained them three times. First the Buddha explained that all beings in conditioned existence in the phenomenal world experience pain and suffering, and this is known as the truth of suffering. We must also understand where the suffering comes from, and this is known as the truth of origin. If the origin of suffering is removed, the suffering ceases, and this is the truth of cessation. Finally, in order to remove the origin of suffering and terminate the suffering, we must find a path, and this is the truth of the path, the fourth noble truth.

The second time the Buddha explained the four noble truths, he explained that we must understand suffering; we must realize what suffering is. Furthermore, we must abandon the origin of suffering. To abandon the origin of suffering, we must follow the path. And having relied on the path, we will come to experience the cessation of suffering.[3]

The third time, the Buddha simply emphasized his previous explanation more strongly. He said that once we understand the truth of suffering, there is nothing more to understand. Once we are able to abandon the origin of suffering, there is nothing more to abandon. Likewise, as long as we follow the path, there is nothing more to practice. And once we experience the cessation of suffering, there is nothing more to experience.

When the Buddha gave his original teaching on the four noble truths, he uttered only twelve sentences, explaining the four noble truths three times. By simply hearing these twelve sentences, all of the five men present attained the arhat level and all the 80,000 gods attained the first bodhisattva level. Why was their experience so different from ours? First, the teacher was different; those words were spoken by the enlightened one, Shakyamuni Buddha himself. Second, the students were different. Because of the prayers of Shakyamuni Buddha in his previous lives, a strong karmic connection had been built between teacher and students. The students were like cultivated grain that had already been growing and was ready to mature. In our time, it is rather different. The teacher is not Shakyamuni Buddha himself, and the students never know whether or not they have had any karmic connection with the teacher in the past. Moreover, we are in a period of greater obscurations and defilements in the world, and as ordinary human beings we take longer to understand. Just hearing these twelve sentences is not enough for us; we need a more detailed explanation of the four noble truths.

The Truth of Suffering

First of all, we must explain what beings experience the suffering (*duhkha* in Sanskrit) of the first noble truth. According to Buddhist philosophy, it is the beings in the six realms who experience suffering. What are the six realms? The lowest is known as the hell realm. From the moment beings take birth in the hell realm until they exhaust their negative karma, they constantly suffer from heat and cold; they experience themselves being burned and frozen. Because the pain of the heat and cold is so intense, they have no opportunity to think about the practice of Dharma.

The second realm is the hungry ghost realm, known in Sanskrit as the *preta* realm. The beings there experience extreme hunger and thirst, from the moment they take birth in the preta realm until their negative karma is exhausted. Their experience of hunger and thirst is so intense that they have no opportunity to practice virtuous actions.

The third realm is the animal realm. Animals live in whatever state they are in, so to speak. If they are experiencing happiness, they live in that state. If they are suffering, they live in that state. Therefore they are blind to spirituality and are unable to practice a path of virtuous action that could eliminate their suffering.

Fourth is our own human realm. Human beings have accumulated both positive and negative karma; therefore, as we all know, we experience ups and downs, the vicissitudes of life. Sometimes we experience happiness, and at other times we experience sorrow and pain. The particular sufferings of the human realm are birth, old age, sickness, and death. In addition, we have the pain of being separated from those we love, the disappointment of not being able to obtain what we want to have, and so forth. Thus in the human realm we undergo hardships, pain, and suffering just as do beings in the lower realms. The difference is that, because of our positive and negative karma, humans have the choice of practicing virtuous or unvirtuous actions.

The fifth realm is the realm of demigods, which is higher

than the human realm. Demigods have also accumulated both negative and positive karma and, in particular, a pattern of jealousy. They do not care to practice Dharma, but because of the strength of their jealousy, they spend their lives fighting and quarreling with each other.

The last and highest of the six realms is the god realm. Beings of the god realm have also accumulated both positive and negative karma, and their pattern of pride is extremely powerful. When beings are in the god realm, they do not experience any suffering at all. They always experience happiness, and because of that, they never think of practicing Dharma. Unfortunately, because they have accumulated a mixture of positive and negative karma, that happiness is bound to end. From their positive karma they experience happiness, but when the positive karma is exhausted, it is too late for them to practice. As a result, they immediately take birth in the lower realms and experience the results of their negative karma. The mixture of positive and negative karma is like a bow and arrow. We shoot an arrow up in the air as hard as we can. From the power of the bow, the arrow goes up a certain distance, but the moment the power of the bow ends, the arrow falls down. It cannot continue to go up. Likewise, by the power of their positive karma, beings take birth in the god realm. Unfortunately, when the power of the positive karma ends, they fall down, just like the arrow.

I have explained the particular type of suffering of the beings in each of the six realms. In addition, the beings of all six realms undergo three general types of suffering. The first is known as suffering on top of suffering, the second is the suffering of change, and the third is the suffering of conditioned existence. Suffering on top of suffering or compounded suffering is experienced by all the beings in the six realms. Sometimes they undergo both physical and mental pain and suffering, which is one suffering on top of another. Mental sadness and physical pain together make double suffering. Examples in which problems are multiplied are so common in our everyday lives that we need not go into more detail.

We can all relate to the suffering of change, the second kind of suffering. As soon as we take birth, we begin to grow and change, and sometimes there is pain in growing. Every moment, we experience changes in our friends, our relatives, our environment, ourselves. When we are experiencing tremendous joy and happiness, we should know that this is bound to be followed by disappointment, sadness, and suffering. It is said that the end of every birth is death, the end of every meeting is parting, the end of friendship is animosity, and the end of love is hate. In the animal realm, the suffering of change is related to the seasons: summer, autumn, winter, and spring. In summer, animals find plenty of food, but in winter, food is very scarce. The hunting season is especially painful for animals. These things come and go, come and go, and that is change.

In the god realm, as we have said, the beings experience happiness. But seven days before their death, the gods experience a tremendous physical change. Their strong magnificent bodies deteriorate, begin to smell, and become unbearable to those around them. Their attendants, relatives, and friends abandon them, and during the seven days, they go through tremendous pain. Because they are in a higher realm, the gods can see all the negative actions they have done in the past, and they can also foresee where they will take birth after the seven days have passed. They are quite certain to be born in a much lower realm, because it is time for them to experience their negative karma. It is very painful for them to see the suffering of beings in the lower realms, like seeing it on television, and know they will go there next. That is the suffering of change in the god realm.

Finally there is the suffering of conditioned existence. As long as we exist, as long as we have a physical body, regardless of whether we are human or animal or any other being, we are subject to pain. For example, if this room were surrounded by your enemies, ready to attack you the moment you opened the door, you would know you were bound to experience pain and suffering as soon as you went outside. The suffering of conditioned existence is that once we exist, we are conditioned to experience pain and suffering. This applies to all the beings in the six realms.

The Buddha said that we must know and understand suffering, and when we understand suffering, there is nothing more to understand.

The Cause of Suffering

The Buddha said that in order to remove suffering, we must first know the origin of suffering. The suffering of the beings of the six realms is not a punishment of the gods, as some people might think, and it is not a curse by demons. It is the result of their positive and negative karma, which they accumulate through the kleshas. No one created us in this form; we ourselves are the creators. Thus the cause of suffering is twofold: one part is karma and the other is kleshas.

What is karma? Karma is the result of our actions in previous lifetimes. When we practice positive or negative actions, we accumulate positive or negative karma. Once the karma is created, the result is infallible. We take birth according to our past positive and negative karma. Positive karma from a past life contributes to a good rebirth, a physical body that experiences little illness or suffering, and continual good fortune. Negative karma from a past life contributes to a poor physical body and sometimes even birth in the lower realms. The result of karma is an individual matter. If I accumulate negative karma, I cannot pass it on to someone else; I am the one who must experience that negative karma. The individual experiences it; it cannot be passed on to anyone else.

What are the kleshas? The kleshas are all the negative emotions or defilements that we have within ourselves in our present state: aggression, greed, ignorance, attachment, jealousy, and pride. Through the kleshas, the actions we perform in the present accumulate both positive and negative karma for the future. You may wonder what causes us to take birth in different realms—sometimes the animal realm, sometimes the human realm, and sometimes even the hungry ghost and hell realms. Strange as it might seem, we all have the seeds for taking birth in any of the six realms. These seeds are the kleshas.

First there is aggression. The negative karma we accumulate through aggression or anger or hatred can become so powerful that it causes us to take birth in the hell realm. The experience of aggression itself is like burning and freezing. We all have the seeds of aggression. If we remove our aggression, the hell realm does not exist. Thus aggression is the origin of the suffering of the hell realm, and when aggression is removed, the suffering of the hell realm does not exist.

Likewise, we all have greed. The negative karma we accumulate through miserliness, through tremendous greed, causes us to take birth in the preta or hungry ghost realm, where we continuously experience a lack of food and water. The seeds of greed exist within us right now. If greed is removed, the hungry ghost realm does not exist; the pain of experiencing birth in that realm does not exist. Next, the negative karma we accumulate through ignorance, through blindness, through not knowing what is good or bad, leads to birth in the animal realm, where we experience dullness and stupidity. In the animal realm, there is no chance to practice.

We are all familiar with attachment. Through attachment, we sometimes perform good actions and we sometimes perform bad actions. The resulting mixture of good and bad karma causes us to take birth in the human realm. We have all experienced jealousy. The mixture of positive and negative karma we accumulate through jealousy leads to birth in the demigod realm. Our pattern of jealousy continues in that higher realm. We create disharmony on all sides and spend our lives quarreling and fighting.

Finally, when we accumulate positive karma by performing virtuous actions, we may develop pride and egotism. We are mainly working to achieve things for our own benefit. That pattern of self-centeredness—wanting to accomplish things solely for ourselves, and developing pride in our achievements—leads to birth in the god realm, where we experience the suffering of change.

We can now understand the meaning of samsara, or *khorwa* in Tibetan. *Khorwa* means circling, or cyclic motion, going around the six realms. The potential to take birth in any of the six realms exists in all of us. We take higher or lower birth according to the strength of our defilements—greed, hatred, ignorance, jealousy, pride, and attachment. We continuously circle in the six realms. If we can remove the kleshas—the six poisons that are the origin of suffering—the suffering ceases. Thus being in samsara is not like being locked in a cage from which we are unable to escape. It is not like being in prison. Samsara is a matter of the mind; it is the defilements we spoke about. When the kleshas have been removed, samsara does not exist; instead there is eternal happiness and peace. When we have overcome the six poisons, no matter how much we search for suffering, we will never find it, because we have completely removed the root of suffering.

In our human realm we often experience suffering. Because we are afraid of it, we work extremely hard trying to end the suffering and prevent it from happening again. However, when we do not understand the causes of suffering, our actions only develop more attachment, jealousy, pride, and aggression, and this causes further suffering. In trying to prevent the experience of suffering, we end up experiencing more suffering.

The Buddha explained that we must understand the root of suffering, and that once the root is removed, nothing more can grow.

The Path That Leads to the Cessation of Suffering

Once we understand suffering, we may try to end the suffering by learning about its origin. However, we cannot achieve the cessation of suffering by simply learning about its origin— the suffering is still there. We must apply a method that gives us the strength and power to abandon the kleshas. That method is known as the path. We cannot take away pain and suffering the way we take off our clothes. The kleshas have been with us for a tremendously long time, and we must work extremely hard to get rid of them. The work of the path is to remove the seeds—the origin of suffering—completely.

Samsara is not an external thing; samsara is internal. The kleshas, the six poisons, are samsara. Since samsara is internal, we cannot escape from it without applying the correct method. We cannot escape from samsara by going up in an airplane or a rocket. We cannot use nuclear weapons to destroy our defilements. That would destroy us but not our defilements. The only way we can liberate ourselves from samsara is to remove the defilements. When we remove the kleshas, we reveal and develop all the positive qualities hidden beneath them: wisdom, awareness, loving-kindness, compassion. We are still in this world, and we are liberated from samsara. Samsara is not external—it is internal.

The Buddha said that following the path requires our individual effort, diligence, and devotion. He said, "I can show you the path, but whether you follow it and reach the destination depends entirely on your effort, your diligence, and your devotion. I cannot take you there; I can simply teach you the path." Actually, by knowing that we possess the six poisons—anger, greed, ignorance, attachment, jealousy, and pride—and thus knowing about the origin of suffering, we have already acquired some wisdom. Through that wisdom, we have removed some of our ignorance and blindness. We can remove aggression and anger by developing compassion. Compassion is having sympathy for someone else's pain and misfortune and, therefore, wishing others to experience happiness. This leaves no room for anger at all, because anger is the opposite wish. Darkness and light cannot exist at the same time; the light automatically removes the darkness. Likewise, if we know how to develop compassion within ourselves, we can effortlessly remove the klesha of anger.

Furthermore, if we develop loving-kindness toward others, we rejoice in their good fortune, and this removes the feeling of jealousy. Jealousy is disliking the fortune and success of others; therefore, loving-kindness and jealousy can never go together. When we know the right method for developing compassion and loving-kindness, we lessen our patterns of anger and jealousy. We also decrease the greed that keeps us from being generous. When we lessen our greed, we are less attached to our possessions and wealth; therefore, we also lessen or overcome our attachment. Not only do we decrease attachment to our possessions, wealth, and property, but we also become detached from our ego, and are thus able to overcome pride and egotism.

We can now begin to understand how to apply the correct path to overcome the six poisons.

Questions

Q: In the story about the Buddha, you mentioned the infant walking and flowers growing just where his feet touched, and also his coming out of the side of his mother. Are these things literally true, or is this just a clever way to tell the story to encourage us to practice?

A: It is really true. It is not a clever way to tell the story. It is evidence of the complete purity of the Buddha, and it truly happened.

Q: From my own experience, I have trouble believing this, or even imagining it.

A: I respect your honesty. To develop faith and confidence in such a story is very difficult, not because the story is untrue, but because we are not familiar with such possibilities. I would like to tell you a story from my own life.

A long time ago, Tibet was a very uncivilized country. Cars, airplanes, and even bicycles were unheard of. During that time, a person came to my monastery and spoke to us about airplanes, which he called flying machines. When we asked what an airplane looked like, he said it was like a house that flies up in the air, in which 100 or 500 people can sit. I thought the person was making up the story. I was fascinated but did not believe it at all. On a second occasion, a slightly wiser person talked to us about the flying house, and when we asked how it was possible, that person gave an example. He said a stone cannot fly, but if you throw the stone, the strength of your hand propels it a certain distance, depending on the force with which you throw it. That gave me some hint that it might be possible. Still, just like you, I was really unable to believe it. Then things changed. I escaped from Tibet and went to India, where airplanes are quite common, and of course, they are even more common here in the United States. Not only do I realize that the story was true, but now I fly almost every day. If someone were to tell me now that a flying house is not possible, I would laugh at that person.

Q: I too find many elements of the story of the Buddha difficult to believe literally, so I tend to give it a symbolic meaning. This applies also to the wheel of life and the six realms. But the story is very beautiful. It evokes an emotional response in me, and I wonder if it is true. This beautiful story is told by Rinpoche as true, and by many other great minds also. When I do not believe this, I wonder what I do believe and why I believe it. What is the basis of my knowledge? What is the basis of knowledge of the Buddhist world view? Is this a valid response, that it makes me question the basis of my knowledge?

A: Shakyamuni Buddha said, "Do not blindly believe what I say. Listen to what I say, examine it, analyze it very carefully, and develop belief yourself." I really do not expect everyone to believe everything I say. I do not want any of you to say, "This was told by Khenpo Karthar Rinpoche, who is a very nice person, so I believe it." Instead, I want you to listen, using your intellect and logical reasoning. Then you can develop belief and trust yourself, without needing to say so-and-so told you.

Suppose I give you an object to take home, telling you it is made of pure gold. You do not have to believe me immediately, but you can test the object to find out whether or not it is pure gold. There are many different ways of testing for gold. A traditional method is to burn the object, and if the color does not change, that is a sign it is pure gold. Another method is to rub the object against a black stone. By looking at the mark on the black stone, a skilled person can tell whether or not it is pure gold. In the modern world, you may have an even faster way. Then to see whether the object is solid gold, you cut it into pieces and look at the inside. Once you come to realize that the object is solid gold, you do not have to rely on anyone else's word for it. You know it from the depth of your heart, from your own experience. That is what we are looking for.

Q: On the subject of doubt and belief and faith, for many years I had heard and read stories of the wondrous miracles of great realized beings. I took them with a grain of salt, thinking they might be allegories or fictions for expanding the mind. However, when I went to Rumtek for the funeral of His Holiness the Sixteenth Karmapa, I saw with my own eyes several miraculous occurrences, such as rainbows appearing when the fire was lit.[4] Later I came back and related these events to people. Those who had not seen them had as much trouble believing they had occurred as I did before I saw them. Yet, because I saw these things with my own eyes, I do believe them.

A: Thank you for sharing your experience. It was very sad for us to lose one of our great teachers. On the other hand, people who were at the cremation developed certainty in the Dharma and about the stories we tell about realized people of the past.

To heighten your confidence and trust, I would like to share some more of my experiences. I had an *aku*, an uncle on my father's side,[5] who was very devoted to the Dharma. Throughout his life he dedicated himself to practice in unbroken retreat. He was a very tall man, about six feet, five inches tall, and very thin, with a red nose. He passed away at the age of sixty-seven, and after a few days he was brought to the cremation. To everyone's surprise, his great tall body had become reduced to a very small size, the length from your elbow to your hand—called a *dukang* in Tibetan. He was sitting in perfect meditative posture, and his body was so small it could be carried on a round tray. If he had been allowed to stay for a few more days, his body might have completely disappeared, which is called being transformed into the rainbow body. This is eyewitness news, not a story from centuries ago.

There was also the uncle of the Very Venerable Deshung Rinpoche. You may have heard of this master, a very advanced scholar and teacher who lived in Seattle. When his uncle, who was equally realized and devoted to the Dharma, passed away, he was in the meditative posture, and he was allowed to stay in his room for seven days. At the end of the seven days, there was no body to be found. The physical body had been transformed completely into the rainbow body. I was twenty-five years old at the time, and I was there. All I could find in the *zen* (the monk's upper robe) was the fingernails and the hair, but no flesh or bones.

It is important to tell these stories to develop your trust and confidence in the stories of past enlightened beings, which sometimes seem to be exaggerated or made up. These are two examples from my own life.

Q: Is it possible for us to be aware of the events in our previous lives that gave rise to our present situation?

A: Unless we are quite realized and advanced practitioners, it is difficult to remember the events of former lives, to know what we have and have not done. An advanced meditator would have insight into the past and the future through his or her own realization, and would not need to depend on the guidance of others. Such a practitioner could say, "This is happening because of what I did in the past. That is happening because of experiences I had in the past." Such a detailed account of our karmic accumulation is hidden from ordinary practitioners like us.

However, there are many things we know, not because we see them, but because of the results that come from them. The experiences we have in this lifetime of happiness and well-being and of pain, suffering, and confusion do not come about merely by chance. They do not just suddenly appear out of the blue. Because we performed wholesome actions and generated good intentions in former lifetimes, we experience harmony and joy in this lifetime. Because of our harmful and unwholesome actions in the past, we experience destruction and disharmony in this lifetime. That is why there is so much disparity in the world. Because everyone's karmic accumulation is not the same, not everyone goes through the same experience. Some people have an abundance of happiness and well-being, and others go through a great deal of suffering. Thus our experience in the present tells us something about what we might have done in past lives, although we cannot pin down exactly what wholesome and harmful actions we have performed in the past.

3 Refuge and Lay Precepts

The first formal step on the Buddhist path is the refuge ceremony—taking refuge in the Buddha, the Dharma, and the Sangha. The Buddha is the awakened one; the Dharma is the teachings of the awakened one; and the Sangha is the assembly of spiritual friends or teachers who have preserved the unbroken line of the Dharma. These enlightened sources of refuge are also known as the three jewels. It is important to understand the meaning of going for refuge, the shortcomings of not going for refuge, the benefits of taking refuge, and the commitments of taking the refuge vow.

A second basic aspect of Buddhist practice is taking and keeping different levels of pratimoksha, or moral precepts. It is important to understand what the precepts are, the significance of the precepts, and the benefits of the precepts, especially in terms of how they support our growth in the practice of the Dharma. If we know the benefits of the vows, it can be a joyous discipline. There is a tremendous experience of joy in being able to live in a dignified and disciplined way.

REFUGE

We have been wandering in cyclic existence from beginningless time, continually experiencing uncertainty and change.

Like the alternating of day and night or summer and winter, we have sometimes found happiness and sometimes suffering. We experience this uncertainty because of our tremendous ignorance and our accumulation of negative emotional patterns, the kleshas. Our greatest ignorance is not recognizing, on the one hand, that we have such negative emotional patterns to work out, and on the other hand, that we have the ability to overcome them. We have always intended to experience complete happiness and perfection, but our activities have not been in a direction that would fulfill that intention. People who are crazy may have the intention of keeping their clothes and bodies clean, but they tend to get into places like mud puddles where they only become dirtier. They fail to act in ways that would fulfill their intentions.

We could also call our behavior crazy. We have not been able to pursue the practice of compassion and loving-kindness, the antidote for the klesha of aggression. Instead, we have been caught up in wanting to cause harm to others. We have developed anger and hatred and have built up the intention to cause harm and conflict in others' lives, in whatever way we can, through our body, speech, and mind. The strongest aspect of our ignorance has been not knowing how to subdue our pattern of aggression and develop patience. As a result of anger, we have experienced birth in the realm of hell, where beings undergo unspeakable sufferings for millions of years.

Another aspect of ignorance is not knowing how to subdue our pattern of greed or insatiable attachment. We want to have all pleasing objects in our possession. What we have is never enough; no matter how much wealth and property we acquire, there is still a thirst for more. We develop strong expectations, constantly failing to know what reasonable limits we should follow. We develop miserliness, becoming so attached to our possessions that we are unwilling to give them to others or even use them for ourselves—we simply want to hoard them. As a result of greed, we have been born in situations of great destitution and poverty, or worse, we have been born, without any choice at all, in the realm of pretas or hungry ghosts, where the suffering of hunger and thirst is unspeakable. Because of our thick pattern of confusion, we have failed to realize that the way to experience wealth, spiritual as well as mundane, is to apply the antidote for greed, which is generosity. Practicing the two aspects of giving—making offerings to the three jewels and giving to those in need—causes us to accumulate inexhaustible spiritual and mundane wealth.

In a similar way, we experience the upheaval of other negative emotions, such as jealousy and pride. Even when we are given guidelines for purifying and removing these negative emotions, the kleshas sometimes intrude, because we have such a strong buildup of them. Clearly we do not need to be encouraged or reminded to bring up the kleshas. We are accustomed to them; they are very spontaneous. Yet, when it comes to compassion and loving-kindness, we almost seem to believe they are not possible for us. We are so unfamiliar with loving-kindness and compassion that we cannot believe they could be a realistic experience in our lives.

When we see things in this way, we might fear there is no hope of our breaking through these patterns of experience, but that is not so. Our failure has been in not linking ourselves with the appropriate support. Having been born in samsaric existence again and again, we have all had moments when we performed virtuous actions. The virtuous actions we performed in our past lives have led us to some temporary experiences of happiness, to certain opportunities and favorable conditions. To enhance these opportunities and favorable conditions and make them meaningful continuously, we must turn to enlightened sources of refuge for support and guidance. Failing to make this connection has led to our continuous birth in cyclic existence. It is like pouring something into a pot without a bottom. No matter what fresh and good and bountiful ingredients we pour in, there is no lasting benefit, because the vessel will not retain them.

In the course of many lifetimes, we must have done some virtuous things. We find ourselves doing positive things now:

supporting our families, helping our friends and relatives, giving to worthy causes in our community. We are generous now, so we must have practiced generosity in the past. However, our attitude plays an important role, and we have not practiced generosity with the appropriate attitude. When we have given to our friends, relatives, and family, our attitude has been, "My friends and relatives are a part of me. It makes me happy to see them better off." We were giving for our own satisfaction so we would feel comfortable and not be bothered by seeing them in need. When we have given to a worthy cause, to carry out some important project in our community or country, we have given with expectations. "Since I have given this help, my name will be well known. I will become a popular figure. I will gain recognition and fame." There is some temporary benefit in giving with such attitudes, perhaps being born once where we do not lack material support, but that is about all.

To make our lives meaningful at this time, we must engage in virtuous activities under the guidance of the appropriate sources of refuge. This is like pouring ingredients into a vessel with a complete bottom: whatever small amount we put in each day is retained and accumulated. What qualities must the enlightened sources of refuge have? First, they must have completely transcended the shortcomings we experience. Second, they must have the ability and the enlightened qualities to help us. To overcome darkness, we use a torch. The torch has transcended darkness; therefore, it is able to bring light into the darkness. Darkness itself cannot bring light. The enlightened sources of refuge are the three jewels: the Buddha, the Dharma, and the Sangha. In the whole world, there is nothing other than the three jewels to which we can truly turn as enlightened sources of refuge.

People often seek security, but out of ignorance, many fail to turn to the enlightened sources of refuge. When they are not successful in their undertakings and are fearful and aware of their limitations, people feel the need to seek protection and security. Some may feel that the trees can help them, or the mountains. Others may rely on persons who are physically powerful or seem to have great vision. Some may turn to beings of the god realm, who have great power but are still within cyclic existence. In primitive societies, people turn to various ghosts and spirits, such as those of their ancestors, for refuge and security. Some even sacrifice the lives of animals to propitiate gods and spirits.

But what benefit can come about from such sources of security? A crippled person climbing a steep mountain cannot rely on a crippled guide for assistance. A blind person wandering in a wilderness cannot hope another blind person will be able to lead him or her. From that point of view, it is extremely important to connect with the enlightened sources of refuge.

What then are the stainless qualities of the three jewels, the Buddha, Dharma, and Sangha? The Buddha signifies the awakened mind, the mind that embodies all-pervading wisdom and omniscience. It is to that enlightened mind, and the possibility of attaining it, that we go for refuge. To begin with, the Buddha himself was an ordinary being exactly like us. He went for refuge to the buddhas of the past and attained the perfect state of enlightenment. The Buddha's attainment of enlightenment was a confirmation that the potential for complete perfection and awakening of the mind pervades all beings. When we go for refuge to the Buddha, we acknowledge that it is possible for us also to be completely awake. Having attained the perfect state of enlightenment, the Buddha is able to benefit sentient beings without fail. He is the example for our own experience of perfection that is without deception and can never fail. Therefore, we go to the Buddha for refuge.

This has come about through the practice of the Dharma, the teachings and methods we work with toward the experience of perfect liberation, and especially the skillful means for developing loving-kindness and compassion. For a long time in the past, the teachings have made it possible for sentient beings to experience perfect buddhahood. The Dharma can be applied universally in the lives of beings, and can be our path to the experience of liberation. Therefore, we go to the Dharma for refuge.

The Sangha is called *gendun* in Tibetan, which means literally "those who have indestructible virtuous attitudes." They have stepped out of the confusion, are now on the way toward enlightenment, and have the ability to help others along the path. The Sangha make it possible for the teachings to be continually available. These spiritual friends have attained the state where they will no longer be overwhelmed by the three poisons. At the same time, they are able to help other sentient beings overcome their confusion. Therefore, we go to the Sangha for refuge.

The Buddha is the ultimate source of refuge, and the Dharma and Sangha are temporary sources of refuge. If we say our samsaric existence is like an illness, then the experience of the awakened mind is like perfect health. The Buddha is one who experiences good health, the Dharma is the medicine, and the Sangha are kind physicians who prescribe the right medicines and courses of treatment for curing the illness. Once we have been cured of an illness and are experiencing good health, we no longer need the physician or the medicine. Likewise, once we have attained enlightenment, we no longer need to take refuge in the Dharma and Sangha, but need only the enlightened mind.

The buddhas and bodhisattvas of the past started on the path by going for refuge. They encountered favorable conditions and were able to recognize the enlightened sources of refuge. Having gone for refuge, they then practiced on the different bodhisattva stages and attained the perfect state of buddhahood. These enlightened beings have gone beyond all suffering and confusion and are able to benefit us and others. We also have met auspicious and favorable conditions. If we now make the appropriate links with the enlightened sources of refuge and have confidence in that, we can experience the same levels of attainment as the buddhas and bodhisattvas. We should feel some sense of encouragement, inspiration, and joy in our circumstances, which can give us the possibility of attaining enlightenment.

In our relationship with the enlightened sources of refuge,

there is much that has to come from us. Although different people may all go for refuge to the three jewels, the results can be different because of differences in their mental capacities, determination, and levels of exertion. Some people go for refuge with a limited purpose. They are sick or have many problems and difficulties in their lives. They want to get rid of their difficulties and diseases and have a more comfortable life. They want a very smooth, safe experience, so they go for refuge. Because of the stainless nature of the enlightened sources of refuge, such a result might be possible, but it is a very limited goal.

Others are a little more farsighted. For them, the purpose of taking refuge may be to be born in their next life as a human being who is physically attractive and who has many possessions and great wealth. Or they may wish to be reborn as some popular person, an important public figure, or a king. They may even hope to be reborn as a god. Because their purpose is limited, because they have failed to envision the possibility of enlightenment and the need to work for that, such people block their chance to experience enlightenment.

Other people are more receptive to the possibility of enlightenment, yet are somewhat selfish in their pursuit of liberation. They have a sense of renunciation, realizing that wherever they go in samsara they will be subject to suffering, so they want to be liberated altogether from samsaric existence. Yet having only the hinayana motivation, they want to be liberated for themselves alone. They want to escape from the situation as soon as possible. They have a sense of urgency, like a thief who has stolen something and immediately wants to run away and be alone so no one else will know. They certainly have a better vision than the first two groups, but it is not complete from the point of view of mahayana principles and attitudes.

If we take refuge at the mahayana level, there is something very dignified we can live up to. By generating the enlightened attitude, we can become worthy of our relationship with the three jewels. This means having a very spacious concern for the temporary and ultimate benefit of all sentient beings. Temporarily we have concern for the happiness, well-being, and harmony of all beings, and it is our aspiration that such happiness may pervade everywhere. Ultimately we wish that all beings everywhere may incorporate in their lives the wisdom of complete enlightenment—not just temporary happiness, comfort, and well-being, but total happiness and complete peace of mind. If we take refuge according to the mahayana tradition, we go for refuge not only for our own benefit, but for the benefit and liberation of all sentient beings without exception. We might not all be able to generate the complete enlightened attitude, but that should be our aim, beginning with whatever attitude we can produce at present. We should realize what stages of development are possible in our relationship with the three jewels.

Taking refuge in the three jewels and generating the enlightened attitude are important steps in our pursuit of perfect awakening. Just one moment's complete enlightened attitude can be immeasurably beneficial in cutting through the patterns of the three poisons. The most appropriate antidote for our pattern of ignorance is recognizing the Buddha, Dharma, and Sangha as enlightened sources of refuge, and linking ourselves with them. The greatest antidote for aggression, anger, and hatred is practicing loving-kindness and compassion toward all beings. Furthermore, we go for refuge with an attitude of doing this for the temporary and ultimate benefit of all beings. We wish that beings everywhere may experience comfort and well-being, and ultimately the perfect state of awakening. Developing such a concern for others is the most appropriate antidote for our sense of selfish attachment. Going for refuge with the enlightened attitude thus helps us remove our pattern of the three poisons—ignorance, hatred, and attachment. The incomparable mahayana teachings make us understand that we can integrate such an intelligence and such a spacious enlightened attitude into our lives.

According to the hinayana tradition, we take refuge from this moment onward until death—for one lifetime. According to the mahayana tradition, we take refuge for the benefit of all beings, from this moment onward until perfect enlightenment. If we take refuge just for this lifetime, we will have to repeat it again in future lifetimes, hoping that the opportunity will come about. It is possible to experience perfect liberation within one lifetime, but only with great intelligence and diligence. According to the mahayana, the commitment is from this moment until perfect liberation, no matter how many lifetimes it will take, no matter how many bodies we wear out. The continuity of the stream of consciousness allows a parallel continuity of such a commitment. It is like sowing the seed of a flower. The seed does not grow into a flower the moment we sow it, but day by day we tend and water it, then shoots begin to come, and finally it develops into a flower.

The refuge transmission must come from an unbroken lineage, in which the teachings and practices have been preserved from the time of the Buddha to this day. It is very important to receive the transmission from a teacher who is authorized by such a lineage. There are several different lineages with which we could make a connection.[6] When we receive the refuge, there is a transmission directly to the mind. If we turn on a light switch, the bulb lights because an unbroken wire runs from it to the source of electric power. An unbroken lineage is like that. If the lineage is broken, the transmission cannot be given, just as when the wire is broken, the lamp will not light.

We are very fortunate to have the opportunity to take refuge from many highly realized teachers from an unbroken lineage. Those who have the chance to be in the presence of a completely enlightened being are especially fortunate.[7] The present opportunity is one of the rarest things that can happen in our lives. It is as if the only jewel that really counts in the whole universe is in our hands. We must realize how auspicious and favorable the present circumstances are. We could not ask for anything more. We have everything we need, including the possibility of the perfect state of enlightenment. This should give us tremendous joy! If we experience joy and a sense of the richness of the conditions and opportunities, our exertion becomes spontaneous. We want to devote ourselves completely to fulfilling this opportunity. As we exert ourselves, we continuously experience results, so the joy and fulfillment give us courage to exert ourselves further in our practice.

When we formally take the refuge vows, the preceptor trims a strand or two of our hair. This signifies that the condition of having to be born in the three lower realms is henceforth cut off. If we are now able to go forward and follow the path, the relationship we are forming cuts off our link to the lower realms from this moment on. We are also given a refuge name, signifying that this is an unforgettable event, a landmark in our lives. With this name we will start a new life, and with this name we will attain enlightenment. This gives us the responsibility to develop ourselves and to experience enlightenment.

When we take refuge, we must make certain commitments. The practice of the Dharma is not just a hobby to do when we feel like it, but it is a way of life. Having taken refuge in the Buddha, we must have respect for any objects, such as images of the Buddha, that represent the enlightened state of mind, placing them in high places, and restoring them if they are damaged. Having taken refuge in the Dharma, we must try not to kill or even harm sentient beings, but to protect them in any way we can. The practice of the Dharma is directed toward the benefit of sentient beings. By working for the benefit of beings, we experience liberation and expand our ability to help others. Therefore we should constantly be mindful to increase the benefit we give to beings and lessen the harm we cause them. Finally, having taken refuge in the Sangha, we must respect all spiritual teachers, and not indulge in jealousy and competition with fellow practitioners. We must have respect for all religions, while following our own spiritual path.

There are also more specific practice commitments. In our living quarters, we should have an image of the Buddha, which can constantly inspire us and remind us how to act. To show our appreciation and gratitude, and to begin letting go of egotism, we should make offerings such as flowers and incense. We should recite the refuge prayer to the enlightened sources of refuge, which includes generating the enlightened attitude toward sentient beings, and we should do prostrations with respect and gratitude.[8] Also, when we sit down for a meal, when someone presents us a gift, or when we buy something new, we should offer the goodness and newness of this to the enlightened sources of refuge before partaking of it. Finally, we should dedicate the merit we accumulate from all these activities and attitudes to the benefit and liberation of all sentient beings, wishing that all beings may experience well-being, harmony, and ultimately perfect buddhahood.

We should also support the refuge vow by taking on various levels of discipline. Without proper discipline, we do not have a foundation for our practice or its fulfillment. If we have a precious seed, just holding onto that precious seed is not enough. For it to grow and bear fruit, the seed must be planted and tended. We can follow the lay precepts, and as we develop we can incorporate further levels of discipline as well as the bodhisattva vow and the samaya vows of the tantra. These will be explained and given at the proper time, when we are able to understand and appreciate them.

People sometimes ask why we must start at this level. We have heard of the bodhisattva and vajrayana paths. Why should we not just practice these paths from the very beginning? That is like asking why a tree cannot grow without being planted in the ground. We must plant the tree in the stable, firm ground. Refuge is the ground for all the other precepts and vows. Without refuge, we do not have the basis for other vows, no matter how advanced we might feel we are.

Questions

Q: Is it just the action of taking refuge that cuts off the possibility of being reborn in the lower realms, or does it depend on our keeping the commitments? We could take refuge and afterwards kill someone. I suppose we could be born in the lower realms if we did something like that.

A: If you take refuge and then keep the commitments and practice the Dharma, your chance of being born in the lower realms is cut off. On the other hand, if you take refuge and then indulge in killing, the fault is even more serious than it would be for a person who has not taken the vow, because you have killed and also not lived up to the vow. Your actions as well as your attitudes must be in accordance with the refuge vow you have taken.

It is important to be consistent in your practice. When you have taken the refuge vow, it is especially important to repeat the refuge prayer every day. It is necessary to purify and renew the vow because, especially for a beginner, there is no guarantee that you will not break any of the commitments. Repeating the refuge prayer renews the vow and purifies whatever violations you might have made.

Q: What can we do when we feel anger, greed, jealousy, and pride, once we have taken refuge? Do you have any suggestions for dealing with these feelings?

A: Certainly we all have these experiences. As discussed earlier, we have been building up habitual patterns for a very long time. Taking refuge does not mean your emotional patterns have ended. It does mean you should sincerely recognize your shortcomings from that moment onward, and understand that it is possible to overcome them. When we indulge in the three poisons—greed, hatred, and ignorance—the patterns and confusion intensify. This is what keeps us in cyclic existence, so it is very important to work toward purifying these patterns. Some sense of discipline and some sense of mindfulness are always necessary.

Although you do your best to live a pure and sane life, you sometimes find yourself overwhelmed by an upheaval of the kleshas. When that happens, you can correct yourself by thinking, "Yes, I have shortcomings to work out." Do not indulge in self-abuse, which is very destructive and makes the situation seem hopeless. Instead, have a sense of humility, seeing your faults but also knowing they can be corrected. You can even go beyond correcting them, so you should have a sense of self-respect. You are capable of not only removing confusion but also being perfectly sane. When you have an outburst of anger or other negative emotion, you should realize that because of these patterns you have been caught up in samsara, and understand that you must let go of them.

Mindfulness is important at all times. Suppose you are very calm and relaxed, you are experiencing peace of mind, and everything is running very smoothly. Even at such times you should be aware that the negative emotions can erupt at any time. You must be mindful and make sure you are always prepared to deal with such outbreaks. Although this may not completely prevent the upheaval of the negative emotions, at least when they come you will have the antidote ready to apply. You will always be mindful that the upheaval of such patterns is possible, and you will be aware of how to deal with them. Also, you should work to benefit beings in whatever way you can.

Q: When you are practicing like this, does a time come when you are able to be completely aware in every situation? You practice watching what emotion is arising and what antidote is needed, until finally in every situation of your life, even dreaming, you are constantly aware of what is negative and how to correct it, so you are not hurting yourself or anyone else. Is this process what is called the enlightened attitude?

A: Yes, it is possible that through the practice, while you may still find the emotional patterns arising, you are always ready with the antidote. You have patterns to work out, but the antidote is at your command. This can be true even in your dreams. When you benefit others and do not harm them, you are developing the enlightened attitude. While the process you mention may not be the complete experience of the enlightened attitude, it is part of its stage-by-stage development.

Q: Would this eventually become spontaneous to the point that habitual patterns cease to exist? Will there come a point when you are living the enlightened attitude?

A: That is quite a long way off. When we cease to have any kind of habitual patterns, that is the state of buddhahood. Having the antidotes at your command is also quite a long way off. If you have reached that point, it is very, very encouraging. Even beings who have reached the first bodhisattva level continue to have certain subtle habitual patterns. When they are in the meditative state, no negative emotions arise and they are mindful of everything that takes place. But in the post-meditation period, though they are not subject to faults, limitations, or further accumulation of negative patterns, there are signs that they still have subtle patterns to work out. For example, if they are in a large gathering, and some people start laughing, they may also unmindfully start laughing, because a pattern similar to that of the other people is aroused.

Q: You said that refuge could be understood and explained at several different levels. Would you tell us more about that?

A: There are no differences in the level of the sources of refuge. The differences are in our stages of development. As we develop, we see that there is more to explore and appreciate. For example, suppose people are out in the brilliant sun on a cloudless day. Some people, because of their deficient eyesight, may find the sun's rays only bright enough for them to make their way around, while others can see more broadly. Still others can appreciate the whole expanse of the region, through the brilliance of the sun's rays. Yet it is the same sun shining in the cloudless sky for everyone.

Traditionally, at the common level of taking refuge, we understand the Buddha as the one who attained enlightenment in Bodhgaya, and we take refuge in that person. We understand the Dharma as the teachings on the four noble truths, and the Sangha as four or more practitioners of this particular teaching. We receive the refuge transmission from four members of the Sangha. Our attitude at this level is only for self-liberation, and the duration of the refuge commitment is from the moment we take refuge until we die. There is a transmission to the physical particles of our body that causes us to receive the refuge, so when our body disintegrates, the commitment ends. This first or common level of taking refuge is much better than blindness, but not as good as full sight.

The extraordinary level of taking refuge can be understood according to the mahayana or the vajrayana. According to the mahayana, we go for refuge not only in the Buddha who incarnated on earth, but also in the more transcendent aspect of the Buddha who has experienced enlightenment from beginningless time.[9] We consider the Dharma to be not only the four noble truths but also the teachings and practices through which we realize the empty nature of all phenomena. The Sangha at this level includes the bodhisattvas from the first to the tenth levels. The duration of our commitment is from the moment we take refuge until we attain complete enlightenment, and we take refuge to benefit and liberate not only ourselves but all sentient beings. When we receive the refuge transmission at the extraordinary level, the wisdom mind of the enlightened ones is transmitted into our mind stream, causing our mind stream to progress continuously and to experience enlightenment. According to the mahayana, we regard ourselves as inferior individuals who need to go for refuge to the three jewels, who are outer sources of refuge. Therefore, this is an outer form of taking refuge.

From the vajrayana point of view, there are outer sources of refuge, but also inwardly our mind, speech, and body represent the enlightened sources of refuge. There is a meeting of the outer enlightened sources of refuge and the inner potential for awakening. A good analogy would be that there is a beautiful form outside us, and our eyes have the ability to see. The meeting of the form with our vision causes us to appreciate the beauty of that form. Or there is something good to taste, and our tongue has the ability to taste it. When these two meet, we experience the taste. Likewise, we have the ability to awaken—to recognize the enlightened aspect of our minds—and this becomes a reality because of our link with the outer enlightened sources of refuge.

LAY PRECEPTS

There are two kinds of pratimoksha vows or moral precepts: the lay precepts and the precepts of monks and nuns. I will not discuss the monk and nun precepts here but will go into the lay precepts, which are fewer in number and easier to keep. They give us the space to live in the mundane world, and they are of great benefit. For laypeople there are three cases. There are the *sojong* precepts[10], which are vows taken for one day at certain auspicious times, and the *genyenpa* and *genyenma* or *upasaka* and *upasika* precepts, for men and women respectively, which are taken for a lifetime. We receive the lay vows and promise to live up to them before a preceptor who holds the transmission in an unbroken line.

Before taking the upasaka and upasika vows, we must first take refuge. Refuge is the ground for all other forms of discipline on the path. The sequence of vows continues in a stage-by-stage manner. After refuge, we take the upasaka or upasika precepts, and we may go on to take the monk and nun precepts. For the bodhisattva vow and the samaya vows in the practice of the tantra, there is further stage-by-stage development. First we take the refuge vows, then some levels of moral precepts, then the bodhisattva vow, and finally the tantric samaya vows. Such a stage-by-stage development is important, just as in building a house. First we must have the ground, then the foundation, and after that we build the first floor, the second floor, and so forth. Once the house is built, we can make it more beautiful by painting and decorating it artistically.

The lay precepts have been used as the foundation for the vajrayana practices by the great masters Tilopa, Naropa, Marpa, and Milarepa of the Kagyu lineage, as well as Drontonpa of the Kadampa lineage and many great masters of the Nyingma, Sakya and Gelug lineages. Other teachers have used the monk precepts as the foundation for the vajrayana samaya vows. For the Nyingmas, this tradition began with Longchen Rabjam, for the Kagyus with Gampopa, and in the Gelug tradition with Tsongkapa. As bhikshus, they practiced the tantra and realized different stages of enlightenment.

The pratimoksha disciplines, the bodhisattva vows, and the samaya vows in the practice of the tantra are names for different stages, but they have essentially the same meaning. Without the ordinary precepts, we cannot master the teachings or live up to the vajrayana samaya vows or the bodhisattva vows, yet the pratimoksha alone will not lead us to the perfect state of enlightenment. We should not regard receiving the pratimoksha vows as completely different from receiving the bodhisattva vow, or the bodhisattva vow as completely different from the tantric samaya vows. They are all interrelated.

There can be a difference in the attitude with which we take these precepts, although the precepts are the same. According to the lesser or hinayana attitude, we take these precepts for our own benefit, and for this lifetime; it is a lifelong practice. However, according to the mahayana attitude, we take these precepts to benefit all beings, because with such a disciplined way of living we are better able to help others. Also we vow to live up to the precepts from this particular moment until we attain enlightenment.

There are five lay vows, four so-called root precepts, and one branch precept. The first precept is not to kill. Specifically, this means not to kill a human being. It is regarded as killing if we kill someone ourselves, if we hire another person to kill someone, or even if we rejoice in someone having been killed. Furthermore, one method of killing is not regarded as worse than another. Whether we use poisons, black magic, different kinds of weapons, or any other means to kill, it is the same.

Although there may be no danger of our killing someone else, there is a chance we may rejoice in someone else having been killed. We must be very careful about this, since it is actually breaking the vow. For example, when our nation is in conflict with another and we hear that someone from that other country has been killed, our hatred toward the other nation may cause us to think, "Oh, that's great." We might have actually wanted that killing to happen. We may also become involved in killing through attachment. For example, because we are not able to take care of a child, we may have an abortion.

The second precept is not to steal, not to take anything that is not given to us. If we are part of a family, we may not have permission from all the people in the family when we take or borrow something, but at least we have some share in it. That is not stealing. Stealing is taking something that belongs entirely to others. It does not belong to us at all, and no one has given us permission to take it. We may see an object that we know very well has not been given to us. If we have a desire for the object, get it into our possession by any means we can (but not of course with permission of the owner), and rejoice when we have it, that is completely breaking the precept. On the other hand, if we simply want something that has not been given to us, or we attempt to steal an object but do not succeed, this is not a complete breaking of the vow, although there is some degree of defilement of the vow.

In killing as well as stealing, it is our intention that makes the difference in whether or not the vow is completely broken. For example, we may be angry at someone and give that person a beating. Because of our strength and the severity of the beating, we may unintentionally cause the person's death. That is not as great a violation of the precept as killing with the intention to do so. Also, perhaps we are shooting or throwing a stone. If we miss the target and happen to hit and kill someone, that is not breaking the precept, because we had no intention to kill. In the same way, if we have a car accident and someone is killed, that is not breaking the precept.

If a person is insane, or becomes irrational through taking drugs or alcohol, and happens to kill someone or steal someone's possessions, that is also not as complete a violation of the precept as when the action is deliberate. In a similar way, it may not be our deliberate will to kill or to steal, but because of certain unfortunate conditions we may be forced to do so by authorities we are subject to. That is also not a complete violation of the precepts, though of course it is a branch violation.

The third precept is not to lie. In this case the precept refers primarily to wearing the mask of Dharma. It is going about saying we can prophesy, we have certain great realizations, we can see things other people do not see, or we can perform many kinds of miracles. We deceive people to draw their faith and attention to us, or to frighten them so they can be under our control. As before, to violate the precept these actions must be intentional. If we dream we have become a realized person or a god, and in the waking state we think we are someone special and say these things out of ignorance, that is not violating the precept. Lying in this context is having the intention to deceive people and telling them things to build up our personal power.

The fourth precept is not indulging in sexual misconduct. If we are married, this means having no sexual relations other than with our life partner. In general, the precept means not having relations with someone protected by the Dharma, someone protected by belonging to another, or someone immature or unprepared. Someone protected by the Dharma would be a person who is following the sojong or precepts for a day, or who is living up to certain precepts for several days, or a monk or nun who is following lifelong precepts. Someone belonging to another[11] would in general be a married person. In marriage, each partner has promised to be faithful to the other, so that we would be interfering with a faithful relationship. A person may be immature or unprepared because of age or because of some sickness that could be aggravated by a sexual relationship. This also refers to the use of force; for example, certain kings might use their power to force a woman to surrender to their wishes whether she is willing or not.

These are the four root precepts. The fifth precept is not taking intoxicants such as drugs or alcohol. This is the branch precept, which is like a fence for the other four. If we indulge in intoxicants and become drunk or stoned, we are in danger of breaking the other four precepts. Thus the fifth vow is intended to protect against damaging the other vows. If we take just one sip of alcohol and do not become drunk, we are unlikely to break any of the root precepts, but we have defiled the branch precept, because we made a commitment not to drink. Furthermore, taking one sip increases the tendency to take more sips, and that could be the gateway to becoming drunk and violating the other precepts.

There are five levels of taking the lay vows, because of the different capabilities of individuals. The first level is taking just one precept. Those who have many limitations and are not disciplined enough to take all of the precepts may take only one. Those who feel able to do a little better than that may take two vows. Others may take three or four or all five, according to their individual ability to live up to the disciplines.

The precepts are laid out in a very skillful way. Some people are not courageous enough from the beginning to take all the precepts. If they had to take all five from the very beginning, they might prefer not to take any of them. Or they might take all five and later violate one of them. If we want to live up to a certain level of discipline but, because of our limitations, cannot take all five precepts, we can start by taking one. If we live up to that one precept very faithfully, that will benefit our practice of the Dharma. However, there are other people who can take all five vows from the very start. If we are courageous enough and our minds are open enough to do that, we have the opportunity to take all five precepts.

Once we have taken the precepts, they are very precious to us—more precious than our lives. If we must, we would choose to give up our lives rather than the precepts. We must die somehow anyway, because the end of birth is death. We cannot continue to live forever; it is only a matter of whether our death is timely or untimely. If we have been faithful in living up to the precepts, through the blessings and the truth of the teachings, we can be certain that a better life is waiting for us in our future rebirth. If we choose to break the vows—for example, if we kill in order not to be killed—this will not prevent us from having eventually to die. Once we die, we will have to go through the karmic consequences of having killed and also of having broken the vow. Also, since we took the vow before the Buddha and the preceptor, we will have to experience the result of having deceived the Buddha. We may be born in the lowest of realms and undergo terrible suffering. That is why people hold to the precepts as more precious than their lives.

Since you might have to make such a dramatic choice, you may think it would be better not to take such vows. But that is not the case. We must take whatever number of precepts we can keep, because discipline (*tsultrim* in Tibetan) is the basis for a better birth, for realization, and for the experience of buddhahood. For example, the teachings emphasize repeatedly that it is impossible to be born as a human being without having followed a discipline in past lives. In our present situation, we have a unique opportunity to practice the teachings in a very effective way. It is very important not to waste our time and our lives.

Hundreds of people may be more popular, powerful, and wealthy than we are, but from the point of view of the Dharma, no one is more fortunate. We have a very precious opportunity to make the best of our lives by working toward the attainment of buddhahood. We have this opportunity because in former lifetimes we made the proper aspirations and followed the proper disciplines. As a result we have obtained this precious human birth and have come in contact with the teachings and spiritual friends. All the favorable conditions are available—we could not ask for more. Yet this is only for a very short period of time. Within this very short time, the best thing we can do for ourselves is commit ourselves fully and wholeheartedly to practicing the disciplines, which are an essential part of the practice of the teachings.

It is important to explain the defects of not having the precepts and of breaking them. If I only speak about the benefits, some people may become very enthusiastic and want to take these precepts that sound so wonderful and profound; yet once they have taken them on, they may realize they cannot live up to them. But when the limitations of not having the precepts and the defects of breaking them are explained, we can sincerely and thoughtfully decide which vows we can take and definitely be able to keep. We must be our own sincere witnesses as to the number of vows we take.

The practice of discipline is very profound. In terms of the effectiveness of the practice of the Dharma, there is a hundredfold difference between someone who follows some level of discipline and someone who does not. Whether visualizing a deity, practicing basic meditation, or reciting mantras, the benefit is a hundredfold greater when we have the ground of discipline. The teachings of the Buddha say that if we take dust from the footprint of a person who embodies discipline and put it on our heads, it is a blessing. Even the king of the *devas* would do that, because of the sacredness of discipline. There is a tradition, followed to this day in India, of touching the feet of a holy person or touching the doorstep before entering his or her door, and then touching our foreheads. This is not merely a cultural tradition, but is acknowledging something very profound.

This has been a short explanation of the Buddhist lay precepts, which begin the practice of discipline for students of Dharma. It is especially fortunate and auspicious for a student to have the opportunity to take the lay vows from His Holiness Karmapa, the main holder of the Kagyu lineage. His Holiness is the undeniable embodiment of the activities of all the Buddhas and is himself perfectly enlightened. It has been prophesied in the teachings of the Buddha that His Holiness Karmapa will appear in the future as the sixth Buddha, whose name is *Sengetal*, which means "the lion's roar." As in the story of Shakyamuni Buddha, if we are able to make a connection with the Karmapa in this way, even if we are not able to live up to these commitments fully or attain enlightenment in the shortest period of time, we may be reborn during the time of the sixth Buddha and become the closest of his disciples.

Questions

Q: Can we reaffirm our vows with His Holiness Karmapa after taking them from another teacher?

A: Yes. Actually there are stages. If you have taken the vows in the presence of just one monk, you can reaffirm them in the presence of four monks, which is a sangha. If you have taken them before a sangha, you can take them from a lama, and then from a higher lama. His Holiness Karmapa is the highest of lamas, so after taking them from him, it makes no sense to go back and take them from someone else. You can go up through the stages, but you cannot go down.

Q: In regard to the fourth vow (about sexual misconduct), if one is married and takes the vow and then for some reason loses one's spouse, can one remarry? I have heard one should become a monk or nun in that case.

A: You are allowed to remarry or form a new relationship in the case of separation from or death of your spouse, as long as it is with someone who is not protected by the Dharma, not protected by family relationship, and not unprepared or immature. However, you should not have casual relationships. After the death of a partner, some people do choose to renounce such relationships completely.

Q: Why is abortion against the precept? Is it also against the precept to prevent conception?

A: Once a child is conceived, it is a being. This means abortion is destroying the life of a being, and one reaps the negative karma of having taken a life. It does not matter what size the being is. Even a small seed can develop into a flower. The consciousness of the child has to go elsewhere after the abortion, and where it goes is uncertain. As for preventing conception, there is no positive or negative karma involved.

Q: I believe you said that any stopping of life is killing, but I am not clear on something like mercy killing in the case of someone who is very sick. Is not the intention different?

A: Ordinarily there is no such thing as mercy killing. Such things are done out of ignorance or what might be called "idiot compassion." Our knowledge is completely limited in this situation. We see only the temporary suffering the person might be going through. We have no understanding of the workings of karma, or what karmic conditions—possibly the most intense suffering—are waiting for this person after death. It would be different in the case of an enlightened person who is omniscient. Such a person might see that the sick person's suffering is very severe yet something better is waiting for him or her after death. Through the connection with the enlightened person, the sick person could be uplifted and helped to experience a better future life.[12]

Q: What about young men who have been drafted by the government and have to kill during a war. Is that breaking the vow?

A: Yes, it is definitely breaking the vow. It might seem that the policies of the government have forced you into that situation. But when you are face to face with the enemy, it is quite certain that wanting to kill instead of being killed will come into your mind, rather than wanting to be killed instead of killing.

Q: Before the Shah of Iran died, I would have been glad if he had been killed. I felt that the Shah was creating a world war, and if someone had killed him, I might have been glad for the benefit of the world. Would that have been breaking the vow?

A: If your vision were clear and you knew for certain that killing the Shah would prevent a war, and if you also had compassion for the Shah as well as others, because you knew he would benefit from not causing such harm, that might have been beneficial. On the other hand, if you wanted the Shah to be dead just because many problems were being created for the American people, and if those problems still came up when he was dead, there would have been no benefit.

Q: I am not completely clear about the notion of being willing to give up one's life rather than kill in self-defense. My first question is, suppose my loved ones are threatened with death, and I have no choice but either to kill the aggressor or allow these people to be killed. If I kill the aggressor to save my loved ones, is that breaking the precept? Or is it as serious a breaking of the precept as other killing? My second question is, suppose I was a French patriot and my country was being overrun by Nazis who were exterminating my people, and their intention was to conquer the entire world. If I took up guns and dynamite to drive them out, would this be as serious a breaking of the precept as going out and fighting over oil fields?

A: There are many things we could say about this from the point of view of bodhisattvas and the enlightened attitude, but we do not have time to go into that here. Basically, in your question about the family situation, you are killing someone to protect someone else's life. That is killing. If you have no precepts, you must go through the consequences of having killed. If you have the precepts, you have broken the precept in addition to having killed. It is like killing a fish and feeding it to a dog to try to keep the dog alive. If you are chasing the Nazis, and you want to kill them so they will not conquer the whole world, it is still killing. If you take the precept and then kill them, that is killing and breaking the precept.

Q: It is killing, but is it as severe as killing out of passion?

A: If you were not passionate, the desire to kill would not arise in you.

The Great Yogi Milarepa

4 Taming the Mind

I will now describe the basic shamata or tranquility meditation practice (called *shinay* in Tibetan), giving instructions for the practice and discussing obstacles that may arise as well as the benefits and results of shamata practice. I will also discuss briefly how shamata practice relates to vipasyana or insight meditation (called *lhak tong* in Tibetan), as well as other more advanced practices on the path. This is an important topic for beginners as well as a good review for those who have been meditating for quite some time.[13]

THE MEDITATION TECHNIQUE

Until we have developed a tranquil and stable state of mind, wherever we go and in whatever way we try to make external things comfortable and peaceful for ourselves, it is not possible to experience true harmony and openness of the mind. We must tame the mind to develop tranquility, calmness, and gentleness, and toward that end the practice of meditation is essential. Without meditation practice, the benefits of tranquility and openness of mind will not come about. Shakyamuni Buddha said in the sutras, "The essence of the Dharma is taming the mind." He said further, "In a quiet, solitary place, on a comfortable meditation mat and cushion, you should sit in the proper meditation posture, your back erect, maintaining the correct position of the body, and engage in the practice of samadhi." I will elaborate on this statement of the Buddha.

First, solitude and quietness in the outer sense means that the place where you meditate must be appropriate. Whether it is in a monastery, a meditation center, your living quarters, or out in the wilderness, it should be a quiet place where you are not subject to many distractions and disturbances. It should also be a place where you can meditate comfortably, without having to worry about being disturbed. A particular place may be very quiet and solitary, but you may not feel comfortable meditating there. You may worry that someone will tell you to leave or that some disturbance will happen. If you are meditating in the wilderness, you may fear that wild animals or strange creatures are nearby. If you have such anxieties, it is not an appropriate place for meditation. Outer quietness and solitude means a place where you can meditate at ease for as long as you wish.

Then there is inner quietness or solitude. When we talk about meditating, it means the mind is focused on the technique of the meditation, and there is a commitment to staying with the technique. You may have a quiet place for meditation, where you can practice as long as you want to, and you may be sitting in some meditation posture, but if your mind is constantly subject to many kinds of distractions, you are not meditating. You are just sitting there. Sometimes your mind is carried away by recalling many kinds of pleasant and unpleasant events of the past—disappointments about things that have happened and expectations that what happened before might happen again. You become completely involved in the past, which has no practical bearing on the circumstances of your present life, let alone on your meditation practice.

At other times, you are carried away by and absorbed in many kinds of future schemes and fantasies. You entertain your mind with some future plan, expanding it more and more, speculating about whether it will work or not work, and what more you could add to it at a later point. If you examine these events of the future, you will often find them quite ridiculous. They have no bearing on what you might really be able to do in the future, let alone on the present time. You become completely absorbed in such distractions and very externally oriented. From the point of view of meditation, your sitting there has had no beneficial effect in your life. You are totally carried away by your mental activity and chatter, stimulated by your emotional patterns.

Inner quietness means removing yourself from these distractions, making a commitment within yourself not to become distracted by events of the past or possibilities for the future. Inner quietness means being able to maintain your awareness and focus your attention on the technique of the meditation.

Having achieved the appropriate outer and inner conditions of quietness, you should sit on a proper comfortable meditation mat and cushion. The meditation mat should be in a level place, so that your body does not tilt to one side or the other, which would be uncomfortable. On the mat, place a meditation cushion three to four fingers' width deep. Sitting on a cushion helps you maintain a better position of the body, such as a straight back. This is important, especially for beginners.

The Seven Positions

Correct meditation posture is described in terms of seven positions of the body. Traditionally, the first position of the body is sitting in the full lotus or vajra posture, in which each foot is placed on the opposite thigh. If this is not immediately possible, you should sit in what is called the sattva posture, with one leg in front of the other and the knees resting on the mat. Or you may simply sit tailor fashion. The vajra posture is called the position of indestructibility, since it creates an element of groundedness and stability.

It is important to keep the body erect and the back straight while maintaining the position of the legs. To help with this, bring the tip of the thumb of each hand to the first joint of the ring finger, fold the fingers inward to make a very gentle, soft fist, place the hands palms down on the knees, and straighten the arms. Putting the hands on the knees with the arms straight keeps you from tilting too far backward, forward, or sideways. It supports the back, keeping you from slouching and helping you maintain a pillar-like straightness of the back. This is the second position of the body.

For the third position of the body, lift each side in turn, tuck the buttocks together, close and tighten the anal sphincter, pull your abdomen and your abdominal organs up with some effort, and then gently relax. This should be done at the beginning of a session of meditation. Outwardly and inwardly closing the organs helps to retain the heat of the body as well as the comfort or sense of well-being the body can generate. Because of the interdependence of mind and body, this contributes to the tranquility of the mind.

After sitting in this way, you may still be slouching, with the lower part of your back somewhat curved out. In the fourth position of the body, you correct this by pulling up and straightening the lower back a little more. You should have the sense of being suspended by a string. This is what the Buddha meant in the sutra when he said the back should be erect. With these four positions, you are able to maintain the proper posture of the body up to your neck.

Your neck and head are part of your body, so their proper position is equally important. For the fifth position of the body, bring the gaze of both of your eyes toward the tip of your nose and, keeping the angle the same, bring the gaze down to a point on the floor about an elbow's length in front of you. Bringing the gaze of both eyes toward the tip of your nose helps keep you from tilting your head to the left or right. Bringing the gaze down to a point an elbow's length in front of you helps keep you from tilting your head too far backward or forward. All this aligns the neck fairly well with the back vertebrae.

For the sixth position of the body, let your tongue rest flatly and somewhat tightly against your upper palate. This keeps you from having to swallow your saliva frequently, and also helps to prevent or lessen coughing. Avoiding such distractions contributes to the tranquility of the mind, and that is the outward benefit of this position.

After you have taken up all these positions, you may still be craning your neck out a little bit, even though you are not tilting your head. The seventh and last position of the body helps you maintain the proper position of the neck and head. Pull the chin back a little, as if you are beginning to rest the chin on the voice box or beginning to make a double chin. When you pull the chin back in this way, you will feel the neck vertebrae coming into alignment with the spinal vertebrae. At this point, you should be in the complete meditation posture.

It is important to use these seven positions to develop mindfulness and tranquility and to meditate correctly. There is no particular sequence to the positions. If you are a beginner, it is advisable to check yourself to make sure all the positions are correct. Later on, you will not even have to check, but as soon as you sit, you will take up the positions properly. There will also be some ease and openness about your posture, which is very important. Maintaining the proper erect position of the back refers strictly to keeping the bone structure straight, and you should not work so hard at it that you find yourself becoming very stiff or tensing your muscles. If you are stiff and tense, it will be quite difficult and uncomfortable to meditate. Even while sitting erect and maintaining an upright posture, you can feel very relaxed and physically loose instead of stiff. This is also why you should make a very relaxed, gentle fist and not let your hands be clenched.

The Buddhist sutras refer to these seven positions of the body as the seven dharmas of Vairochana. The word *dharmas* relates to the activity of taking up the positions, and the term for Vairochana in Tibetan is *Nam nang*, which means having a clear view of things, a clear insight. Things appear to us the way they are, not as an illusion of what they are. We have insight into what things really are; we are not deluded about what things are. The seven positions are referred to in this way because they contribute to our seeing the true nature of the mind. For many centuries these positions have been the wealth and unique heritage of the Kagyu lineage. For the many great masters, yogis, and mahasiddhas who have been produced in the Kagyu lineage, these positions of the body have been an important instrument for developing true insight and realization.

Furthermore, it is said in the teachings that keeping the back straight and maintaining the proper positions of the body make the breathing regular, which tends to stabilize the mind and keep it from wandering. When we are breathing gently and our breath is following a very normal and steady pace, the mind conforms to that, and the correct positions of the body are very important for giving the breath such a steady and normal pace. It is like shooting an arrow at a target. It is not enough to have a good aim; you must also have a very straight arrow. If the arrow is not straight, no matter how well you aim it, you are unlikely to hit the target.

Relation of the Positions to the Wind Energies

Having explained the outer importance and benefit of the positions of the body, I will now introduce some aspects of the inner benefit of these positions. Why do we need to sit in these positions? Is this a tradition or some cultural thing? Is the purpose to make us look different from other people? What are the internal benefits, if any, of these positions?

The physical body is basically a combination of elements. When we suffer physical pain and sickness, it is caused by an imbalance in the elements of the body. When we talk about the elements in the present context, we are not referring so much to the flesh, blood, fluids, and so forth as to the so-called five wind energies. We say "wind" because there is motion, and "energy" because there is some activity or power that has beneficial or harmful effects. There are four peripheral or branch wind energies and one central or life wind energy. When we are able to retain these four wind energies and bring them closer to the central wind energy, we experience good health and a sense of comfort and well-being in our lives, both physically and mentally. If the four peripheral wind energies can be directed into the life wind energy, we begin to have great meditative realizations. When these wind energies are not properly balanced and retained, we are susceptible to many kinds of sickness and many kinds of distractions and conflicts. This results in chaos and confusion.

The seven positions of the body are important because they help retain the wind energies. Simply assuming these positions correctly, without focusing the mind on any particular object of concentration, brings about an air of tranquility, an air of harmony and openness. Three of the positions of the body contribute to retaining the so-called all-pervasive wind energy. These are: bringing the gaze of the eyes down in front of us, sitting in the vajra posture or the sattva posture, and putting the hands over the knees. This wind energy pervades the whole body and corresponds to the water element. For example, the ability of the body to produce heat and the functioning of the circulation are due to the all-pervasive wind energy.

The position of closing and tightening the anal sphincter and pulling our abdominal organs upward contributes to retaining the so-called downward-moving wind energy. Retaining this wind energy contributes to the taming of the mind and to developing tranquility and openness. The downward-moving wind energy corresponds to the earth element. Its activity is, for example, responsible for causing us to have bowel movements.

The position of correcting the slouching of the lower part of the back and raising the back to a straighter position contributes to retaining and properly balancing the so-called wind energy of metabolism. Retaining this wind energy contributes to the tranquility of the mind as well as to physical health and well-being. The wind energy of metabolism corresponds to the element fire, and its activity affects, for example, the digestion of food.

Finally, the two positions of placing the tongue against the palate and pulling the chin back to align the neck contribute to retaining the so-called upward-moving wind energy. This wind energy corresponds to the element air, and retaining it also contributes to the tranquility of the mind.

These are the four branch wind energies. When they are properly retained and directed, it is possible to have physical health and well-being as well as mental harmony, tranquility, and openness. The development of different stages of meditative advancement and realization is related to the central wind energy. The more we are able to retain the four branch wind energies and direct them into the central wind energy, the greater is the tranquility of the mind and the greater is our realization and insight. The central wind energy corresponds to the element space. The present instructions are for shamata or calm-abiding meditation. This is basic sitting practice for developing tranquility and openness of the mind, without which true insight is not possible. When is true insight attained? The experience of vipasyana or panoramic awareness takes place when the four peripheral wind energies enter the life wind energy.

In the life stories of great yogis and meditators, it is often said that the older a certain meditator became, the more youthful she or he looked. When we hear such things, they do not make much sense in our ordinary way of understanding things, but they describe how people have worked with the wind energies and what state they have achieved in this way. As far as time is concerned, they are getting older, but because they are retaining and balancing the wind energies, their appearance is more youthful, more glowing, and more healthy.

When a great meditation master or yogi passes away, for three or four days afterwards, he or she remains in the meditation posture. This is quite well known among Tibetan Buddhists, especially in the Kagyu lineage. The person's regular respiration has stopped, there is no movement of the body and no pulse, so the person is dead. Yet the body is still in the meditation posture, and even after three or four days, it does not smell or start to decay. The person looks more alive and glowing than ever. Being around the body would not make us feel uncomfortable, because it does not have the look of a corpse. Because the yogi practiced meditation based on the seven positions, he or she has been able to direct the peripheral wind energies into the life wind energy. Normally, when people die the glow or lively aspect of the body disappears, and the body becomes pale and sunken and begins to smell. This happens because the wind energies become dispersed and the system is out of control.

The positions of the body are thus very important for meditating properly and attaining true realization. For the great masters of the Kagyu lineage, the positions have proved to be indispensable for their effective advancement in meditation. Because these positions have played an important part in the lives of many meditators, we put great emphasis on them.

The above brief explanation of the meditation positions and their benefit and importance is mainly according to the sutras and somewhat according to the tantras or the vajrayana practice. However, much of the explanation of the wind energies and how they operate is according to the Tibetan medical system. The practice of Tibetan medicine is unique in that diseases are diagnosed primarily on the basis of the working of the wind energies and the condition of the elements of the body, and not so much on the physical aspects of the body. Also, descriptions of diseases are given in terms of imbalances in the wind energies.

Treatments given by Tibetan physicians do not cure a person immediately, because they dig down to the roots of the disease—what imbalances of the wind energies have caused the disease, and how these wind energies can be restored. Tibetan medicine takes time, but once the disease is cured, it is cured permanently, not just temporarily. When some of the medicines are given, the pain increases instead of decreasing, because the medicine stirs things up. The physicians are usually quite pleased when they see that the treatment they have given is causing a reaction from the wind energies. Seeing the effect of the treatment, in addition to examining by feeling the pulse, gives them a better understanding of which wind energies are in a state of imbalance.

Following the Breath

Having obtained the proper conditions for the effective practice of meditation, you next attend to where you should focus your mind—the meditation technique. Up to this point you have been preparing an appropriate vessel. If you want to pour something into a vessel, you must first make sure that the vessel is sound, with no cracks or holes in it, and that it is well placed, so it can hold whatever you put into it. Then you begin to pour the substance into the vessel. What do you do with your mind? First you should put yourself into the seven positions and sit with these positions for a moment. By simply sitting in this way, you should feel an air of tranquility, a very open and harmonious atmosphere. This is true unless you are feeling some discomfort in your body, which may happen when you are taking these positions for the first time. When you are familiar with the positions of the body, just sitting in the meditation posture will produce an atmosphere of openness and tranquility.

You cannot remain in this state for long, however. You are so accustomed to the activities of the mind that, stimulated by emotional patterns, you soon become distracted and begin to have various thoughts. When thoughts begin to arise, you should make no effort to discourage or encourage them. But when you notice the thoughts, take a slow and gentle breath into the nostrils and let the breath go down just below the navel. Let the mind follow the breath, let the mind be with the breath. Center yourself in this way. Do not hold your breath, but breathe out slowly, and follow your breath all the way to where you have directed your gaze on the floor in front of you.

After the first long breath, follow the normal pace of your breath. Do not try to make it faster or slower—just go with its normal pace. When you breathe out, your mind follows the breath out. When you breathe in, your mind follows the breath in. When the mind is following the breath, thoughts dissolve by themselves; they are self-liberated. It is the nature of thoughts to arise and disappear. Thoughts are not substantial; we create the substantiality and reality of thoughts. You do not have to try to suppress or reject any thoughts, or to encourage and entertain yourself with thoughts. Simply follow your breath, and the thoughts will dissolve automatically.

Following the breath in and out in this way is important and appropriate for beginners. You have two reference points, two objects of concentration: following the breath out and following the breath in. It is not advisable to begin immediately to meditate without any object of concentration. That would be difficult and ineffective. Even having only one object of concentration is difficult. It is more appropriate and effective to concentrate both on the breath going out and on the breath coming in.

When your mind becomes distracted by thoughts, you should not be discouraged by this. Do not be disappointed if they are so-called negative thoughts, and do not be inspired or encouraged if they are so-called positive and wholesome thoughts. Whatever your thoughts may be, do not entertain them. Simply come back to the breath. Come back to breathing in and out normally and following the breath.

Some of you have been meditating for some time. When following the breath in and out in this way, you may hardly be distracted by thoughts. If this is the case, you could use just one object of concentration. Focus only on the fact that you are breathing, not on breathing out and breathing in. You do not need to have a sense of going out with the breath and coming back in with the breath, but simply be aware that you are breathing. Alternatively, you may follow only the outgoing breath, which would also be just one object of concentration. Again, when your mind becomes distracted, bring it back to the breath in a very relaxed and easy manner.

Questions

Q: How long does it take before the meditation posture becomes comfortable?

A: The time it takes to become familiar with the positions depends mainly on two factors. One is the general flexibility or suppleness of your body. To tell you honestly, I have a hard time getting into any position. My body seems to have its own way. The other important factor is perseverance, being willing to go through a little discomfort or pain because the practice is worthwhile. People in the West, especially in the United States, are rather susceptible to pain, because they are accustomed to having things easy. They are reluctant to go through hardship and discomfort, even for something worthwhile. In other countries, where people often face hardships, they learn to accept difficulties even for things that do not benefit them. Such people are willing to bear some discomfort for something they know is worthwhile.

Perseverance can play an important part, especially sitting consistently. It is advisable for a beginner to sit very frequently and for short sessions. Trying to do a long session is not helpful for the practice or for the posture. Sit for a short session, take a break, and then sit for another short session. As you become more and more familiar with the practice and the positions, you can extend the time. Another way to handle pain is to work mainly with the positions of the body as explained, but once in a while to stretch yourself a little, or bring your knees up for a short moment, or change your position a little. Finally, the most common method for becoming comfortable with meditation is to use a combination of sitting and walking meditation practice. You are meditating at both times, but the walking meditation helps ease the physical discomfort. Then when you go back to sitting, there is a freshness about it. With the combination of sitting and walking, you do not break the meditation mood and environment.

I have noticed that when new students of mine practice meditation consistently for about a month, they are doing much better and their complaints are much fewer than at the beginning. When they have practiced consistently for several years, they are proficient in the positions. If you have some physical problem such as a deformity or an injury, and if sitting in this posture seems to aggravate the problem, then it is not advisable to keep working on the positions. But if you do not have such problems, and the trouble is only that your feet fall asleep, or your ankles or hips or something hurts, or the nerves seem to be pinched, then do not be concerned about it. It is simply a matter of becoming familiar with it.

Q: Some people have physical handicaps such that they are unable to assume the meditation positions, yet their minds are working. Is it possible for such people to do meditation practice?

A: The positions of the body are certainly very important. For those who have the ability, it is worthwhile to work at mastering the positions because that is the most effective way to do the meditation practice. However, a person who has some degree of handicap, yet whose mind is basically clear and sound, can definitely meditate. To the extent that he or she is not able to assume all the positions properly, there is some limitation, but it is certainly not a hopeless situation. What is most important is the mind and how well the person is able to focus her or his mind on the technique of the practice.

Because of disease or old age, some people are unable to sit upright. Most of them just try to sit however they can, and there is certainly some benefit. Some very diligent practitioners who want to devote their lives to practice find ways to sit straight. For example, they put a board against the back and tie a belt around the body to keep themselves erect. They use a "chin raiser," a cushion and stick to raise the chin up. It is arduous, but these people, knowing the importance of the positions, are willing to do this to improve their meditation practice. However, if a person cannot assume the positions at times, that does not mean he or she has to be deprived of the benefits of meditation.

Q: Do you recommend that we work on achieving the full lotus posture, or is it sufficient for us to use the sattva position?

A: That depends on how it feels for your body, and also on how dedicated you are to the practice. You should try the vajra posture, and if you can do it without much difficulty, you should use it. Otherwise, if the basic meditation practice and its benefits are what you want, sitting in the sattva position is good enough. However, if you are young and your body is flexible, and you really want to engage in the highest of practices, it would be very helpful to work on the full lotus posture from now on. For example, if you ever have an opportunity to do such practices as the six yogas of Naropa, sitting in the vajra posture is indispensable. Some practices can only be done in the vajra posture.

Q: If meditation is the way out of confusion, what hope is there for individuals who are autistic or mentally retarded? Because of their limitations, it is impossible to communicate any of this to them.

A: It is very unfortunate, but Buddhism in general and meditation practice in particular requires an intelligent mind, so that what is communicated can be understood. If there is need for clarification, people can ask for it, so they can get a sense of exactly what to do and can do it. People who are unable to communicate and understand the teachings cannot learn the practice. To help such people, you can give them consolation, companionship, friendship, and whatever else seems necessary. You can generate the wish that things may become better for them. We are very fortunate not only to have been born as human beings, but also to have our senses intact and to have come in contact with a proper spiritual path. Not taking advantage of such an opportunity could be a karmic condition that would deprive us of such precious opportunities in the future.

People who have difficulty communicating and understanding things on a mundane and material level would find it harder to communicate and understand the Dharma. The Dharma certainly is not easier than the mundane world, as many people think. Some people feel they just cannot cope with their responsibilities in life, so they try to escape by participating in spiritual life and practice. This is not a very sound idea. We should become involved in the Dharma when we realize the futility of mundane activity, even though we can do well in it, and when we see the goodness of the Dharma.

Q: In some traditions of meditation, the hands are placed palms up in the lap, with the thumbs touching. Does that do similar things to the energy as the hand position you teach?

A: Folding the hands in the lap as you describe has the same effect of maintaining control of the wind energy as placing the hands on the knees. It is known as the samadhi mudra, or the meditative gesture of the hands. If you have meditated for quite a long time and have no problem in sitting straight, then placing the hands in this way is fine. However, if you tend to slouch easily, the hand position we teach gives a very good support for maintaining a straight posture, in addition to controlling the wind energy.

Q: Do the wind energies and channels have anything to do with the nervous system?

A: The wind energies affect the proper functioning of the nervous system. Some of the wind energies help in circulating the blood. Some help in circulating the air or energy, and some the bile. There is a complex, detailed explanation about the relationship of the wind energies not only to the nervous system as a whole but also to various parts of the nervous system. This relates more to the vajrayana aspects of the Buddhist teachings, which will be explained at the proper time to those who are engaged in the advanced practices. Such practitioners will understand and benefit from hearing these teachings. Right now it is best to say that the four branch wind energies contribute to the health and well-being of the body as well as the tranquility of the mind. In regard to the life wind energy, there is nothing inside the central channel other than air or wind, and because there is activity in this wind, it is referred to as wind energy.

Q: From reading books on yoga, I have the impression that the central channel can be identified with the spinal column. Is that correct? Inside the spinal column, there are nerves.

A: The concept of the central channel in Buddhism is very different from what might be described in Hindu yoga or our modern physical view of the nervous system. The life wind energy or central channel we are talking about here is not like a material nerve. As we work on more advanced practices, and the description of that wind energy is given, it does not correspond to any part of our physical, material body. It is something we develop through meditation practice. An expert physician cannot locate the central channel with all the instruments he or she can attach to the body. When we are examining with a material object, it is difficult to find something nonmaterial. However, simply because we cannot find it materially is no logical reason to conclude that it is not there. We know about the transference of consciousness.[14] What happens in that process cannot be determined by a physician's instruments.

Q: So, it is nonmaterial?

A: Yes. If you look at the tiny seed of a flower, no matter how many pieces you break this seed into or how carefully you slice or peel it, you will never find the beautiful flower or the stem or the leaves. But even though you cannot detect the flower, the stem, and the leaves in the seed, you cannot say this seed will not produce such a flower, because it clearly will.

OBSTACLES TO PRACTICE

I have explained the positions of the body and how they contribute to a more tranquil state of mind as well as to health and well-being, and also how following the breath lessens distracting thoughts. When you practice meditation, in addition to using the correct posture and technique, it is important to have guidelines for overcoming obstacles to the practice. There are two obstacles in particular that you may encounter quite frequently, not because of the meditation practice itself, but because of other activities and circumstances you are involved in. The first obstacle is dullness or drowsiness in your meditation, and the second is restlessness or wildness. I will now explain why these two obstacles come about and how to apply the antidotes for them.

The first obstacle, drowsiness or dullness, may be encountered because you are meditating in a dark room. It may happen when the weather is hot and humid, or when it is cloudy and rainy outside, so the atmosphere is close or heavy. You might be meditating after eating a very large and rich meal or after being involved in tiring activities. When you try to meditate in any such circumstances, you may not be able to maintain the positions of the body effectively or follow the breath effectively. You try to sit in the proper upright position, but without being able to help it, you begin to droop and slouch. You have no discipline or control over your body. As to following your breath, sometimes it seems to be happening and sometimes it does not. Sometimes you are not quite sure whether anything is happening at all. There is a sense of dullness and vagueness, to the point that you feel drowsy and sleepy. No true meditation is taking place; there is just some clumsy, vague state of the mind. If you continue to sit, it will not be beneficial. Quite possibly you will fall asleep. If you encounter this obstacle, your meditation practice will not be effective unless you apply the antidote.

To apply the antidote, you should raise your body up with some effort and sit very straight. Instead of holding your head and eyes in the standard meditation position, raise your head and look up. Also, if it is a warm day, it is helpful to sit where there is a cool breeze. If there is bright light to the front and above you, that is very good, but if not, you can visualize a brilliant light. When you exhale, visualize your breath as a very brilliant flow of light going up. When you inhale, visualize the brilliant light coming in and lighting up your whole inside, like a lamp being lit.

Sit in this very straight position and follow the breath in this way for as long as necessary. As a result, you should become more and more awake and feel more and more normal. When you feel normally awake, return to the standard meditation posture, breathe normally, and simply follow the breath as was explained earlier. The technique just described should only be used as an antidote for drowsiness, not for regular meditation practice.

The second obstacle is wildness or restlessness of the mind. This may be encountered because prior to practicing meditation you were involved in some kind of disturbing activity, perhaps an argument, and you are still carrying the excitement with you. Perhaps you took part in some exhilarating sport, or had some kind of experience that caused you anxiety. Restlessness can also be caused by an emotional pattern that you are repeating, such as a feeling of anger toward someone or a feeling of resentment toward some person or object. If this happens, although you sit in the correct posture, you may not be not able to follow the breath. You are distracted, you feel agitated and keyed up, and there is no tranquility or stability.

To meditate properly, there must be tranquility, stability, openness, and a degree of clarity in the mind. Feeling too drowsy and dull is not appropriate for meditation practice, nor is feeling too agitated and restless. There should be a combination of alertness and tranquility. If you try to meditate when your mind is restless, you will have difficulty bringing your mind back to the breath. In response, you may try to put more effort into it, correcting your position and being more disciplined in following the breath. But often that makes the situation even worse, and it may cause you to develop a backache or headache. If you continue to practice without understanding what else can be done, you may become very frustrated and disturbed, which is the opposite of practicing meditation.

At such times, you should relax your body from the normal erect meditation position. Loosen up your muscles and even your bone structure. Slump and bend forward, not all at once but slowly and gradually. Do this very gently, so your body is very relaxed and at ease. You should also close your eyes gently—not immediately or tightly. Then breathe very gently. Visualize your breath coming out like a black string and going down to the invisible depths of the cracks in the earth, getting subtler and subtler and tinier and tinier like the point of a needle. As you inhale gently and slowly, visualize your breath coming inside you like a black string, and imagine you are pervaded by darkness like an empty bottle being filled with black ink. If you repeat this several times, you will become more and more settled and grounded.

As you feel more settled and grounded, raise your body up gradually—not immediately or all at once but very gently and slowly. Then begin to assume the proper positions for meditation. When you are rather well settled, begin to follow the breath in the usual way. This technique can be a valuable antidote for the obstacle of restlessness.

RESULTS OF PRACTICE

As I have mentioned several times, if you practice shamata meditation, you will experience many benefits from the practice. Developing tranquility, stability, and simplicity in your mind is helpful in your day-to-day activities, in your relationships with others, and of course in the practice of the Dharma. You may wonder what specific experiences you will encounter. Does anything happen immediately, or do the results take a long time? The results of Buddhist meditation practice are very simple and very sane. You should not expect anything colorful or dramatic to happen—this is not important. You will not immediately see colors, have visions, appear in two different places at the same time, or have many kinds of different sensations. That is not the nature of Buddhist meditation practice, which is basically very simple and straightforward.

However, you will experience beneficial results even at the very beginning of your meditation practice, which you must learn to recognize. The more you meditate, the more you will experience beneficial results. You will be able to tell for yourself what results you are experiencing, without needing to have them confirmed by anyone else.

There are several levels in the practice of shamata meditation. When you first begin to meditate, you may expect that through the practice you will become less and less distracted, and have fewer and fewer thoughts, and this will result in a clearer, calmer state of mind. However, when you try to meditate, you find you have many kinds of distractions, many kinds of thoughts. You experience quite a conflict, trying to follow the breath and having to deal with all these distractions and thoughts. You may wonder whether you are doing the meditation properly, or whether meditation is as helpful as it is supposed to be. When you were not meditating, you did not seem to have so much distraction and so many different thoughts, but now that you are trying to meditate, you are filled with thoughts and distractions. You may even think it might be better if you did not meditate.

When you find yourself facing this problem, it is important to understand what is happening. Most of the time we are distracted by many kinds of gross and subtle thoughts. Our senses project outward and come into contact with the different sense objects, and this stimulates many kinds of thoughts. We are so constantly entertained by thoughts and distractions that there is no gap where we can see how incredibly distracted we are. In meditation, we are trying to direct our thoughts into just one thought—following the breath. When we try to do this, it becomes very clear to us how distracted we are. We begin to pay closer attention to what has really been happening all along. If we find we are distracted even when we try to focus our attention, there is no need to say how distracted we are at other times.

When there is a great deal of water in an open field, we do not notice how much water there is because it is spread out over such a wide area. However, the moment this water is brought into a drainpipe, we see the quantity and power of the water. The same amount of water was present while it was in the field, but only when it comes into the drainpipe do we begin to notice how much there is.

This initial encounter is itself a beneficial experience, because you begin to recognize how distracted you are. To treat a disease properly, a physician must first make an accurate diagnosis. That is exactly what you are doing when you begin meditation—getting a correct diagnosis of the problem. Now you know what you must work on. This first step is a beneficial sign, and with this explanation you will not have mistaken ideas about it. Do not feel discouraged or disappointed. Realizing that you have to work, continue to practice. This first stage you encounter in the practice is referred to as the waterfall level of meditation. There is tremendous activity going on in the mind, like water constantly pouring down in a waterfall.

Without becoming annoyed or disappointed at the number of distractions, you should resolve to continue the meditation practice. Neither encourage the thoughts nor try to suppress them, but simply work on coming back to the breath. As you continue to do the practice, you will begin to notice a change. While thoughts are still arising and you still encounter distractions, they are not as frequent as at the beginning, and not as gross or as powerful. You are not so shaken up by the distractions but are able to come back to the breath quite easily. This is the second phase in the basic meditation practice, the second sign that the practice is going properly. This phase is said to be like a meandering river in a valley. Sometimes the valley is wide and the ground is level, so the water runs very smoothly. Sometimes there is a turn or the ground is uneven, so there is play and activity in the water. Likewise, you are sometimes able to follow the breath for some moments without any distractions. Sometimes you have distractions, but you are not overpowered by them. Again you are able to come back to a stretch of calm and tranquil mind, staying focused on the technique of following the breath.

As you continue with the meditation practice, you will notice further change taking place. In the third phase that you encounter, you are able to maintain the awareness of following the breath most of the time, but once in a while there are some distractions. At this point, there is not so much shakiness or uncertainty in your meditation practice. You begin to feel a sense of confidence and trust in yourself and in the practice. This phase is said to be like the ocean with waves. While most of the time the ocean is tranquil, once in a while a large wave arises and then gradually settles back down into the ocean. For a time the ocean takes a rest. After a while another wave arises, and again it goes back into the tranquil ocean. At this stage of meditation practice, there is still some distraction. This shows that more refinement is necessary, but you have certainly come a long way.

As you continue to practice, the basic shamata meditation finally becomes stabilized, and you experience the fourth phase of meditation practice, which is likened to a windless, waveless ocean. No matter how long you meditate, you can sit without distraction. There may still be some subtle thoughts, but they do not take you away from following the breath. The technique of following the breath is dominant at this point, so that as long as you want, you can sit continuously, without being interrupted, shaken up, or carried away by distractions. To reach this level requires consistent and diligent practice over a long period of time, going through the various stages. At this point your shamata meditation practice is very reliable. It is not subject to change, not better today and worse tomorrow. Whenever you sit, you can practice the technique, be at ease with it, and have good control over it.

Having reached this level, what is the benefit of all of this practice? As I said earlier, there is a great deal of benefit. Developing such an open and tranquil state of mind does not result in completely uprooting your negative emotions or completely developing your wholesome potentials. However, the meditation practice and the openness and tranquility developed in the mind certainly have the effect of subduing and diminishing the intensity of your negative emotions and bringing your wholesome potentials more to the surface. When you have developed a calm, stable, open mind, the qualities of consideration for others, compassion, gentleness, tolerance, patience, and diligence are closer to the surface. You can relate to things, live, act, and think more intelligently. Altogether you become a saner person, which is very rewarding and very beneficial. Your neurotic patterns, whatever they are, have less say in your life. Although they are not totally uprooted, they are not so dominant and overpowering as before. Faced with a situation in which you previously would have become very annoyed or frustrated, or even angry and aggressive, you are now able to tolerate and absorb it instead of creating a conflict. This comes not from trying to suppress or control your emotions, but from being more tolerant and patient.

Although it is the nature of water to be clear, if muddy water is stirred again and again, you cannot see and appreciate the clarity and beauty of the water. The water is not usable or drinkable. When the water is not stirred or disturbed, the mud and dirt settle to the bottom, and the water on the surface becomes clear. It has the good characteristics and benefits of water, and it can serve the purposes of water. Likewise, when the mind is disturbed, filled with anxiety, restlessness, and irritation, it is useful neither to you nor to others. However, when the mind becomes calm and clear and stable through shamata practice, it is very pleasant for you and for those you are with. In this way, meditation practice and the qualities you develop through it can be very beneficial in your day-to-day life and very beneficial to your further growth, enabling you to live your life in a sane and joyful way.

Clearly, there are many benefits from shamata practice, but you must understand that tranquility of the mind is not the final goal. Shamata practice and the experience of a stable, tranquil, and open mind lay the ground for the experience of vipasyana or panoramic awareness—*lhak tong* in Tibetan, which literally means "seeing beyond." There are also specific vipasyana practices that you may be introduced to once you have stabilized the basic meditation practice so that, any time you sit, your meditation is very reliable and trustworthy.[15] Continued practice with the proper guidance and techniques lead to the vipasyana experience. Through vipasyana, you can not only diminish the intensity of your negative emotions and bring wholesome potentials to the surface, but also begin to uproot your negative emotions and perfect the wholesome potentials. Then true sanity, insight, and wisdom can begin to develop.

However, to have true insight—enlightened insight—it is not enough to practice meditation. True insight cannot be attained without meditation practice, but it cannot be attained through meditation practice alone. The great bodhisattva Maitreya, the future Buddha, said in a text that true vipasyana, the enlightened state of the mind, is developed through the inseparable accumulation of wisdom and merit. On the side of wisdom is the meditation practice, and on the side of merit, or positive qualities, is developing loving-kindness and compassion toward others. We vow to generate the enlightened attitude, the mind that is inseparable from loving-kindness and compassion toward all beings. Along with that are the practices of generosity, patience, and so forth. The practice of generosity includes making offerings to worthy causes such as preserving and supporting the Dharma and making gifts to people in need of food, shelter, or guidance.

There are also more formal practices for developing merit, traditionally known as the four foundation practices. These involve going for refuge with devotion to the awakened ones for the benefit and enlightenment of all beings, going through the appropriate procedures of purification, accumulating great merit through profound ways of making offerings, and finally supplicating and receiving the blessings of the great masters of the lineage. Through the accumulation of merit and wisdom, by means of meditation practice and such practices as compassion and loving-kindness and the four foundations, we can give birth to the true enlightened state of mind.

In order for seeds to grow and produce fruit, there must be the proper ground, a soft ground that can be plowed. But this is not enough. For the seeds to grow, there must also be water, proper temperature, manure, and other conditions. With

the help of the soft, plowable ground and these other requirements, the seeds can grow and produce fruit. In the same way,
through the tranquility and openness of the mind that develops
through meditation practice (which is like the soft, plowable
ground) coupled with the accumulation of merit (which is like
the water and other requirements for growing crops), we can
develop true insight and enlightenment.

Questions

Q: If we encounter many distractions in our meditation practice, but we still continue to sit with all sorts of things coming
up, does the practice of itself correct these distractions?

A: For someone who has been meditating consistently for quite
a long time, it is very possible that persisting in the meditation practice, repeatedly coming back to the breath, will make
the distractions subside. Therefore it is important to carry on
with the meditation practice, understanding its benefits. However, in the case of a beginner, if many distractions come up,
it is somewhat difficult to continue the sitting practice. It is
very important not to become upset or disappointed about the
distractions. Whenever you notice you are distracted—it could
be after a very short moment, it could be after some time—
simply come back to the breath. Bring your mind back to the
breath repeatedly, not feeling upset about it, not feeling frustrated or disappointed, and not feeling alarmed as if something
absolutely terrible had happened.

   If coming back to the breath seems to be quite difficult, there
is something else you can do. Just as at the beginning of a
meditation session, do not do anything with the thoughts, but
simply take a deep, slow breath into your nostrils, and follow
that breath down just below your navel. This is very effective
as an antidote for distraction. It is like making a fresh start.
Since you have not continued to entertain yourself with them,
the distractions subside. Following the breath in this different way brings your mind back to the breath, and then you
can return to following the normal pace of the breath.

Q: When I focus my thought in some direction, another thought crops up, and I cannot seem to see where it came from. Is that my thought?

A: Yes, when a thought arises from your mind, it is certainly your thought. The thought may be stimulated by your senses. Your senses come into contact with different sense objects, and this contact is kept up by the consciousness. In this way, thoughts arise repeatedly—subtle thoughts, gross thoughts, sometimes a chain of thoughts. Sometimes they seem just to come out of the blue. These thoughts that arise may involve something happening right now or something you have speculated about in the past. This explains the importance of meditation. Through meditation practice, you develop simplicity, precision, and efficiency. You develop the ability to direct your mind wherever necessary and to continue to direct it without being interrupted by thoughts. These are the basic benefits of meditation practice. The interruption of your practice by thoughts and distractions demonstrates the need as well as the importance of meditation.

Q: When your senses send a message to the brain that they have perceived something, is that not a thought? Especially with regard to vision and hearing, is not every impression a thought? Do you ignore what you see and what you hear? Do you see it without seeing it?

A: The contact of one of our senses with an object is not a thought. The consciousness sometimes goes after the contact, and then thoughts are produced, but the contact by itself is not thought. When your eyes see things or your ears hear things, this does not necessarily produce thoughts. Suppose your attention or consciousness is focused on a particular thought, and at that time you hear a sound. Though the sense of hearing is operating and you hear the sound, that sound does not stimulate any thoughts. The sound and the sense of hearing have come into contact, but you have not responded. The consciousness can only be in one place at a time, and this changes from moment to moment. It might seem to you that the consciousness is involved with many things at the same time, but it is not the same time. It happens at different moments. If the sound is very loud or clear, you may think, "Ah! There is a sound," and then you begin to think, "That is a beautiful sound!" Now you have responded to the contact, and your discrimination about it begins—it is loud or soft, it is good or bad. That is thought. However, just hearing or seeing does not necessarily produce thoughts.

Q: Can you be conscious of the breath and at the same time be aware that your legs are hurting?

A: Two thoughts cannot take place together, so you cannot focus on both your breath and the pain in your legs at the same time. However, the change happens very fast from the breath to the pain and back again, so the two thoughts appear to happen simultaneously.

Q: When following the breath as you described, if I tend to focus on just one aspect at a time, like first noticing the sound of the breath, then noticing how the breath feels, and sometimes visualizing the breath going down, is that being distracted?

A: Yes, there is some distraction here because the focal point should be the sense of the breath going out and coming in. As the breath goes out, you have a sense of it going out. As it comes in, you have a sense of it coming in. It is a distraction to have sometimes a form of the breath going out and coming in and sometimes a sound of the breath going out and coming in. You are beginning to entertain yourself with something more colorful than just the sense of the breath going out and coming in, which is simple. It may not be entertaining but it is very effective. In the sutra, the Buddha said, "When your mind is distracted by thoughts, know your breath; know your outgoing breath and know your incoming breath." This means you are aware of the fact that you are breathing out and breathing in—nothing more, nothing less.

Q: When you are doing shamata and you are distracted, and then you recognize that and return to the breath, is that the same thing as cutting off thoughts?

A: It is more like transferring the attention from the distraction to mindfulness. It is not repressing thoughts.

Q: How loose or how tight should our awareness of the breath be? Should we follow every single breath? Or should we sometimes be loose and space out a little bit and then come back to the breath when we remember it?

A: There should be some openness about the way you follow the breath, an open awareness. You are barely aware of breathing out and in. It is not vivid and specific. You should make sure you are noticing the breath and are not distracted. It is as if you are holding an egg. If you hold it too tightly, you will crush it. If you hold it too loosely, you will drop it. In either case it will break, which is not what you want. You have to hold it in a balanced way, with a sense of moderation. In the same way, you should not try too hard at the practice. It is more like allowing it to happen than forcing it. Just follow the breath in and out in quite an open way, not being worried about when you will get distracted or how long it will be before you notice you are distracted. Simply be casual and at ease. When you are distracted, notice it and do not get too upset about it, but gently bring your mind back. As in the example of holding the egg, you should not be too casual about it, as if you were not interested at all, but neither should you be waiting for distractions to happen.

Q: When I breathe in, I find that if I visualize the air passing through a point in the back of my head and falling down, it has a pretty relaxing effect.

A: If you examine whether the air really goes there, you will probably come to the conclusion that it does not, so this is your imagination. Sometimes people become involved in speculations, ideas, and entertainment. This does not really help you become relaxed; it helps you become distracted. Since we are more familiar with distraction, that seems more relaxing than nondistraction at this point. It is a familiar home ground. For example, people who are addicted to very bad habits talk about how good they feel when they indulge in them. Someone who is not involved in such bad habits may try to indulge in the same things and feel miserable. So this is entertaining you—not relaxing you—because you are familiar with this distraction.

According to the instructions, you use the breath as an object of concentration, and initially you concentrate on the breath going down below your navel. Actually the breath does not go down below your navel; it just fills up your lungs. When you inhale, the diaphragm pushes the organs down, giving a sense of expansion or inflation below the navel, but your breath does not really go all the way down below your navel. Concentrating in this way has proved over a long time to be beneficial for centering and turning inward.

Q: Is there any positive or negative effect in doing hatha yoga or trying to do some of the Tibetan Buddhist exercises we read about in books, like breathing techniques, moving a little white dot up and down the spine, or realizing warmth while we are doing meditation?

A: Hatha yoga is more according to the Hindu tradition, and I cannot say what good or harm it would do for you. However, practicing hatha yoga as a physical exercise may help with the meditation positions.

As for the different practices you may read about in books on Tibetan Buddhism, it is generally not at all advisable to try to do a practice from a book, because there are many ways to go wrong. The most common thing is that you make your own interpretation of what is being said, rather than understanding what it really means. Furthermore, most practices must be preceded by certain preliminaries and followed by certain conclusions that should be done to complete the practice. You might try to jump into the middle of the practice, which is like trying to sit in mid-air—not very effective. The practices you mention, especially moving little dots up and down, are actually very advanced. If you try to do them now, at best nothing will happen. Later on you may have the opportunity to receive the transmission and complete instruction regarding such a practice. At that time it will not be as effective as it should be, because you have played with it, in a sense. So I strongly advise you not to try to learn practices out of books.

Buddhism is well known for having vast and profound methods, with different levels of practice for different types of individuals. The very advanced methods are also very delicate. To practice them, you must have the proper instruction and authorization from an experienced teacher, who can tell you what kind of experiences you will have, what preliminaries you should go through, what you should do after the practice, and so forth. If you try these practices without the proper instruction, they could be harmful, not because their nature is harmful but because you will not know how to handle them. If you wish to shoot a bullet at a target, you should put the bullet in a gun and then shoot. If instead of putting the bullet in a gun, you hold the bullet in your hand and hit it with a hammer, hoping it will go toward the target, other things might happen. You have the idea that the bullet has something to do with shooting and hitting a target, but you do not know how to handle it.

5 Entering the Path of the Bodhisattvas

GENERATING BODHICITTA

To enter the path of the bodhisattvas, we must generate the enlightened attitude, or bodhicitta. With this most profound and important attitude, seeing that beings all around us are caught up in many kinds of confusion, suffering, and difficulty, we have the spacious and courageous aspiration to work for the benefit of all these beings. Temporarily, we long to help eliminate the pain, problems, obscurations, and sickness beings are going through and give them happiness and well-being. Ultimately, we long to help all beings transcend cyclic existence entirely. This means not only helping beings to be born in the human realm or the realm of gods, but helping all beings attain all-pervading wisdom and enlightenment. This is our purpose in receiving and practicing the Buddhist teachings.

The effect of generating the enlightened attitude is eternal, because it implants the seed that enables us actually to work for the benefit of others, and it ultimately causes us to experience perfect enlightenment. If we can generate bodhicitta, we are awakened to travel the path of the mahayana. We are blessed to be practitioners of the greater vehicle.

We should remind ourselves to turn our minds toward the

Dharma at all times. At the present time, we have obtained a precious human birth and have found favorable conditions for the practice of the Dharma. This opportunity is extremely rare because, unfortunately, very, very few beings can obtain a birth in the human realm. In the future, there is no guarantee that we will be born where we have such favorable conditions to practice the Dharma. Yet when we think about it, the ways in which we could lose this opportunity are innumerable, and there is no certainty as to when the end will come. Therefore, we must be diligent and prompt to take advantage of this opportunity. We must make a sincere commitment to ourselves that, before this precious opportunity disappears, we will make sure we are fully devoted to learning and practicing the Dharma. Without such a sincere commitment, our practice of the Dharma will lack effectiveness and consistency.

Such a complete sense of commitment and discipline is very important, and it is a personal responsibility. Since we have many kinds of neurotic patterns, if our commitment and devotion are weak and our understanding of the Dharma is not clear, a sudden upheaval of our kleshas will separate us from the practice of the Dharma. We should realize that the practice of the Dharma is the only effective means we can apply for both our temporary and ultimate benefit. And the most effective way to practice the Dharma is to travel the path of the bodhisattvas and generate the enlightened attitude for the benefit and enlightenment of all sentient beings. The practice of bodhicitta is the only way to transform our kleshas and uproot our gross and subtle neurotic patterns. We are very fortunate to have the opportunity, the motivation, and the ability to do this, and we must take advantage of it fully. Otherwise, even though the blessings of the buddhas are continuously present everywhere, there is no certainty that we will find ourselves connected to them and able to receive their blessings. Even though the sun shines brightly and all-pervadingly at all times, if we become blind, we cannot enjoy the brightness of the sun's rays.

Ordinary sentient beings and enlightened beings equally possess the buddha nature, the all-pervading seed of enlightenment. The buddhas were originally ordinary beings like us. How is it then that the buddhas experienced the perfect state of enlightenment, while we have remained ordinary sentient beings? The difference is that the buddhas practiced bodhicitta. Through practicing bodhicitta, through completely dedicating themselves toward the benefit and enlightenment of beings, the buddhas experienced the perfect state of enlightenment. On the other hand, we have always engaged in selfish pursuits, seeking to fulfill our selfish desires. As a result, we have been caught up in samsaric patterns. Now that we have the opportunity, we must realize that it is necessary for us to remove and transform these patterns.

Ordinary sentient beings are like those who have not yet entered school, have not studied anything, and have not developed any qualities. The bodhisattvas who have generated bodhicitta and are on the different paths and stages are like those who have completed different classes, and the buddhas are like those with a full doctorate—the highest degree. The potential is the same; it is just a question of how much study they have done.

In the continuous line of the Buddha's teachings, from the first sermon on the four noble truths to the teachings on the practice of the tantra, there was a parallel continuity of emphasis on generating bodhicitta. Because of differences in the mental capacities of beings, there were different levels at which they were taught to generate and develop the quality of bodhicitta. Those who needed to give rise to and practice bodhicitta were given teachings on that. Those who had given rise to bodhicitta but needed to develop it were given practices accordingly. Those who were developing bodhicitta but needed to experience awakening were helped toward fulfillment. But always, on all levels, the teachings included the practice of bodhicitta, because when the Buddha was an ordinary sentient being, that was his approach to the path. That was the way he experienced enlightenment and was able to work toward the benefit of beings, and that was his way to help beings travel on the same path and experience the same realization.

For thousands of years, from the time the Buddha attained the perfect state of enlightenment to this day, he has been working untiringly for the benefit and enlightenment of countless beings. He has helped countless beings travel the path of omniscience, the path of all-pervading compassion. In all future times, he will also work for the benefit and enlightenment of countless beings. We are able to receive and understand this teaching through the boundless compassion of the Buddha. Only through bodhicitta will we also transcend samsaric existence and give birth to buddhahood. By generating the enlightened attitude, we can experience perfect enlightenment and work for the benefit of beings constantly and untiringly, like all the buddhas.

According to the compassionate teaching of the Buddha, there is no discrimination as to who can practice bodhicitta. Anyone whose mind is able to generate such an attitude—whether male or female, no matter what race, background, or age—can do this practice. If everyone practiced bodhicitta for the benefit and enlightenment of all beings, could there not be peace, harmony, friendship, and openness? If everyone generated bodhicitta, this would give rise to an enlightened society. If everyone practiced bodhicitta, there would never be war, conflict, misunderstandings, or hatred.

When we generate bodhicitta, our names and our purpose in life become transformed. Up to this point, we are called the ordinary neurotic sentient beings we truly are. After generating the enlightened attitude, however, we can proudly proclaim ourselves as bodhisattvas, because anyone who embodies such an attitude is a bodhisattva. Bodhisattvas are altogether dignified and impressive, like chakravartins.[16] Our activities are also transformed. Up to this point we have been caught up in many kinds of selfish pursuits that have caused us confusion and difficulty and have led to further intense suffering. From now onward, we are removing such patterns and developing clarity and the ability to benefit beings.

We can also say that our bodies are transformed, although

they may not immediately look larger or more glorious or have special physical attributes. Because of our attitude, because of the name we are living up to, we become worthy of respect and devotion not only from ordinary beings but from such powerful beings as Brahma and Nagaraja.[17] The change is not only temporary but ultimate, since we will continuously live up to the enlightened attitude until we experience buddhahood and acquire all the physical and mental marks of enlightenment. This is the opportunity we have.

The bodhisattvas are even respected and upheld by the buddhas. A son, no matter how handsome, famous, or popular he becomes, is always respectful to his mother. He realizes that he has such qualities only because of the kindness, guidance, care, and concern his mother has given to him. In the same way, the buddhas' experiences of enlightenment have been caused by bodhicitta, so bodhicitta is the mother of the buddhas. Therefore the buddhas respect and uphold the bodhisattvas.

It is very important to generate bodhicitta in our practices at all times. Unfortunately, we have always been caught up in selfish pursuits. We have undertaken many different activities, trying to fulfill our needs and selfish desires, thinking this was the best way to help ourselves. But this has only caused us more confusion and more suffering. The only cure is the practice of bodhicitta. The only way to remove our neurotic patterns is to practice bodhicitta, giving birth to and developing the enlightened attitude for the benefit and enlightenment of all beings. The practice of the Dharma is the practice of bodhicitta. Training our minds with such an attitude is the only purposeful way to practice if we are to benefit beings and experience enlightenment.

When we travel the vajrayana path, we may engage in various secret and advanced practices, such as the visualization of deities and the recitation of mantras. Without bodhicitta, however, no matter how advanced our practices are, they will not help us experience enlightenment. Neither will they contribute toward removing our neurotic patterns. Because of these secret and advanced techniques, we may for one lifetime or so experience beauty of form or some kind of comfort and luxury. On the other hand, we may not even have that result, because without bodhicitta, we have not transcended our neurotic patterns. A sudden upheaval of aggression could cause us to take birth in the lower realms and experience intense suffering and confusion. If an advanced practice has only helped feed our pride, it has not served its purpose; we have not used this tool in a meaningful and effective way. Therefore, it is most important to incorporate bodhicitta in our practices.

The deity practices of the vajrayana are certainly profound. We are most fortunate even to be able to hear the names of such practices. But without bodhicitta, these practices do not make much sense, because there is no basis for them. By incorporating the practice of deities into our lives, we could experience enlightenment within one lifetime, within three or seven lifetimes, or when we are in the state of the bardo (the intermediate state between death and rebirth). Such a result is possible when our practice is united with bodhicitta. Bodhicitta is like a fire that is burning. If we want the fire to spread and blazing flames to rise, we pour on gasoline or oil, or we cause more air to come toward the fire. That will make the fire spread and the flames rise. The vajrayana practice of deities quickens and enlarges the process, but there must be a process to enlarge. That process is the practice of bodhicitta.

No ordinary being can express in words the effect of the practice of bodhicitta. From the moment we generate bodhicitta, with the continuity of our minds, this effect continues and multiplies, because the attitude is so profound.

If we truly and sincerely wish to work for our own benefit, the practice of bodhicitta is also the way to do that. It is the way to transcend and transform our neurotic patterns without having to suppress them. Generating bodhicitta spontaneously transforms our neurotic patterns. The more we wish to benefit beings, the more our neurotic patterns diminish. We do not necessarily have to work with a particular klesha, saying we must purify this, avoid this, get rid of this. If we generate bodhicitta, that in itself transforms our kleshas. If we bring a lamp into a dark corner, the lamp brings light, so we would not say, "Now we must take away the darkness." The darkness is already taken away when the light comes in. Likewise, when the sun rises, and the bright rays of the sun pervade the world, we would not say, "Now the darkness must be taken away." For our own benefit and the benefit of beings, for the purification of our negative emotions and the removal of our neurotic patterns, we must develop bodhicitta.

When we lack bodhicitta, we have difficulty liking beings and opening ourselves up to them. If bodhicitta becomes the dominant aspect of our lives, we begin to like all beings equally, without discrimination, because we realize that sentient beings contribute as much toward our experience of enlightenment as do the buddhas. If there were no beings, toward whom would we generate bodhicitta? Sentient beings cause us to generate bodhicitta; therefore, we must have as much appreciation, concern, and respect toward sentient beings as we have devotion toward all enlightened beings. If we understand that without sentient beings we cannot attain enlightenment, how can we not like and respect them?

When someone shows us aggression, the practice of bodhicitta means practicing compassion and patience. If this aggression does not arise, how are we going to practice patience? If no one gives us any challenge, we may presume we have patience, but when someone directs aggression toward us, we have the opportunity to practice patience, or to learn that we need to develop patience. The practice of patience through generating bodhicitta gives rise to our experience of enlightenment. Therefore, instead of hatred toward the person who shows us aggression, we should have a sense of gratitude for the opportunity to see clearly how challenging the practice of bodhicitta is. The hungrier we become, the more clearly we are able to think of food. The colder we feel, the more precisely we are able to think of clothing. Likewise, the more we realize our limitations and shortcomings, the more we realize the need for practice. If we are practicing bodhicitta, every person is worthy of respect.

Questions

Q: In our interactions with other people, how do we keep from getting caught up in their neurotic patterns, which are related to our own neurotic minds?

A: In practicing bodhicitta, the way we can relate to other people, without getting caught up in their neurotic patterns, is first to have no expectations. The purpose of generating the enlightened attitude and practicing the Dharma is to attain enlightenment for ourselves and all sentient beings. Right now, we should not expect anything from the immediate situation or from the people we relate to; thus we will not give way to the intrusion of other people's neurotic patterns.

Second, when we are practicing bodhicitta, we see the neurotic patterns others are caught up in. When we see that a certain person has weaknesses and limitations, we must be very careful not to become caught up in feelings of pride and superiority. That only causes further confusion and suffering. We should instead have compassion for that person. If, through our understanding and ability, we can help, that is most wonderful. If not, we should at least generate compassion, hoping that the person will be able to transcend such neurotic patterns and confusion. We should refrain from pointing to the faults of others while seeing ourselves as spotless.

Q: Would you explain more about the meaning of bodhicitta?

A: The first important understanding we should have is about the aspiration aspect of the practice of bodhicitta. When we are sitting down to do a formal practice, we should have the aspiration that we are going to do this practice for the benefit and enlightenment of all beings. We think, "All sentient beings are going through many kinds of confusion and bewilderment, and it is important that they be helped; therefore, I will do this practice for the benefit and enlightenment of all beings." With that attitude, we do whatever formal practice we are doing. When we finish the practice, we dedicate whatever virtue and merit we have accumulated from this practice completely and sincerely for the benefit and enlightenment of beings, thinking, "May this benefit beings; may it bring them happiness and well-being, and may it ultimately bring them the experience of enlightenment."

At other times, when we have a moment to ourselves in the general pace of life, we might notice that all beings around us are going through many kinds of suffering, confusion, and bewilderment. We should think, "May I be able to work for the benefit of all these suffering sentient beings." Looking around, we think to ourselves, "The only solution is the experience of enlightenment, and may I be the pioneer in this project." Reminding ourselves with such an attitude is very important. If we train ourselves with that attitude, at a certain point it will become spontaneous, a living quality in our being.

Second, it is very important to take the bodhisattva vow, and connect to the unbroken lineage of bodhisattva vows taken by countless beings on the path toward enlightenment. However, if we do not have such training at the beginning, it is difficult to keep the vow. In one second we might receive the vow, but in the next second we might break it. Therefore, it is very important first to train our minds with the enlightened attitude. Once we have taken the bodhisattva vow, if we think of the enlightened beings and the lineage and make supplications to them, they can support us in this project. Right now we should simply train our minds in this way, during formal practice and in daily life.

Q: Is bodhicitta an intrinsic quality of enlightenment?

A: Bodhicitta is like a spark, an intrinsic quality we can develop as we work toward enlightenment. When we have experienced enlightenment, this intrinsic quality is all-pervading. The spark becomes a blazing flame.

SENDING AND RECEIVING

In addition to gaining an intellectual understanding of bodhi-citta from the teachings, it is important to have a practical experience of the practice of bodhicitta. To that end, there is a meditation practice called sending and receiving (*tong len* in Tibetan) that can help you develop the enlightened attitude.

When you do this short meditation, first sit in the meditation posture, relaxing your body and sitting rather comfortably. Then breathe normally, following the natural course of your breath. Imagine that with the exhalation of your breath, whatever merit you have accumulated from beginningless time, are accumulating now, and will accumulate in all future time, radiates toward all sentient beings. Just as when the sun shines, the rays of light radiate toward all places, so with your exhalation, these positive qualities radiate, bringing happiness, well-being, comfort, health, and longevity to all beings without discrimination.

Then when you inhale, imagine you are inhaling all the suffering, confusion, sickness, turmoil, and conflict of sentient beings. All the suffering and turmoil of sentient beings merges with you, and this uproots the suffering and confusion of the sentient beings. Because of the strength of bodhicitta—the power of your sincere attitude of wanting to benefit beings—as soon as the suffering merges with you, it dissolves into nothing and disappears. It is just as if you had collected some dust together into a little pile and a strong wind blew it away. Inhaling and exhaling in this way, meditate for a short time.

After you have meditated in this way for a short while, let go of the mental focus and let your mind rest in a state of awareness. Attempt to have the sense that there are no sentient beings to meditate on, there is no person meditating, and there is no act of meditation taking place. Try to transcend these three, which are relative, and give birth to something ultimate, something effortless and spontaneous like the arising and disappearing of clouds in the sky. Just remain in a state of clarity. There is no act, no thought of doing something outside or inside, no you doing something. Just cut off all that and remain in a state of awareness.

In order to give birth to bodhicitta, we must accumulate merit or positive qualities on the relative level and also on the absolute level, the level of wisdom. The desire to benefit beings accumulates merit on the relative or physical level, since we think of doing this in a substantial or physical way. We imagine all sentient beings everywhere. We generate love toward all the beings and think of helping them in this way; we generate compassion toward all the beings, and think of taking away their suffering and confusion. The inner aspect of the accumulation of merit comes through developing wisdom, which transcends any fixed, substantial focal point. Wisdom is understanding that, in ultimate reality, the practice transcends any idea of other beings on whom we need to focus, the self as the one who is focusing, and the very act of focusing.

It is possible to transcend these, because in ultimate reality the true nature of beings is not suffering; it is not the upheaval of neurotic emotions. Certain causes have evolved in such a way that beings now experience suffering and confusion. They experience a feeling of solidity and, therefore, a feeling of insecurity that this solid entity might be jeopardized. All of this takes place, but in reality it is like the appearance of clouds or rainbows. Clouds and rainbows appear in the sky but they are not part of the sky. They appear suddenly and disappear suddenly, from various causes. In our situation also, suffering and confusion are not innate qualities; they are not something substantial with us. When we understand that, we transcend the act of focusing, someone to focus on, and someone who is focusing. We just maintain a state of clarity, meditating in a state of awareness and spaciousness. This is a very, very important aspect of the practice.

There are different names for these two practices—the practice of focusing on an object and the non-focusing practice of awareness. They are called relative and absolute bodhicitta, method and wisdom, or merit and wisdom. Whatever name they are given, both practices are very important for practitioners of the Dharma on the way to developing the qualities of a bodhisattva.

We must always be aware that at some point we will experience the perfect state of enlightenment. At that point, nothing special or unique will come into our being. No particular magical factor will be transmitted to us from the earth or from the heavens. It is just that we have the potential to awaken, and because we have met the proper skillful methods and have put in the necessary effort, we experience enlightenment. It is important to remember this, because sometimes we lack confidence. We rely on some being or quality to come to us from the outside, and we think that if that outside quality does not come into us, we are helpless. In this way we discourage ourselves. But the buddhas, who have realized the perfect state of enlightenment and are able to perform many kinds of immaculate, miraculous activities, have experienced the full blossoming of certain seed qualities that were innate in them. Since these qualities are also innate in us, we must be confident of our qualities and our potential.

In all past times we have been caught up in many kinds of confusion because we have always had selfish pursuits. Now also we are caught up in many kinds of confusion. We put in a great deal of effort, time, and energy, but again it is for selfish pursuits. We are making the situation darker and darker, building up thicker and thicker layers, because of our self-centeredness in trying to do everything for our own benefit. Some clearing away is now very necessary. The difference between the buddhas as enlightened beings and us as sentient beings seems to be vast and absolute, but we have the same abilities as the buddhas, and the same methods are given to us. If we make the effort to put those methods into practice with diligence and confidence, we can also awaken and blossom forth like all the buddhas.

This potential to blossom forth into enlightenment is a quality inherent in each one of us. For example, when a piece of metal has been exposed to water and dirt, it becomes tarnished. But after cleaning and polishing, it will become bright and shiny. Likewise, when a piece of cloth has become dirty, it can be laundered and become clean. Now this cleanness of the cloth or this shiny quality of the metal is not something added to the object. The cloth itself embodies the quality of cleanness, and the metal embodies the quality of brightness. It is necessary to put time, effort, and diligence into the practice of the Dharma, in order to clear away our neurotic patterns. The experience of enlightenment means the clearing away of our neurotic confused patterns. The more we are able to clear away such patterns, the more we will find the space and ability to help sentient beings. If we can completely purify our neurotic patterns, we can benefit sentient beings limitlessly.

If we wish to experience permanent awakening and happiness, and if we truly wish to benefit beings, the practice of the Dharma is our greatest individual responsibility. Just as the buddhas of the past applied the Dharma to purify and transcend their neurotic patterns, so must we apply the Dharma for the same purpose. As we follow the path of the bodhisattvas, there are specific practices to follow stage by stage in order to transcend our neurotic patterns. These are the six *paramitas* or six perfections, which are described in the following chapter.

In addition to applying the methods of the Dharma, the buddhas prayed and made obeisance and supplications to the buddhas of the past. Likewise, we make obeisance to the buddhas and to enlightened beings, asking them for their blessings and their protection. In this way we make ourselves open to their accumulation of merit and their blessings.

This discussion of bodhicitta may seem very repetitive, but that is necessary. This very profound teaching must penetrate into our beings so we can feel it, experience it, and express it.

Questions

Q: Do you recommend that we do the sending and receiving meditation as a regular practice?

A: Yes, you can incorporate this meditation into your daily practice. It is good to follow some kind of sequence in the practice. You can start with some basic shamata practice, following the breath or another technique. After doing that for a little while, then do the sending and receiving meditation. The shamata meditation is mainly to develop stability and tranquility in the mind. The sending and receiving meditation has a two-fold effect. Since you are following the breath and maintaining some kind of focal point, it has the same effect as shamata meditation, but the attitude gives it an additional quality. Because you are generating kindness and concern, it is more effective, so it is a very special practice.

Q: What happens if you meet someone who wants to give you a present or a good feeling?

A: We must make a distinction between what is mundane and what is spiritual in helping beings. If you ask someone to give you something to please and comfort you physically or mentally, and your purpose is just to fulfill your desires or the needs of your senses, that is rather mundane. On the other hand, it may be a spiritual need. You may ask for something from a certain person in order to bring greater clarity and stability to your mind so you can help others and cut through your neurotic patterns. For example, if you want to ask a teacher for spiritual guidance, encouragement, or inspiration, you should have the courage to ask without hesitation.

From your side, the practice of giving to others is very important, but what is pleasing to someone is not necessarily what is beneficial and harmless for that person. Without being judgmental, be careful to give what will have a positive effect and will not cause further accumulation of negative patterns. If someone is dying of starvation, with nothing to eat, and you are able to provide that person with food and other basic needs, willingly and without expectations, that is proper giving. It is beneficial as well as pleasing to that person. In the same very simple way, if someone is sick and going through many emotional and physical problems, some gentle sincere words of love will give consolation to that person's mind. If you find a person who is very cold and in a helpless state, you can provide something warm in a careful and safe way.

On the other hand, if it is something that will harm the person, or something the person will use to harm other beings, it may not be advisable to give it, even if it pleases the person. For example, someone may come to you and say, "I like fishing, but it is difficult for me to find a worm to put on the hook. I would be very happy if you would provide me with a worm so I could fish." You would have to think about whether to provide that worm. The fish is going to be harmed, and the worm is going to be harmed, so is it worth pleasing that person?

Q: I have difficulty doing the part of the meditation in which we rest the mind in awareness. Either I have thoughts or I am in a trance-like state—I am not sure what it is, really—and I spend a lot of time in the middle. I find it very hard to get to this state, and I wonder if you can help me.

A: I do not wish to discourage you, but because this practice is very profound, it is very difficult for beginners. Still, we cannot leave it out or postpone it, because then you may never get around to doing it. We have to try, and we do have the ability to develop.

Think of an infant. When you look at an infant, it is quite difficult to imagine it growing and being able to walk. Some motion is taking place though, so it seems hopeful. As the child grows, it starts to crawl, and later on there is more falling down than walking, but eventually the child will be walking independently. Likewise, right now we are very much at the infant stage. We are trying to walk on the path of the enlightened ones, and it is very much a beginning. But we must keep trying; it is important to keep up with our practice.

If you are focusing on an object, such as following the breath, a moment may suddenly come like the breaking of a thread, when you know the past and the future are cut off, and you remain in the nowness of the present. When you let go there is a gap for just one second, or possibly longer, in which there is awareness but no thought. To keep up with that awareness and remain in that experience may be difficult, yet you have to try. As you say, a lot of thoughts come up, but do not be worried about having thoughts. Before this, we did not realize that thoughts were coming up constantly, but now this constant motion is a bit clearer.

When a thought arises, just notice the thought. Watch the thought. It is the nature of thoughts to arise. Just be aware of the thought, not suppressing it or encouraging it in any way, or regarding it as a good thought or a bad thought. This thought has no shape, no form, and no color. While you are noticing the thought, it disappears. Remain again in a state of awareness. This may last only for a second before another thought appears. Notice that thought just as you did before, continuing to practice in this way. All you have to do is notice and not become distracted. If you are distracted, then after three or four thoughts you will realize those thoughts have gone by, so notice that and be mindful. One thought comes and you just watch the thought. Then the thought disappears, and you are in a state of awareness. Another thought comes, then disappears, but you maintain a state of mindfulness and awareness. The arising of thoughts is not significant, but it is important to notice the thoughts and then to continue with awareness.

BENEFITS OF TRAINING IN BODHICITTA

I have explained the importance of developing bodhicitta, and especially the sending and receiving practice, which is generating the attitude of giving comfort and happiness to all sentient beings as well as taking on their suffering and confusion. This practice is very beneficial to us, and in the long run it is beneficial to all beings, but you may wonder how it works. You may wonder, "How can I possibly generate such an attitude of benefiting all sentient beings, or taking on the suffering and confusion of beings?" You may think, "I am trying to work to cut through my own suffering, confusion, and neurosis. What sense does it make to take on the suffering and confusion of other beings?'' You may ask, ''Even if I generate such an attitude, I am not really giving anything to sentient beings or taking anything from them. How can this be beneficial to myself or to others?'' These questions may come up in your mind. If they do not come up right now, they may arise later in the course of the practice. To answer them, I would like to give a brief explanation of the benefits of developing bodhicitta and what positive effects it brings to the practitioner as well as to others.

If we examine ourselves, we find that up to this point we have been caught up in many kinds of selfish pursuits. This habitual tendancy is very strong. We want to protect ourselves. We want to do everything we can to benefit ourselves and fulfill our selfish desires. We have trained ourselves in this way for countless lifetimes, so during this lifetime, we need no more training in this direction. We are already well prepared. It is like water running down from a higher place. We do not have to make it run down; the water can follow the downward slope without any assistance. Because of the strong training we have had for a long period of time, we are still to this day caught up in habitual patterns.

We now realize that although such training was aimed toward our benefit, protection, and security, it has not fulfilled these aims; in fact it has been in the wrong direction. Our minds have been trained in a confused way, and we now understand that we must transform that pattern. To do that, we must train ourselves to think about others and have concern for others as much as we have thought about and had concern for ourselves. We need to direct our thoughts and feelings toward the benefit of others more than toward our own benefit. This training is a skillful method for cutting through our neurotic patterns. Our neurotic patterns are not tangible things we can throw away, but they can be transformed and turned toward positive purposes. Understanding that this is possible and beneficial, we must turn to this different way of training the mind.

You may think that, since we are so involved in our neurotic patterns, the training must be very difficult. Actually it is not so difficult; in fact, it is rather simple. We come across many different kinds of people. Suppose we know that our country has very friendly relations with a certain country. We have never seen the people of this other country. We have never met or talked to them. But suppose a person is introduced to us as being from that country with which we have such friendly relations. Although we have never seen that person before, we will immediately extend a friendly smile and show respect toward this person, as if we have had a long friendship with him or her.

On the other hand, suppose a certain country has been labeled as our enemy because there is some kind of conflict between the two countries. Just as in the other case, we have never seen or talked to any of the people or had any conflict with any of them directly. Even so, we have a sense of aggression and negative feeling toward them. When someone is introduced to us as being from that country, we have an immediate sense of suspicion and doubt about that person, even though we are seeing the person for the first time. Now suppose a treaty is signed between our country and the country with whom we have had the conflict. At that very moment, there is friendship. Now when we meet people from that country, we extend the same kind of smile we showed toward people from the other country. Clearly, the way we feel toward others depends on how our minds have been trained.

Training the mind toward negative effects and further confusion is of course very easy, but training the mind toward positive, awakening effects is also very possible. It is not only possible but necessary, because our intention is not to build some temporary treaty or to be able to smile at someone. Our intention is to awaken our minds to a state in which we can experience ultimate, unending peace and happiness. We can then radiate an equal amount of warmth, peace, and harmony to help other beings feel happiness. This training is not just for a mundane purpose; it is for the temporary as well as the ultimate benefit of beings.

According to the traditional stories of the Buddha's previous lives, at one time when he was an ordinary sentient being, he was born into the noble and wealthy family of a merchant. For generations, the men of this family had been merchants and had gone to sea to collect many kinds of jewels. His grandfathers had all gone to sea and had drowned, and the same thing had happened to his father. His mother, understanding that all generations of men in that family had died in the sea, feared that if this son of hers was to follow the same kind of trade, he would also die. Therefore, she gave him a girl's name, trying to prevent him from following the merchant trade, and she took him away to a very remote corner of the land, where they would be little noticed.

When the future Buddha was old enough to work, since the family was much in need of basic sustenance, he went out to collect firewood to sell. Because of his good fortune, he was able to find large bundles of firewood, more than anyone else who collected firewood. He was able to sell more firewood than anyone else and thus to provide very well for his mother. However, the firewood-gathering people soon expelled him from their community. They told him he did not belong a family that did this kind of work.

He next joined another group of people who collected and sold grass for animals. Again he was able to collect more grass and sell it faster and more efficiently than anyone else. He was then told by these people, "You have no right to be with us, because you do not belong to a family that does our kind of business. You belong to a family of merchants."

When these things took place, the Buddha went to his mother and told her that none of the trades would accept him, but they all told him he belonged to a much nobler family. He asked his mother to tell him the truth, precisely the truth a mother should tell to her son if the bond of mother and son was not to be violated. The mother wept for a long time. She then said, "You belong to a noble family. To save your life,

I have kept this from you, but it seems to be no longer possible," and sorrowfully she told him about the family's history.

At that time, he happened to encounter some other sons of merchants, who were all surprised to see him. They told him they had thought he was a daughter, and therefore they had not contacted the family to ask him to join in their trade. Now that they found there was a son to follow the noble family's heritage, they gave him many words of advice and encouragement. They said, "You must not waste your time; we must immediately go into business together." When the Buddha— who was at this time just an ordinary merchant's son—heard this, he immediately went back to his mother and said with great excitement and enthusiasm that he wanted to go into business with these people. His mother wept and begged him not to go, because his life would be in danger. She insisted many times, and he insisted just as much that he must go. His mother tried to hold him back by the mantle of his robe saying, "You cannot go." Finally he became very angry, kicked away his mother, and left.

He went to sea with his new friends and, of course, as his mother feared, their ship was wrecked and they were all drowned. After they all died in the sea, the future Buddha was in the state of the bardo, the intermediate state between death and birth. He felt that he got on a plank from the broken ship and floated to shore. In this bardo or dream experience, he found himself in a very beautiful palace, surrounded by four beautiful maidens, who had many kinds of offerings for him. This was because, when he was collecting firewood, he was able to give his mother four coins every day to provide for her food and basic needs. He lived in that palace for a long period of time, but he always had the desire to go to the south. The maidens warned him not to go toward the south, but this longing was very strong, and he finally left.

After traveling for a certain distance he found himself in another palace bigger than the first one. There he found himself surrounded by eight beautiful maidens, who welcomed him and made many kinds of offerings to him. This was because, when he was collecting and selling grass, he was able to give his mother eight coins every day for her food and basic needs. But still his yearning to go toward the south was very strong, and though he was warned not to go there, one night he took his leave.

After traveling a long distance, he found himself in front of an enormous iron building that reached from the earth to the sky. Because of the huge size of the building and the vibrating sound that came from it, no one, no matter how brave, could keep from shivering in intense fear. (Remember, this was all happening in the bardo state, so it was all in his mind.) In front of the gate stood a huge man dressed in black. He asked the huge man who he was, and learned that he was the one who takes account of the karmic consequences of the actions of sentient beings.

When the future Buddha entered the enormous iron building, he saw a kind of machine in one corner, with a wheel projecting down from it. A man had been tied up with his head under the wheel, and as the wheel turned, his brains were being thrown about here and there. When the Buddha asked the huge man why this was happening, the man said that during his past life this person had kicked his mother on her head, and this was happening as a consequence. At that point, a voice came from above and said that the one who was tied must be untied, and the one who was untied must be tied. As soon as he heard that voice, the Buddha found himself in the machine, under the wheel, going through the same process he had witnessed. At that moment, instead of being completely caught up in frustration and fear, he had this thought: "Not just I, but many sentient beings have mistreated their mothers, and possibly in worse ways. May this suffering I have to go through be the embodiment of the suffering of such beings who have mistreated their mothers." With the arising of that attitude in his mind, he found himself being born in one of the higher god realms. That was the first moment in which the Buddha generated bodhicitta when he was still a very ordinary person.

When the future Buddha generated that attitude, it was a very simple thought. He realized that the pain was going to be very severe for him as well as for other beings, so his thought was, "May this be the embodiment of the pain of such beings." He did not have the further aspiration of wishing that through whatever merit he gained with such an attitude, all sentient beings might attain the perfect state of enlightenment. It was just a momentary wish about sufferings that beings would go through as result of mistreating their mothers. It was not a very cosmic attitude. Still the fruition was that he was born in the god realm, and from there he was born in the human realm.

In his next birth in the human realm, the Buddha was born into a brahmin family. Because he had mistreated his mother, the family he was born into was very poor. However, at that time the Dharma was prevalent, and he was able to make an offering of one bowl of soup to the buddha of that particular time, Dipankara Buddha (*Ösung* in Tibetan). This was not the buddha before Shakyamuni, who is also called Dipankara; this Dipankara lived many, many eons before that. After making that offering and thus making a connection with Dipankara Buddha, he was able to generate the complete attitude of bodhicitta for the benefit and enlightenment of all beings. From then on he continuously followed the path of development and fulfillment and gradually reached the perfect state of enlightenment. Now he remains in the perfect enlightened state, helping countless beings in most profound ways.

Our present opportunity may actually be much more favorable, since we find ourselves more aware of what is possible than the Buddha was when he first began. Therefore, it is very important that we practice bodhicitta. When we go through any kind of problems, suffering, or confusion, instead of being filled with selfish ideas as to how we could get rid of this suffering and pile it on someone else, our attitude should be, "May this be the embodiment of the suffering and confusion of beings." In addition, we should have the sincere wish to take on whatever suffering and confusion of beings we can.

At the same time, whenever we are experiencing happiness, well-being, satisfaction, and contentment, instead of trying to protect this happiness, we should think, "May this happiness and well-being be experienced by all sentient beings equally." We should couple that attitude with the wish that the merit we accumulate from such attitudes may lead ultimately to the enlightenment of all sentient beings. If we do our practice in this way, it is not possible that we will have to return repeatedly to cyclic existence, or else this ageless wisdom lacks the truth.

A sincere examination and undertaking is necessary. If we think this does not apply to us or work for us, that means we question the validity of the ageless wisdom. The practice of bodhicitta is extremely important. Bodhicitta means happiness, it means contentment, it means clarity. When we are able to do this practice, no matter what situation we find ourselves in, we always have a sense of peace, contentment, and happiness in our minds and in our lives. For example, by generating bodhicitta, we transcend jealousy. If we enjoy the happiness of others, how can we be jealous about their success and well-being? With bodhicitta, when we see a person doing very well in some undertaking, we are very happy about it and feel that this must be a result of the great accumulation of merit the person has earned. Our attitude is, "May this person continuously be able to accumulate such merit and continuously be happy, and not only have temporary happiness but realize the perfect state of enlightenment."

Also, when we encounter poor, helpless beings, we will have no sense of pride. How can there be pride if we have a strong sense of compassion? If we always want to work for the benefit of others and to eliminate their suffering, how can we think, "These people are going through many kinds of suffering, and I am not, because I am so intelligent and efficient." How could we have such a sense of superiority? Our attitude is that these beings are going through such suffering and confusion because of their negative intentions and actions of the past. We try to help them in whatever way we can, thinking, "In the future, may these beings never again be involved in such negative intentions and actions.''

With this attitude, there is some clarity, because we are content. When we see situations in which something is lacking, we are able to see what we can do to help. Having this selfless attitude at all times is very, very important—always wanting to give, always being open. If our minds are trained in this way there is great joy, and our body and speech are able to cooperate with such mental activity. There is willingness and spontaneity, and when we give, there is no sense of expectation. We give with the wish, "May whatever merit I gain from this particular gift contribute to the happiness and enlightenment of all beings." There is no experience of anything substantial. There is a total letting go, a powerful sense of awakening.

Such selflessness and openness is extremely important in the kind of world we live in, which is filled with jealousy and hatred. The first and second world wars began because of the negative intentions of just a few people, and they culminated by bringing suffering to countless beings. This suffering was intended to benefit those few people, who had in their minds such an epitome of confusion that they thought overpowering and conquering many people and killing them would lead to peace and happiness for them, their country, and their people. What it brought instead was suffering, death, and loss for people in other countries and their country and for themselves. The temporary suffering was constant, and the consequences of their intentions—the experience of suffering they will have to go through in different lower realms—is beyond expression in human terms.

To this day such things are happening. We see and read about the kinds of conflicts and wars that occur and the kinds of suffering that take place because of people's negative intentions. If everyone were filled with such negative intentions and such confusion, there would be no chance for peace among humanity in this world. But something very sane, something very awakening, is available to us in the practice of bodhicitta.

We have the opportunity to participate in this, so we must take this opportunity seriously.

I have talked very briefly about the benefits of the attitude of bodhicitta and the defects of not practicing it. These teachings are very easy to understand—I have tried to put them in the simplest way possible—but the most important thing is to practice them. It may be difficult to practice bodhicitta, but we must do this practice. We must try to work toward transforming our mental patterns. This is extremely important. This subject is the core of the Buddhist teachings. Many explanations can be given as helping hands, and there are many different methods, but you need to understand the essence of the teachings.

I would very much appreciate it if you would sincerely ponder what has been explained. The main thing is to put it into practice. I have sincerely tried to impart to you my limited understanding of this teaching. If you put this into practice, it would be most beneficial for me, because it would make it worthwhile to have imparted these teachings and I would accumulate much merit through your practice. It certainly would be very beneficial for you, so I would like you to think deeply about this teaching and practice it as much as possible.

DEDICATION OF MERIT

I will now give a brief explanation about the importance of dedicating merit. When we receive teachings or practice meditation, it is very important to include the dedication of merit as part of the practice. There is a relative aspect and an absolute aspect of dedication. Right now, we are able to practice the relative aspect. We should dedicate whatever merit we accumulate from any formal practices we do, such as individual or group meditation, and from any informal practices we do, such as virtuous actions or the generation of virtuous attitudes. If we know of specific beings who are suffering, we dedicate the merit of our practice for the benefit of these beings in particular and for the benefit of all beings in general. We say,

"Temporarily may this merit eliminate the sufferings and difficulties these beings in particular, and all beings in general, are going through. Ultimately may it bring about perfect enlightenment for all beings."

The dedication of merit is very important. We begin our practice with the attitude of doing it for the benefit and enlightenment of all beings, and while we are doing the practice, we do it for the benefit of beings. Therefore, we may wonder why it is necessary at the end to dedicate the merit of the practice for the benefit of beings. All three of these aspects of the attitude are necessary in the practice. First, we have the aspiration aspect, the attitude that we want to do the practice for the benefit and enlightenment of all confused and suffering sentient beings. Second, while we are doing the body of the practice, we remind ourselves that we are doing this practice for the benefit and enlightenment of beings. Third, having done the practice, it is important to dedicate the merit of the practice for the benefit of beings.

Suppose a person has a precious jewel and has acquired a very good box in which to put the jewel. He or she has also lined the box so the jewel can be held very securely inside. After doing so much work, it would be very foolish of this person not to close the box. The jewel is put inside the box to keep it secure, but it will only be secure if the box is closed. Dedicating the merit at the conclusion of our practice is like closing the box.

Furthermore, we are ordinary beings with many limitations. We may begin to do the practice for the benefit of beings, but by the end we might be expecting to get something out of it for ourselves. We might be thinking we should experience the fruition, which makes it a selfish pursuit and hinders the development of our practice. Also, because of our limitations, we may at some point have a sudden upheaval of aggression or some other neurotic pattern. If we are trying to hold onto the merit for ourselves, the accumulation of merit will be destroyed at that point like a piece of wood that is burned when we put it into the fire.

If we have a drop of water in our palm and we try to hold onto it, this water will certainly evaporate. We might turn the hand over and spill the water, and it will also evaporate. On the other hand, if we carry this drop of water and pour it into the ocean, our drop of water will become a part of the ocean. As long as the ocean remains, that drop of water will also remain without drying up. In the same way, once we have dedicated the merit, it is ours. If we have not dedicated it, there is no certainty it is ours. If we dedicate the merit, it becomes inexhaustible, but if we do not dedicate the merit, it is likely to be exhausted because of our limitations. We dedicate whatever merit we accumulate in order to make it inexhaustible and beneficial for us as well as for others and, ultimately, in order to experience enlightenment and thereby benefit countless sentient beings. Because the dedication of merit contributes toward such realization and awakening, it plays as important a part in the practice as does the main practice.

There is something profound and even magical about dedication. It is certain that from beginningless time, while we have done much to develop our neurotic patterns and defilements, there have also been occasions when we developed virtuous intentions and performed virtuous actions. Yet we may not have dedicated the merit we acquired from this, so the nature of that merit was exhaustible. In future times, we may also perform virtuous actions and generate positive attitudes, yet somehow not have the wisdom to dedicate the merit. At this time, when we have the good fortune to receive the instructions, we can dedicate not only the merit from this particular practice and all our virtuous actions and attitudes of this lifetime, but whatever merit we have gained from beginningless time in the past or will gain in all future times. We dedicate this total accumulation of merit for the benefit and enlightenment of beings. Thus within just one short moment of dedication, we can cover an immense span of activities and practices. This is the most important aspect of the practice. It might be called the pith instructions. Nothing more profound than this comes to us.

There is also the absolute aspect of dedication, which comes about through transcendental wisdom. Even though we do not have the transcendental wisdom to make such an absolute dedication ourselves, there is a way to make our dedication of merit into an absolute dedication. Having dedicated in the ordinary way, we dedicate the merit again in the way the buddhas and bodhisattvas dedicate their accumulations of merit in the present as well as in all past and future times. We say, "May the buddhas and bodhisattvas of the past, present, and future grant us their permission and blessings, so our dedication takes the same direction as their stainless and profound dedication." In this way, our dedication becomes absolute.

The dedication is very simple and does not take much time or effort, but it is effective and profound. We can have an attitude of dedication even if we do just one prostration, just one recitation of a mantra like *om mani peme hung*, or just one moment's virtuous action. No practice of the Dharma is insignificant. Any practice of the Dharma is worthy of dedication and should be dedicated to make its effect inexhaustible. Thus in our daily lives, it is very important to remember to dedicate the merit of whatever formal and informal practices we do.

Questions

Q: It seems to me that before we can go from anger and jealousy to compassion, there has to be a period of repenting, and sometimes before that there is guilt and self-hatred. Would you talk about this?

A: It is very important to have sense of repentance, but this can easily be misinterpreted. Much of our time has been wasted in futile activities that have intensified our neurotic patterns. Therefore, we must change our ways. We should have a sense of regret because we have done many negative things. We must review the situation, but this must be done with the understanding that we have the potential to change, to develop ourselves and transform the patterns. It is self-hatred to say, "I am really bad and I cannot change." That is of no benefit. We should repent by thinking, "This is not the way, because I have other abilities and potentials. It is stupid to waste my limited time. Now that I understand this, I will not continue to be caught up in such activities." This kind of repentance will inspire us to appreciate our potential and commit ourselves to the practice.

When you are feeling relaxed, it is very important to review the ways you have wasted time in unnecessary activities, and resolve to work toward some kind of discipline from this moment on. When you are in the midst of turmoil, however, if you try to review and regret, it may not operate in the right way. Instead, it may lead to frustration, self-hatred, and guilt.

There are also different kinds of guilt. If you continue to feel guilty about something without doing anything about it, that is pointless. But sometimes you are able to change the situation because of feeling guilty, so in those cases guilt may be helpful.

Q: Would you give some basic rules for those practicing Dharma?

A: The most important rule is that, having taken refuge, you should at all times have respect, confidence, and devotion toward the Buddha, Dharma, and Sangha. You will not go for refuge to any other beings or things, no matter how powerful and glamorous they may seem. This is the most important discipline and provides the basis for any other level of practice.

Second, having committed yourself to the Buddhist path, you should develop the attitude that you want to benefit others, as we have been discussing. This is not a law that you have to follow because you belong to a certain tradition. It transcends barriers of tradition. If you are a rational, thinking being, you will realize that it is important to help others. Right now you may not be able to make a complete commitment that from now on you will not harm any beings and, at the same time, you will benefit all sentient beings. But you can resolve to work as much as possible to benefit beings and to lessen the harm you cause beings. In this way, you pave your path. This is very, very important in the practice of Buddhism.

We have put so much emphasis on the attitude you should have and the kind of mental work you should do, that you might feel there is no need to do anything physical. We emphasize the mental practice because if you develop the right motivation, you are happy about doing the physical work and you are able to do it effectively. If you have mental reservations, but you are forced to do physical work, you might give it up later on, when you find it to be boring or tiring. If you give something out of a sudden feeling of compassion or generosity, you may later regret it. Therefore, you must first train your mind to develop the attitude that you will benefit beings untiringly and never harm beings, no matter what inconvenience or discomfort you might have to go through. Then when you actually do these things, you will have that unflinching attitude. The practical side is as important as the mental side, if not more so, but first you must train your mind so you feel comfortable in helping or giving.

The third basic rule for Buddhist practitioners is to work for your future benefit and well-being more than for your happiness in the present. For the present, if your need for basic sustenance is met, you should be satisfied. That is all you need, and whatever time and energy is left should be directed toward your future benefit. For almost every one of us, the future may be rather bleak. There are specific disciplines that you can practice (such as the lay vows), and if you are able to follow these disciplines, it is beneficial for you. There is not some strict law that if you are a Buddhist, you must always follow these disciplines. Practitioners take on the disciplines as a practice, realizing that this is for their benefit. When you are able to see the situation clearly, you may see the importance of taking on such commitments, feeling comfortable with them and not suppressed. In specific situations and with specific vows, the kind of discipline you need to follow will be explained.

Q: Why should we visualize deities, and what is the meaning of that?

A: There is much profound wisdom in the visualization of deities, but I will answer briefly. One reason we visualize a deity is that the mind is pulled in all directions by distractions and emotional upheavals. It is quite uncontrolled. To help our minds become less distracted and more concentrated and focused, we use the visualization as an object of meditation.

Furthermore, the deities you visualize not only symbolize the teachings, but are also in fact the figures of enlightened beings. When you attain the perfect state of enlightenment, you will become like one of these beings. This fruition is becoming the path in your visualization right now, so you are developing an affinity and a familiarity with what you are going to be. As an illustration, suppose you are painting a picture, such as one of the thankas. Even if you have only painted a small corner of it, the full image of the deity in the thanka is in your mind. In the same way, what you visualize is the fruition, although right now you are only beginning on the path.

Finally, you invoke the essential qualities of all enlightened beings into the visualization you have made of the deity. What you have visualized is created, but you have created something that holds truth. Then you invite the essential qualities of enlightened beings into the deity you have visualized. Because of the transmission of enlightened qualities (called the *jnanasattva* in Sanskrit) into this visualization (the *samayasattva*), you can use it to practice purification and to receive the blessings of enlightened beings.

The Bodhisattva Chenrezik

6 *The Six Perfections*

When we enter the path of the bodhisattvas and begin to practice at the mahayana level, we generate the enlightened attitude of wishing to give happiness and joy to all beings, to remove their pain and suffering, and to establish them all in a state of unchangeable happiness. As we travel this path, there are specific mahayana practices that we develop. These are the six perfections or six *paramitas*: generosity, discipline, patience, enthusiastic effort, meditation, and wisdom. These six practices include everything necessary to follow the path of the bodhisattvas. None can be omitted; they all must be practiced and, ultimately, perfected.

THE PERFECTION OF GENEROSITY

There is a particular order for the practice of the six perfections, and the practice of generosity is presented first. If we cannot begin to let go of our involvement in mundane existence at least to some extent, it will be quite difficult to undertake any spiritual journey at all. Letting go of our involvement in mundane affairs does not mean giving up eating or wearing clothes. We can lead a comfortable life and have enough to meet our needs without being dominated by the material world. By developing generosity, we are letting go of material things, which seem especially real to us. This is something we can all do and understand at a beginning level. Practicing generosity helps us accumulate merit or positive qualities, and this lays the foundation for undertaking the spiritual journey.

There are two external objects toward which we should practice generosity. First, we should make offerings to the Buddha, Dharma, and Sangha, for example by preserving and upholding the teachings, supporting teachers, and helping enlightened qualities increase and spread. In addition, we should help beings in great need, whenever we encounter them. Giving to those in need and making offerings to the enlightened sources of refuge are both essential practices of generosity. In order for us to develop the positive qualities necessary for effective spiritual practice, it is actually more important to make offerings to the three jewels. However, on an ordinary level, it may seem more satisfying and realistic to fulfill people's needs, because when we help someone we can see immediate results. To accumulate an abundance of merit, we practice generosity toward both these objects.

In practicing generosity, we must distinguish between pure and impure offerings. For example, it would be impure to offer to the three jewels the blood of animals or humans that have been sacrificed. This unfortunate custom is practiced in certain societies in order to propitiate high and powerful gods. Even if we made such an offering to enlightened beings, it would be inappropriate from a Buddhist point of view. The aim of Buddhism is to benefit all sentient beings. It would be completely inappropriate to kill an animal and offer it to someone who is committed only to benefiting beings. It is also impure to offer to the three jewels something that is stolen. That is hardly proper even for an ordinary recipient. Also, if another person is extremely unwilling to part with some object, but we force him or her to offer it, that is inappropriate because such a gift is not given with sincerity. We should avoid making such impure offerings to awakened and compassionate beings.

Furthermore, when we practice generosity toward beings in need, we may become caught up in "idiot compassion." For example, we might help a person harm another being. Perhaps we feel pity for a very weak person who wants to take revenge against someone else, so we give that person poison or a weapon with which to kill his or her enemy. We might provide the means for a person to commit suicide, or we might take objects stolen from one person and try to be generous by giving them to another. These are examples of unwholesome or impure offerings to beings in need. Because they are directly or indirectly harmful to beings, they are not acceptable.

We must also distinguish between pure and impure attitudes with which we make the offerings. We may make offerings to highly awakened beings, to the shrine, or to a temple. These are appropriate objects and the offerings may be very suitable, but we may have a thoroughly wrong attitude. Perhaps we hope to gain some kind of status. We make the offerings in an effort to gain popularity, to show how well off we are, or to make ourselves known as being very kind and generous. Perhaps we want to embarrass someone by making glorious and elaborate offerings, knowing the other person cannot afford to do the same. Or we may believe that if we do not make as many offerings as other people do, we will not be included in the group of virtuous people. We make the offerings to avoid feeling left out. If we make offerings with any of these unwholesome and impure attitudes, the offerings are incomplete and inadequate.

Further, we may practice generosity toward ordinary beings we know are in need, giving whatever we can and giving something that really helps, but our attitude may be impure. For example, we might be generous with the expectation that the recipients will repay us for the favor we do or the gift we give. We expect them to be grateful to us, to respect and honor us for our generosity, or to serve us in some way. We may give with the hope that other people will think we are very kind and generous, because they realize that the recipient needs a lot of help. We are not personally interested in helping—we do it so others will have a good opinion of us. Rather than a genuine wish to benefit others, this giving involves selfishness that is not material but psychological. Again, we may give to people in a condescending way, with the attitude that they are inferior and incapable of even meeting their basic needs. These are all examples of impure attitudes. They are very enticing, and we all have patterns that could lead us to be involved in them.

In the Buddhist practice of generosity, those to whom we make the offerings must be appropriate, the objects we offer must be pure and appropriate, and we must have a proper and pure motivation. We should make offerings to temples, shrines, and enlightened beings with sincerity and devotion, and with gestures of respect. We should practice material generosity toward others fully, with kindness, compassion, and respect, knowing that these people need what we give. We should make the gift with our own hands, gently and kindly, with appropriate gestures and words. It is important to involve ourselves fully and not to give in a curt or casual manner.

We should also give fully in the sense that we give not only for the good of one person, but with the motivation of wishing to benefit all beings. We give with the enlightened attitude, understanding that countless beings undergo immeasurable suffering in different realms of existence, and wishing to help all these beings. This makes it a total giving with no "strings attached." Sometimes when we make a gift to someone, we do not give it fully. Our attention is still on it. We may say, "I did not expect this person to give my gift to someone else." If we have given the gift fully, it does not matter what the person does with it. We have made this person happy, and when this person gives it to someone else, it might make that person even happier, so that is all the better. With the proper attitude, we give completely and permanently.

In the many places I have visited in this country, and with the many people I have met, I have been encouraged by observing that people are kind to animals. They like to have animals and birds as their pets, and they give grass to animals and seeds to birds. That is a very good custom; it is definitely a practice of generosity. However, this practice of generosity can be made more complete by not only thinking that we have benefited these beings, but also dedicating whatever merit we might gain from this toward the benefit of all beings. We have the wish, "May this merit temporarily bring an abundance of happiness, well-being, and peace to all beings, and may it ultimately bring them unchangeable happiness." Such an attitude helps us develop the perfection of generosity.

In the ordinary practice of generosity, we may help one individual—we have the ability and resources to do that—but that does not mean we have fully eliminated our negative patterns. At one moment we may be very kind, compassionate, and generous toward one individual, but in the next moment we may become aggressive and harm someone else. This destroys whatever good qualities we have gained through our generosity. However, if we dedicate whatever merit we have gained through this practice of generosity to the temporary and ultimate good of all beings, then the benefit of the practice can never be fully destroyed.

The practice of generosity has several aspects. The first is the practice of generosity through material giving. While there may be differences in how much we can give, this is something we can all understand and practice. It is the first stage of training, and the principle is not how much we give but how well and how completely we do it. Giving the proper objects to the proper recipients with the proper attitude, words, and gestures is more important than giving something extravagant but lacking any of these essential features. We do not immediately have to give away everything. We would not be able to do this; it would too painful, because our neurotic patterns would rebound. We begin at whatever level we can. We give whatever we can fully let go of, even if it is a very small thing, so long as we have confidence in the benefits of the practice.

In Buddhism, when we give examples of the practice of generosity, we may describe how bodhisattvas first gave all their material possessions and belongings to others and then gave away their relatives and friends.[18] They gave everything, including their bodies when it was necessary, for the benefit of others. The more they gave, the more they had to give, and the more developed they became. This gives us a picture of the possibilities, but when we practice, it is a different matter. What level of practice can we attempt? Do we have the courage, determination, openness, and understanding to develop to the point that giving becomes spontaneous, and the more we give, the more we find we can give?

When we talk about bodhisattvas giving even their bodies to beings, cutting off whatever pieces are needed, it is quite difficult to imagine. But bodhisattvas realize that the body is illusory and the nature of phenomena is altogether dreamlike, so whatever they give is replaced. There is actually no concept that one thing should be kept and another given. They can give all the time, because whatever they give is an illusion. Knowing that the nature of phenomena is a dream, they can recreate that dream at any time.

Beginners in the practice of generosity are not all alike. Some people have very little courage, and for them a gradual approach is beneficial. Others are immediately very courageous—they can do anything. Do we have the courage to say, "Yes, I can give this up, I want to give it for the benefit of others"? If so, we do not have to hold back because we are beginners. If we feel absolutely sure what we are doing is appropriate, we should go ahead and give.

The second aspect of the practice of generosity is generosity of protection or refuge. This can be done in different ways and on different levels in various situations. For example, statues of buddhas and bodhisattvas have been made and volumes of Buddhist scriptures have been produced. These give tremendous inspiration and confidence to many people. If any such statues or scriptures are lying in places where they could easily be destroyed by fire or water or other means, we can build a shelter to save them from such destruction, so people can take advantage of them in the future. This would be offering protection.

If practitioners of the Dharma are engaged in the solitary practice of meditation and discipline, and there is danger of their practice being disturbed, we can protect them from such disturbance. If the peace, harmony, and friendship of the sangha is in danger of being disrupted by misunderstandings and conflict, we can protect them from such disharmony. If certain great practitioners are living up to many profound precepts, and there is a danger of their being caused to violate their discipline, we can protect them from such violations. In this way, we can offer different levels of protection.

Unfortunately, many undesirable things take place in mundane society. People sometimes use their power to frighten, torture, and harm others. We can try to protect beings from such fears, dangers, and insults in whatever way we can—physically, through words, or by using our wealth. We can protect those in the midst of worries and sadness by giving them consolation and attention. We can protect those who suffer from terrible sicknesses by providing treatment.

We might find two ignorant animals, one killing the other. One is killing in fear; the other is being killed in fear. We can intervene, protecting the one from the fear of having to kill and the other from the fear of being killed. We might come across animals who have wandered onto the road unknowingly, or who are stunned and lying on the road, and we can pick them up and move them away. Someone might be about to kill an animal, and we can buy that animal and let it go. In all these unfortunate situations, we can practice giving protection to beings.

The third aspect of the practice of generosity is giving the gift of the Dharma by making the teachings available. Through the Dharma, we can bring understanding into the lives of others and help them remove their patterns of ignorance. We do not have to be great scholars to practice generosity through the Dharma. We may know just one line of the Dharma, but if we know that one line clearly and correctly, we can genuinely express it to others and help them. If we know four lines of the teachings, through those four lines we can help to clear up someone's ignorance or lessen someone's problems and sufferings. What counts is not how much we know but how correctly we know it and how sincerely we use it to help others. We should not wear the mask of the Dharma, pretending we know a great deal and are doing great things, while hiding ugliness inside us.

When we give the gift of the Dharma, we should give it tirelessly. One explanation may not be enough. The other person may not understand it, or we may not arouse the interest of that other person. If we really wish to benefit others, we should not give up but should continue to explain the teachings many times in different ways and in different situations. Of course, this should not be done with any impure attitude, such as wishing to be regarded as very knowledgeable, to be honored as a teacher, or to be served and presented with many good things. All that should matter to us is benefiting others. Finally, we should dedicate the merit of this practice for the good of all beings. In these many ways, we can benefit others through the gifts of the Dharma.

The fourth aspect of the practice of generosity is giving loving-kindness and tenderness. If we are kind and compassionate toward others, we are being generous because we are not harming others as we might otherwise be doing. This feeling of loving-kindness and tenderness is not just extended toward our friends and associates—people we feel close to. We have equal concern for all beings, whoever or wherever they are, no matter what their background. All beings desire happiness and do not desire suffering, so what difference is there? We extend loving-kindness and compassion toward all beings, thinking, "May all beings be happy. May all beings be without suffering." This is generosity in the sense that we are not harming others, and we are therefore not harming ourselves, which is very wise.

This is a very brief explanation of the practice of generosity in general together with four specific aspects of the practice of generosity.

The Six Perfections 149

Q: Is loving-kindness just an attitude?

A: Yes, it is basically an attitude. If we have a kind and gentle attitude, that will bring about a very healthy and pleasant atmosphere. We will extend a quality of warmth that makes other people feel relaxed and comfortable. Since we are members of society, this will contribute toward a more pleasant and livable society. As a simple example, if our leaders are very kind, compassionate, loving people, and they go away for a time, when we hear that they are coming back, we feel very happy. We want to celebrate that day in some way. There is warmth and openness, and everyone's spirits are lifted up. But if our leaders are very aggressive and angry, when they return after an absence, our reaction is to look for a place to hide and do our best to avoid them. If loving-kindness is in our hearts and we sincerely mean it, we will express it with our words and gestures. That will bring about warmth and friendship.

Q: Rinpoche, you spoke about helping prevent one animal from killing another animal. In the West, we believe that for certain animals, their nature is to kill, and they would not be able to eat if they did not kill other animals. Would you comment on that?

A: Yes, it is true that certain animals are born to survive by killing others. This very unfortunate pattern comes about because of past karmic conditioning. These animals have no wisdom; they just immediately kill other animals. Not only have they taken a very unfortunate birth in this lifetime, but this also signals a worse state of existence in the future, since killing others can only result in more suffering and pain. As people who are living up to the bodhisattva attitude, we should have equal compassion toward the one being killed and the one doing the killing.

It is very unfortunate to be killed, to be the victim, but it is equally unfortunate to be the killer of another being. As a result of killing, one will have to go through immeasurable suffering. It is really not worth it. If one had the choice and realization, it would be much better to starve. If we are in a position to prevent this killing from happening, we should do so with equal compassion and concern for both beings. This does not mean we are causing the animal to starve when we stop it from devouring another one. We will not always be able to keep it from feeding. It will find more prey, but we will have done our part.

Ordinarily, when we talk about being compassionate, we are frankly not being compassionate at all. When we say we hate a person who has killed or beaten another, that is not compassion but aggression and attachment. We hate the person who killed because we had attachment toward the person who was killed, so where is the compassion? Compassion is having an equal concern for both. It is just as unfortunate to be the killer as to be the victim, if not more so. Our idea of suffering goes only so far. There is much more we cannot pretend to comprehend, so it is important to have equal compassion toward all beings.

THE PERFECTION OF DISCIPLINE

The second of the six perfections is discipline, which is *shila* in Sanskrit. Discipline has three aspects. The first is not harming others or ourselves, the second is doing what is wholesome and virtuous for ourselves, and the third is helping others.

The first aspect of discipline is making a commitment not to do harmful things to ourselves and others. When we become practitioners of the Dharma, we are expected to change our attitudes and conduct from what they were before we practiced the Dharma. Our behavior is expected to become permanently more wholesome and virtuous. When we did not know about the wholesomeness of the Dharma, we were swayed by our patterns of aggression, attachment, and ignorance. We engaged in many kinds of activities that were harmful to ourselves and harmful to others. Now we are practitioners of the Dharma. With the knowledge we have now and the transformation we are trying to bring about in ourselves, it would be quite foolish to repeat the same mistakes.

This commitment not to engage further in harmful activities can be practiced both informally and formally. Informally, as we begin to understand the Dharma and develop a little wisdom, we begin to have a saner sense of discrimination. We see how ridiculous it would be to do a certain negative action and to keep repeating it. We will not do this any more. We will not repeat this ever again, because it is so harmful to others, so harmful to ourselves, and so destructive. We realize that this activity is a weakness. We understand that because of a long history of attachment, it is very difficult to abandon this activity, but we will try diligently to give it up. In this way we transform our pattern of activities.

The formal way of ceasing to engage in harmful activities is to take some level of moral precepts, vowing never to do particular harmful acts again. For example, we may take on one or more of the lay precepts (not killing, not stealing, not indulging in sexual misconduct, not lying, and not consuming intoxicants). In formal as well as informal ways, we discontinue our old patterns of harming ourselves and others.

Because of the compassionate nature of the teachings, the methods are very practical and versatile. As far as formal disciplines are concerned, we can take anywhere from one to 253 precepts.[19] If we take one such precept, it does not mean we have to take all 253 precepts. The precepts range from one to 253 because not all people are equally determined or equally courageous in taking on such disciplines; therefore, we take whatever precepts we can keep. The more we take, the better, but if we take even one precept, we take on a discipline that serves as a basis and a support for more effective practice of the Dharma.

Also, there is ample room for adapting the precepts to whatever period of time we are able to follow such a discipline. There are precepts we can take for just one day, for overnight, for several days, for a year, for several years, and for a lifetime. Again, it depends on how determined we are in our commitment. Once we have taken on whatever disciplines we can, the benefit they give is real. It is like a texture that will continuously affect our practice of the Dharma, giving a helpful and effective tone to our practice.

The second aspect of discipline is making a commitment to do what is wholesome and virtuous for ourselves. For example, we may make a commitment to get up earlier than usual in the morning to do a certain practice, such as prostrations. Or we may resolve to go to bed later so we can practice meditation in the evening. We may resolve that, while today we were unfortunately not able to do much practice, tomorrow we will definitely do a certain number of hours. Perhaps today we have been able to do quite a lot of practice, so we resolve that tomorrow we will make it a point to do even more. In this way, we make a commitment to be more sincere and diligent in our practice, and thus to become more involved in wholesome activities for our own benefit.

The third aspect of discipline is making a commitment to help others, particularly from the point of view of the Dharma. In whatever way we can help others with their practice of the Dharma, we do so tirelessly. If one effort does not give others enough help and encouragement, we continue our efforts to support and inspire them. We encourage others in any way we can, practicing together with them or doing whatever seems to help them with their practice.

The least we can do to help others is to dedicate the merit of whatever practice we have done toward the benefit of others. We extend the attitude, ''May this merit help others become connected with the Dharma. For all those who have made a connection with the Dharma, may their practice continue unobstructed for the benefit of beings.'' In this way, we can help others by dedicating our merit toward their benefit.

Questions

Q: When we practice a sadhana, the dedication of merit is written into the text. If we practice something such as a mantra, and we want to dedicate the merit, can we make up a dedication of the merit for the benefit of all sentient beings, or does it always have to be a formal prayer?

A: The most important thing, of course, is the attitude. If you are doing a particular sadhana, you say whatever dedication prayer is incorporated in the text. Otherwise, you can make something up or you can generate the attitude. As long as you have an understanding of what you are doing, you can just dedicate the merit mentally. If you want to express it in words, you can also do that.

When you have done a certain practice, you do not hold onto the merit and keep it to yourself but dedicate it for the benefit of beings. You give it all up for the benefit of beings, with the attitude, "May this merit cause beings temporary and ultimate benefit. Temporarily may all beings—wherever they are, whatever they are doing—experience happiness, well-being, satisfaction, harmony, and goodness, and may everything run smoothly for them. Ultimately, may this merit cause beings to experience complete liberation, so that they no longer have to be subject to cyclic existence." With that attitude, you dedicate the merit of your practice.

Q: I have heard stories of meditation masters who get drunk in public and have sex with their students. This disconcerts me and makes me very uneasy with the practice. Sometimes it even breaks my confidence in the practice. I wonder if such a person can speak the truth. Am I being too judgmental or too naive?

A: As students and beginners, we must learn not to judge a teacher but rather to judge the teaching. We must examine the teaching, analyze it, and see whether that teaching is suitable for our minds and our lifestyles. If we see a fault in an individual teacher, we should not mix it with the teaching. This is very important. Some people, seeing the faults of an individual teacher, think the teaching itself is mistaken. Many teachers are at a very beginning level. Take me for example, an unqualified teacher, ignorant, possessing all the kleshas, yet trying to give people teachings that I myself am not certain about. It is important for us to examine and judge the teaching rather than the teacher. If the teaching is suitable and helpful, follow it and forget about the teacher's behavior.

It is especially important not to judge realized beings by ordinary standards. If you read the life stories of the eighty-four mahasiddhas, you will find that their behavior was unbelievable—they killed, they had sex, they drank alcohol—yet their teaching was effective. We cannot take the behavior of such enlightened beings in the same way as we do the behavior of ordinary people. At the same time, we must be careful not to indulge in this negative behavior ourselves. A realized person may sometimes have to perform different kinds of negative or positive actions in order to tame the mind of a student. As students, we should take everything in the behavior of the teacher as a way of taming our minds, and we should take the teaching itself—the Dharma—very seriously.

THE PERFECTION OF PATIENCE

The third of the six paramitas is the perfection of patience, which has three aspects. The first is having patience with the various problems and difficulties we go through in life, so we can accomplish our goals. The second is having patience with the practice of the Dharma until we reach the point where we have genuine experience and confidence. The third is having patience and tolerance when others harm us or give us any kind of problem.

Patience in Everyday Life

The practice of the Dharma is important in the mundane aspect of our lives as well as in the spiritual aspect. In fact, the practice of the Dharma is a way of life. Sometimes we have the idea that spiritual is on one shore and mundane on the other, so the two can never meet. Of course, if we become completely engrossed in mundane affairs and indulgences, we will have no understanding of spirituality. However, that is not because the two cannot go together but because we are not open and intelligent enough to work with both of them. In order to follow the path of the Dharma, we do not immediately have to renounce the world and leave everything behind. As we continue to practice the Dharma, we will begin to realize how trivial and unimportant many of our worldly pursuits are. We will see that the practice of the Dharma is all that really matters. At that point, we can discard what is unimportant, not because we were forced to do so but because we are able to manage our affairs well.

If we take a look at the ordinary world, we may see people with many advantages—wealth, popularity, and education— who do not accomplish as much as they could. They make a great commotion with what they do, becoming frustrated and upset and often not finishing their work. There seems to be no point in their being such popular, rich, and intelligent people. We may see others who are poor and deprived of opportunities for education, wealth, and popularity. They have difficulties, feel downtrodden, and are full of self-pity, and also do not accomplish much. Either way, there can be a problem. It is like the play of the scales. If we put a little more on one side, they go one way; if we put a little more on the other side, they go the other way, never staying still. This is because people do not have patience or understand the benefits of moderation.

Sometimes we have problems, worries, and suffering, simply because we did not have the patience we needed to succeed in what we were doing. If we have patience, when we set out to accomplish a particular project, we work on it steadily and carry it through until we finish it. If we do not have patience, we touch one thing a little and we fiddle with another, and suddenly we find there were many things to do, but none of them is done. We are full of frustration, very mixed up and upset. Trying to find some place to put the blame does not help. We continue to suffer, because we do not have patience. At other times we do succeed in finishing some project, but then begin to take on more and more projects, beyond what is necessary and reasonable. This is because we do not understand the benefits of moderation.

Furthermore, we often encounter disappointments. When something goes a little wrong we become upset, because we have no patience. We have no idea of the benefits of patience or even what patience is. We become bothered, agitated, and nervous when any small disturbance occurs. This is totally unnecessary. Actually, we have used this situation as a kind of feedback. We have intensified and amplified the situation through our own patterns. It seems almost as if it were necessary for us to become nervous and frustrated. Of course, the experience is not at all pleasant. We want to justify blaming things on someone else, so we make it painful for ourselves. This is quite unrealistic and in some sense totally ridiculous.

If we develop patience and some understanding of moderation, we can accomplish what we set out to do, and we can put up with the pain we make for ourselves as well as any intrusions made by others. If we have a strong wish to benefit others, we have about us an air of gentleness. As we practice the Dharma, we bring some degree of firmness to this gentleness, being able to tolerate any difficulty or interference, because we have a commitment to benefit others. If we always live up to our commitments, we have dignity and are worthy of trust and respect. The practice of patience is important in our lives, no matter who we are or what our background is. At the beginning, we may not always be completely patient, but with practice we can learn.

As practitioners of the Dharma, we must be sincere, diligent, and intelligent. We must know what is truly important and sensible to do. Sometimes we think of the Dharma as a kind of last resort, turning to the Dharma when we do not succeed in the world. That idea is completely wrong. Many practitioners of the Dharma have become highly realized because they could handle not only their mundane responsibilities but also their spiritual responsibilities. Spiritual practice is much more difficult than any kind of mundane undertaking. These people practiced the Dharma, not because they were running away from things they could not handle, but because spirituality was the most significant element in their lives. For us also, the practice of the Dharma is an important element that can make our lives more complete and meaningful.

Patience in the Practice of the Dharma

The second aspect of patience is patience in the practice of the Buddhist teachings, such as meditation practice. As ordinary beings we are sometimes able to be kind and open to others and to tolerate whatever harm is being directed toward us, but we cannot do this all the time. We do not at this point have such indestructible qualities that we can always benefit others and that no harm can bother us. The practice of the Dharma is directed toward developing such qualities, and this practice requires patience.

Suppose we are in a situation where we and many other people are afflicted by a particular disease. We are distressed by the suffering everyone is going through and we develop the conviction that something must be done about it. We might study medicine and work toward being able to practice it. Not only would we train ourselves about medicine in general, but also about what kind of medicine works for which ailments and how to give the correct treatment. If we did this, we could eliminate the disease that is afflicting so many people.

Similarly, we may have a sense that, from the point of view of the ordinary world, people are quite intelligent and capable of taking care of their needs, but most people have great confusion, frustration, and worry. No matter how precisely things are done, and what methods and approaches are used by various people, we sense that something is missing from their lives and ours. The remedy is none other than the practice of the Dharma—the path that leads from confusion and suffering to happiness and clarity.

As I have said, the practice of the Dharma demands a certain amount of patience. First, we must hear the Dharma. Then we must study the Dharma, not just enough to have some idea of what it might mean but enough to know and understand the meaning completely. Furthermore, we must investigate how the teachings relate to our lives. Hearing and studying the Dharma is not enough, however, just as knowing about various medicines is not enough. We must take the medicines, and learn how to administer them to others and what kind of effects they will have. Likewise, once we know the Dharma, we must practice it diligently. Understanding and practicing the Dharma requires a certain amount of patience.

In order to fulfill this important task, we may have to give up some things we enjoy and we may have to give up some time. We may have to go to particular places at particular times to do specific practices or hear certain explanations. Some physical and mental work may be required, and there may be some expense. Studying the teachings once may not bring a complete understanding; we may have to continue to study. Practicing a given meditation once may not bring the desired realizations; we may need to practice consistently. If we are to meet the necessary requirements and experience the real benefit, we must have patience.

Patience does not mean simply tolerating our suffering and the suffering of others, but it means working to eliminate suffering through the practice of the Dharma. We must always be concerned not only with eliminating our own suffering, but also with liberating others from various kinds of suffering, both physical and psychological. This should be more than an aspiration. In addition to having the wish that beings not experience certain kinds of suffering, we should train ourselves so we can actually help others. In order to accomplish this, simply hearing about various aspects of the teachings and various possible methods is not enough, nor is it enough to understand and know the conceptual meaning of the teachings. We must have some direct experience of the meaning of the teachings.

For example, if we are to help others with the philosophy or the psychology of the Dharma, we will not be able to bring about an effective improvement in someone's life by simply knowing the words. We must know the meaning of the words, and we must also have a certain amount of experience. Only then will we be able to give guidance as to the possible sidetracks and the most effective way to approach the practice. We should be able to give not only one instruction, but also further instructions in what might happen, what might not happen, and so forth. If we do not have the experience ourselves, we will not be able to give such practical explanations and information. From that point of view, we must study, understand, and practice the Dharma both for our own benefit and for the benefit of others. This certainly demands patience.

You may have heard the names of the incomparable forefathers of the Kagyu lineage. Marpa, one of the great masters of the lineage, studied and practiced the teachings for forty years before he gave teachings, instructions, and transmissions. Through his great learning and experience, he became one of the most prominent holders of the Kagyu lineage, the treasury of teachings and the profound path that we have the opportunity to hear and experience even to this day. Marpa's foremost disciple, Milarepa—also one of the exceptional holders of the Kagyu lineage—studied and analyzed the teachings for many years. He then went into intensive non-stop practice of the teachings for twelve years, twelve months, and twelve days. Because of his patience and endurance in the practice of the Dharma, Milarepa's tradition is still very much a living practice, even though centuries have passed. To this day, disciples go back to the inspiration and examples manifested through the lives of such beings.

We have the same potential for practice and realization within us. The more we study and understand and practice the Dharma, the greater will be our appreciation of the Dharma as a tool for eliminating suffering and confusion. The more we realize this and begin to taste the possibility of liberation from suffering, the more we will long to continue the practice of the Dharma and the more effective our practice will become. In the beginning stages, a certain amount of diligence, commitment, and patience is necessary.

We should understand that Milarepa began as an ordinary human being. He was not some exceptional being who had all the realizations from the very beginning. Like any other human being, he had emotions, feelings, sensitivity to heat and cold, and so forth. Yet he lived in a cave in the coldest of places, with no mat to sit on or sleep on, hardly anything to wear, and only nettles for his food. He did not do this because he was helpless or could not take care of the mundane side of life. He was not running away from the responsibilities of the world. He could have done much better than most of us. The fact was simply that he understood the Dharma and saw in it something far more profound than is found in all other endeavors. The more he practiced, the greater was his experience of joy, sanity, and tranquility. The more he experienced these qualities, the less he needed to be concerned with other things, and they became very much secondary.

Like Milarepa, in order for us to appreciate the nature of the Buddha's teachings fully, we need to commit ourselves to understanding and practicing them. Without sincere, correct, and diligent practice, it is not of much practical use simply to witness certain sessions of teachings or study the teachings for a short time in an intellectual way. We should have a sense of aspiration that we sincerely wish to benefit other beings. To benefit others, we must practice the Dharma. To practice the Dharma, we must understand it first. By going through these stages, we can benefit both ourselves and others.

Milarepa said that what is rare is achieved through endurance and patience. This is true of anything we are involved in, whether mundane or spiritual. In our ordinary world, many people may be engaged in a particular field or profession, but only a few succeed. Only a few have sufficient perseverance and patience to pursue all the necessary studies, activities, or projects. Those who do not have enough diligence and patience do not succeed. They do not achieve what is rarely achieved. Likewise, there are very few people who truly, sincerely wish to benefit others and have the ability to do so. All of us have the potential, but most of us fail to recognize and acknowledge that potential and put it to proper use. We must learn to have confidence that we can actually benefit others through the practice of the Dharma. To have confidence in the Dharma, we must study and understand it. In this way, we can develop our potential.

When we engage in the practice of the Dharma, we may encounter obstacles, hindrances, or interferences, and we must have patience to overcome them. Sometimes we feel insecure and are afraid we lack the capacity for Dharma practice. Sometimes we feel we cannot understand the teachings, or we develop fear of emptiness. But if we are diligent practitioners, we can tolerate such obstacles and go beyond them because we appreciate the importance of the task we are engaged in. We begin to develop such patience that no interference or distraction can hinder or stop our work.

Actually, for a true practitioner of the Dharma, obstacles can be used as vehicles for further progress on the path. For example, when Milarepa was meditating in his cave, there was once a great snowfall that lasted for eighteen days and nights. Whatever birds and animals could escape the snow did so, and those that could not escape were buried under the snow. For a long time he could not hear anything from outside—no sound of birds, no sound of animals, no sound of other human beings, nothing. Instead of bothering Milarepa, this outer silence gave him an opportunity to work on inner tranquility. It was terribly cold during the many days of snow, but instead of filling him with frustration, this outer cold gave him an opportunity to experience the inner heat. The storm also made it quite impossible to obtain ordinary food. This gave Milarepa the opportunity to practice living on the food of meditation. Milarepa was of course an advanced practitioner; nevertheless, this story shows how any obstacle can be used as an opportunity rather than a hindrance in the life of a practitioner.

Patience When Others Cause Harm
The third aspect of patience is having tolerance whenever any harm or disturbance is directed toward us by others. With

patience, we are not motivated to take revenge. Sometimes, even if we do not or cannot fight back with our bodily actions or speech, there is a plot or a strong wish to retaliate in our minds. With patience, we are not motivated to take revenge through our bodily actions and speech, or even to plot revenge in our minds.

How can we experience such a quality of patience? First we must realize the benefits of the practice of patience. We must understand that the other person is projecting the disturbance and harm toward us, not because it is a pleasant experience or of great benefit to him or her, but out of utter confusion. When a person is already going through a great deal of confusion, how can we add to that confusion by retaliating? From that point of view, there is no sense in taking revenge or making any kind of aggressive attack. Also, what benefit do we gain from retaliating? It really gives no benefit at all, so the attempt would not be worthwhile.

It is very clear to us that we long for happiness and peace and we do not long for sufferings of any kind or in any measure. As much as this is true for us, it is true for all other beings without exception. It is very important to understand this. As much as we do not wish for suffering and confusion, as much as we wish for happiness and peace, that much all beings wish for the same thing. From that point of view, how could we harm others? How could we bring afflictions into the lives of others when we know how much they wish to experience happiness and well-being and not to experience suffering? If we try to protect ourselves from experiencing suffering and confusion, we should also be responsible for not causing any harm to others.

For example, because you like your left hand so much, you would not pinch or cut your right hand. It feels pain just as much as your left hand. It would be foolish to say you have greater admiration for one hand than the other, or one is more valuable than the other. Such a distinction makes no sense at all. The wish to experience happiness and peace and not to experience suffering is the same for all beings. If we harm someone else, it is like harming a part of our own body, because the experience of pain is the same for all beings.

Second, we must realize the shortcomings of aggression. Aggression is a very destructive pattern in our lives that we must learn to control and uproot. We have never heard of a person who was very happy because he or she experienced aggression. When we are overwhelmed by aggression, we cannot appreciate our food or even taste it. We cannot communicate properly. We cannot even rest or sleep because of the upheaval of this negative emotion. It can reach the epitome of ignorance in which a person overwhelmed by aggression takes his or her life, mistakenly thinking this is the best way to end things. Such a person has not the slightest idea of the future consequences and does not even understand the negative and destructive nature of such an act. Is it worthwhile to let ourselves be overwhelmed and imprisoned by the pattern of aggression?

Aggression makes life unpleasant not only for us but for others. It interferes with our relationships. We may have a very pleasant and wonderful friendship, but it can all be destroyed by a sudden upheaval of the pattern of aggression. In a family, tremendous pain and confusion result when aggression is projected. For example, when a family member who is filled with aggression has gone somewhere, the family is filled with laughter and joy, and good things happen. As soon as this person comes back, everyone becomes quiet. Things become cold and frozen. On the other hand, when a person known for gentleness, loving-kindness, and patience goes away, this person is missed. When this person comes home, there is a great welcome, not because he or she is bringing big presents or rewards to anyone, but simply because the person's presence is very enjoyable and pleasant. Thus on a very basic level, we can begin to understand how destructive aggression is both to us and to others.

The psychology and practice of aggression takes us even further than that, however. Developing and intensifying such a pattern can result in being born in the lower realms, where we undergo various kinds of intense psychological suffering.

The different realms, the heavens and hells, are not places someone has prepared for us. Whatever birth we experience, with its psychological sufferings or happiness, is of our own making. We do not go to a particular place where suffering or bliss is planned for us. We cause ourselves to enter a certain kind of psychological pattern. If we find ourselves in a situation where there is tremendous confusion and unspeakable suffering, it is caused by nothing other than our own pattern of aggression.

Because of our pattern of aggression, we often become overwhelmed by anger. If we examine what causes us to become so angry and aggressive, even in a mundane context, we usually cannot find a valid reason for putting on such a show. If we became angry and aggressive because someone harmed us, caused us physical pain, or robbed us of our wealth, then in a mundane context, there would be a reason for it. Although it is far from the most wise or beneficial thing to do, there is some logic to it. However, most of the time there is no reason at all.

For example, suppose someone came to me and said, ''I think you are a terrible person.'' I might become so upset and defensive, so overwhelmed by anger, that I would harm this person for saying that. But in reality, what have those words done to me? Have they caused me an untimely death of some kind, robbed me of my wealth, hurt my body, or made me uglier? Those empty words have actually made no difference at all. In such a situation, we are confused. We feel that some irreparable harm has been done to us. Actually, the words have not done the harm; we are doing the harm to ourselves. The harm is from our pattern of aggression, not from the words. It is as if we need an excuse to become angry, which makes no sense because all we do is harm ourselves.

On the other hand, if we tolerate the words and pay no attention to them, we feel more comfortable. We do not have to beg for praise and attention. Other people will naturally say, ''Oh, what a patient, tolerant person.'' Even the person who spoke the words may say at some future time, ''Yes, it really makes sense that this person did not react angrily to the stupid way I acted." Without any argument about who is right and who is wrong, our very behavior would give the best answer.

Furthermore, as responsible people we must learn to accept our faults and limitations instead of trying to project them onto someone else. A person may say something about us that is not very pleasant but is actually quite true. If someone says the truth about us, how can we argue? For example, suppose someone came to me and said, "You look dumb." I would say, "How? I talk; how can you say I am dumb?" The person would respond, "Because you cannot speak English; you cannot communicate with me." And that is quite true. When it comes to the English language, I might as well be dumb. I must accept that; it would not get me anywhere to argue. Many times we have difficulty accepting our faults. We think others are responsible for anything we do not want to deal with. This is very unfair and selfish.

In another situation, a person might say to me, "I think you are blind." I would become very upset and ask, "Why do you think I'm blind?" The person might say, "Because you do not see as I see." Now that person is in no position to say any such thing, but is saying it out of ignorance and stupidity. The person really cannot know what I see or how I see. That puts me in a position to generate compassion for the one who is making such an ignorant statement. When a person is confused, how can we add to the suffering and, by doing so, actually make the situation harmful to ourselves?

The experience of nonaggression will not be achieved overnight. The pattern of aggression has been deeply ingrained in our minds for a long time. However, it is possible to change it. This is a real psychological possibility that human beings can commit themselves to. It is not some kind of mystical transformation. You can begin to change the pattern of aggression by understanding how pointless it is to project such a negative pattern and become so overwhelmed by it. You must remind yourself of the beneficial nature of patience and the harmful nature of aggression, and train yourself in a proper, wholesome attitude. You must do this individually. No matter how much money you are willing to spend, no one can put patience into you. It is an individual matter.

The mindfulness must be there before a situation arises that could produce an upheaval of your pattern of aggression. In the midst of an outburst of anger, you may suddenly have the thought, "This is not right. This is a very futile thing to do," but you will not be able to stop the intense emotion. In fact, you may become even more frustrated. On the other hand, if the antidote is invoked before something happens that could stimulate your pattern of aggression, you are prepared to handle the situation. You will not become completely overwhelmed by anger.

The experience of aggression produces a kind of blindness, in that we see the faults of other people but never see our own. When we are filled with aggression, we think one person is wrong, another has done harm, or another is not being honest. The fault is all with others and none is with us. This blindness induces many unpleasant feelings, doubts, and suspicions. We suffer because we feel others are against us and are deceiving us, but the fault is actually ours.

For example, if we have very bad eyes, whatever we are looking at seems to be defective in some way. One object is not very clear. Another does not have a good shape. Something is wrong with everything we see. There is not really anything wrong with the objects; we simply have bad eyes. We need to treat our eyes, not change the objects. If we work on the objects, that will not help. The objects will still look bad, because the problem is not there but with us. To bring about changes that are necessary and possible, we must understand what really needs to be done.

Some of you may conclude that, while all of these arguments sound good and seem to make sense, they are not realistic. You may say, "I cannot change. I have been like this all of my life; it is my personality. This behavior is natural to me." You have many excuses and rationalizations, but what you are saying is not the truth. If you cannot change, you would have been angry every moment of your life. Obviously you have not been. Sometimes you have been aggressive and angry, and sometimes you have been full of joy, even wanting to help others. The idea that you cannot change comes from ignorance and a wish to make excuses. If anything can change, it is certainly the mind.

The mind is very flexible and changeable. One moment we are happy and excited, full of wonderful plans. The next moment we are upset and anxious, with no sense of ground whatsoever. Suppose for some reason you have just projected your anger toward someone, and that person says, "I am sorry, it was my fault. I apologize." The anger and aggression disappear. You say, "Oh, that is all right, I am fine," and it is gone. Clearly, anger is not a fixed pattern of your personality. Suppose you are full of joy and full of life, and then someone says something rude to you. You become very upset. It does not take drastic measures to stimulate your negative patterns. At the same time, it is not very difficult to release or diminish such emotions if you have a correct understanding, know the proper techniques, and apply those techniques sincerely.

We must understand that the experience of nonaggression is possible, then train the mind toward such an experience. Once the mind is properly trained and controlled, the body and speech will naturally follow the discipline and direction of the mind. On the other hand, if the mind is going wild, trying to discipline the body and speech in a strict way will leave us feeling very tight and imprisoned. Because the mind is not established in a state of peace and tranquility, we will have many complaints, such as "I feel very sick from trying to do this." It is very important to know how to work with the mind, and this is an individual responsibility.

Through the understanding and practice of Buddhist psychology, it is possible to bring about peace in the world. This will not happen magically, but very simply and realistically, through individual practice. If you have developed patience, your experience of nonaggression is a contribution toward the peace of the world. There is a tremendous amount of chaos, conflict, and warfare in the world, and this is all because the world is filled with aggressive people. If you are an aggressive person, it is like having a contagious disease. You are never welcome anywhere. Wherever you go, you bring discord. You say, "Oh, the country is no good, the people are no good." Actually, what is wrong with the people? If anything is wrong, it is with you. You have the greatest faults yet make the greatest complaints. If you are aggressive, no matter where you go, you will be a problem to yourself and to others. When many aggressive people meet together, there is conflict and warfare. You are part of the world, and you have an individual responsibility not to misuse your role in it. Rather than projecting aggression, if you experience peace in your own mind, this will help more to bring peace to the world than any superficial talk about peace.

Buddhist psychology is very practical. There is tremendous respect for the individual. No one has to take responsibility for you; you are capable of being a dignified and gracious person. You must learn to do that by yourself. If you are a person with great patience, a nonaggressive person, no matter where you go, you will be welcome. Everyone will speak highly of you; everyone will love you. No matter what culture or tradition you encounter, you will fit in. It seems almost miraculous, but it is simply the practice of patience.

It is very important to know and apply the methods for subduing the pattern of aggression. We must realize that there is nothing in the world so demonic or terrible as aggression. This is not an outside force. We worry about being harmed by outside forces, but no outside force causes more harm than we cause ourselves through aggression. We have the potential for quite a different experience. To make this a reality, well-designed methods have been practiced, experienced, and confirmed by people in many walks of life. Instead of finding ways to blame others for our problems, instead of postponing the opportunity that is available, the practical thing is to pursue these practices. In the beginning, it is important to have a correct understanding and confidence in the methods. Diligence and discipline are required, along with a commitment not to turn back. Then gradually the practice will become easier, because we will experience the benefits of patience. We will appreciate the practice more, and it will make sense.

Every day we interact with many kinds of people. Not all people are perfect; in fact, almost everyone has some kind of imperfection. To begin applying the techniques to develop patience, resolve with a sense of mindfulness that today, no matter what accusations, insults, or rude comments come your way, they will not bother you or overwhelm you. If you go about the day with this attitude and with an understanding of the defects of aggression, things will be quite different. Some person may say unpleasant things to you, but it will not be a painful shock. You will be able to tolerate it. Some empty words may be said, but you will not become totally overwhelmed by them. On the other hand, if you are the usual sensitive and defensive person, any insult will shock and offend you, and you will be full of anger. It is just a matter of training yourself to bring about some element of change.

The next step is to ask the question, "Why am I aggressive?" The upheaval of aggression takes place because of your egoistic patterns. Because of ego-clinging, you have the idea that everything good should happen to you and no harm should come to you. However, the real world is quite different. You go about with a blind expectation that everyone will be kind to you and do good things for you, and no one will harm you. When a person says something harmful to you, and does not do good things for you, you become angry and aggressive toward that person, because you never expected this. Surely you must realize that you live in a world where many negative things happen. Because of the circumstances of your birth and your individual make-up, you are actually quite a vulnerable and fragile being. If you have done nothing noble or profound yourself, you cannot expect never to experience harm or disturbance from others. When you experience these things, you feel it is very unfair to be put in a position of harm. It is not that anyone is actually being unfair. You become anxious and upset because events go against your expectations, which are based on ego-clinging.

To undo the pattern of ego, with its tremendous clinging and selfishness, it is important to generate loving-kindness and compassion toward others. What does this mean? Loving-kindness is wanting to do good things for others instead of expecting to receive all the good things from them. Compassion is wanting to eliminate the sufferings of others instead of blaming others for all the suffering you experience. There is some sense of responsibility for others, wanting to benefit others and eliminate their pain.

At this point, you are not doing these things, but you are at least generating the attitude and looking at the possibilities. Right now, you have not taken on anyone's sufferings and you have not given anyone great happiness. But you are training yourself with the attitude and trying to make it familiar, so you may be able to put it into action in the distant future. At that time, you may in fact feel quite comfortable doing beneficial things for others and eliminating the suffering they are going through. This is an individual responsibility, but it is not really a great burden. I am asking you only to do what you can. At least acquaint yourself with what is possible and train yourself. Generate good intentions toward others, have compassion toward others, and envision the possibility of benefiting others and eliminating their suffering.

To develop loving-kindness and compassion, it is important to do the *tong len* or sending and receiving practice (described in the previous chapter). You imagine that you are extending loving-kindness and goodness toward others, and that others are experiencing goodness and happiness. You also imagine that you are eliminating the suffering of others. This practice is done by working with the breath, simply to train the mind. You are not really eliminating harm or bringing happiness, but you are training with the possibilities so that at some point you may be able to put some of these intentions into action.

In the Buddhist practice of patience and other related practices, the emphasis is on developing such internal qualities as genuine simplicity, compassion, kindness, and patience. When you have developed and experienced such internal qualities, you can help others. You can be very understanding, loving, kind, and compassionate with your family members: parents, children, husband, wife. You can be kind, compassionate, and gentle with your friends and associates and with people and beings in general. You can do this not with arrogance, but with humility and simplicity.

As a result of the practice, you experience a sound state of mind, more mindful, precise, and composed and less distracted in any situation. Buddhist psychology involves a simple, practical, straightforward practice, nothing really mysterious or mystical. We do not expect you to shake your body, roll your eyes, see lights, or generate rainbows from your body. What good would these do for you? In addition, if you always want to be by yourself and not associate with anyone else, you cannot claim to be practicing Buddhist psychology. Perhaps you just keep to yourself because you feel superior to everyone else, or perhaps you are a "dropout" who cannot associate with others but only with nature. This is not where Buddhist practice should lead you. Buddhist practice should help you integrate more with society and be responsive to people, something you can afford to do if you have patience. A person who does not experience patience says, "I cannot stand it; I want to be by myself." That is usually selfish. Saying this is not meant to criticize anyone, but it is simply the nature of the Buddhist practices of patience, sending and receiving, and loving-kindness and compassion to bring you closer to others.

Patience is like a beautiful ornament. When you become a person with great patience, it brings a certain element of charm to your life. You are loved by others, and you give no problems to your friends. You bring an element of joy, happiness, and calmness to other people's lives—your friends, your family, and the community. You do not have to ask to be accepted; everyone longs for your presence. Everyone looks up to you and respects you, not because you have worked for that or expected it, not because you were competing for their favor, but simply because of the nature of patience. You are respected and trusted, and you acquire dignity with the practice of patience. When you are honored, it is with sincerity, and it is something you can live up to.

I have explained certain important qualities of patience. The perfection of patience is quite a different matter and deserves more explanation; yet all of this must begin with basic meditation practice. Just hearing about patience does not mean you are experiencing it now or will easily develop it. To lay the ground for training the mind, you must first tame the mind. To tame the mind, it is extremely important to do the basic shamata practice, which develops calmness and tranquility. Then you can add the practice of patience, understanding the benefits of patience and reminding yourself to take advantage of the available antidotes. With the practice of sitting meditation and the practice of patience, it will be easy to practice the other perfections. You will feel very comfortable with the other practices. However, until you develop a calm, clear, tranquil state of mind and some degree of patience and tolerance, no matter what other practices you claim to be doing, they will not be realistic.

Questions

Q: What happens to the energy of aggression when you apply patience and other practice and study? Would you discuss the transformation of that energy of aggression?

A: When you are experiencing aggression, you sense that it has tremendous energy. Right now you are not experiencing aggression, so there is also no energy of aggression. The energy of aggression is only there when you are in a state of aggression. When the aggression goes away, the energy of the aggression does not stay with you so you could do something else with it. In terms of removing the pattern of aggression, through consistent practice you become less and less aggressive and more and more patient. This is a sign that you are applying the antidotes more and more effectively. On a more advanced level, there is another explanation that you may be given later when the right time comes.

Q: Certain associates can say things to me that spark an aggressive reaction. Why is it so easy to spark this feeling of negativity if there is not an accumulation of energy behind it?

A: This is because of your pattern of clinging to the idea that you should have all the good things, and nothing that bothers you should ever happen, as I explained earlier. This is wishful thinking, because the nature of the world is not like that at all. The ego game you have planned is itself the explanation for how easily your anger is sparked. Because you have planned such a delicate, impossible game, and there are many things that can happen, anything that jeopardizes the plan of your ego upsets you. It is not an accumulation of energy but the pattern of clinging that is at fault.

Q: Can we actually uproot negative emotions?

A: What happens is that you apply antidotes, which help prevent further upheaval of such kleshas. As the upheaval of negative emotions becomes less and less frequent and powerful, you are able to control the negative emotions, but that does not mean you have uprooted them. As you apply the antidotes further, you begin to uproot the negative emotions.

Q: Many people live in situations that are hostile to the Dharma. They have friends, roommates, parents, or spouses who are very frightened and cause obstacles, such as interrupting their privacy with television and radio. Would you give us some help in dealing with that?

A: The practice of patience definitely comes in here. We might become very upset and blame these people for everything, but that would not be fair. If you take a close look at them, you may find they have a certain amount of confusion. If they understood things better, they would not cause such obstacles. You can afford to practice patience and develop compassion.

You can think, "May they make a connection with the Dharma themselves. May I help open them up to wider perspectives about what is possible in their lives. May I do something good for them, benefit them, and be patient with them." You are being presented with an opportunity, and it is important to do whatever you can to tolerate the situation.

You have the idea of doing a particular practice. If you are completely involved in the practice, any interference that occurs may not bother you at all. If the interference does bother you, you are not limited to this particular practice (for example, sitting meditation). Now you have an opportunity to practice patience and compassion instead, so you turn to these aspects of skillful means and practice them.

Through the practice of shamata meditation, you will experience calmness of the mind, and gain insight and a better perspective on things. You will begin to see the possibility of patience, and develop confidence in your ability to integrate it into your practice. Then you will find you have become quite different. You will be able to tolerate situations you could not have put up with in the past. You will find it unnecessary to complain or to blame others, which does not help at all. If you blame others you are being inconsiderate because, as we said earlier, if the other person knew any better, he or she would not do something that bothers you.

For example, if you have a friend who is drunk, and you fight with him or her, what is the difference between you and the drunk friend? If you are considerate, you would try to keep this person from getting into trouble. If you think this drunk friend of yours should not do something, it makes no sense to become angry and start beating him or her. Instead, you would give the person a lot of space, watch the situation, and bring up whatever matters you can.

If others are involved in a certain amount of confusion, and you know something to say that you are quite certain would help to change things, then say it. If there is no room for that, attacking them or threatening them will not benefit the situation. So skillfulness is important.

THE PERFECTION OF ENTHUSIASTIC EFFORT

The fourth of the six perfections is diligence or enthusiastic effort. Thus far I have covered the perfections of generosity, discipline, and patience. The sequence is important in terms of ground, path, and fruition. It would be difficult for a beginner to develop the perfection of wisdom immediately. We begin by working on the material level, which is familiar to us. We practice generosity by learning to give to others more freely, by becoming more hospitable, and by helping others. When we are able to be kind and generous to others, a sense of openness arises naturally. Because of the benefits of generosity, we become less entangled in the enticements of the material world, and this lays the foundation for discipline. Discipline means not being swayed by the objects of aggression and attachment, not being controlled by gain and loss, love and hate, and so forth. When we acquire discipline, we can manage our affairs more effectively. We are more collected, because our minds are not scattered everywhere with many preoccupations.

When we understand generosity and discipline, we can better comprehend the idea of patience. Having developed generosity, we have a desire to help others, so we would never want to harm others or create problems for them. Even if others give us problems and difficulties out of ignorance, we can be patient with them. Having developed discipline, we have more virtuous attitudes and actions, and thus we can cultivate patience.

Discipline and patience contribute to a rational and wholesome way of life. Things begin to come together and run smoothly in a very dignified manner. This is a joyful and uplifting experience. With this joyful experience, we want to make our practice more consistent, extensive, and successful. No matter how much we perform generosity or discipline or patience, it is a joy rather than a burden. In this way we begin to develop diligence, which is joy in the practice of virtue.

Diligence is a very sound practice even in mundane life. Although we may have a difficult project that requires a great deal of work, we have no resentment. It is a pleasure and a joy for us to do this kind of work. When we have a sense of openness and acceptance, we are able to accomplish even the most difficult project. As we work, we experience happiness rather than aversion, resentment, or exhaustion. On the other hand, when we are reluctant and resentful, doing a project against our will, even the smallest task brings many complaints, and we may do the job badly. There is no joy in the work, because we cannot accept the assignment openly.

As we practice the Dharma, we find a vast amount of material available to study that we are able to understand and appreciate. As we develop an understanding of various aspects of the Dharma, we experience joy. When we practice the Dharma with joy, we do not have problems. Indeed, we find it a most invigorating experience!

There are two aspects of diligence. The first is carrying out our responsibilities consistently and regularly. For example, if there is a piece of work we should do every day, this aspect of diligence means we will do it without fail. It is important to have a commitment to keep it up. If we are responsible and trustworthy about our commitments, we will do our work every day without excuses or complaints. We make it clear to ourselves that we will definitely carry it out, no matter what happens.

This aspect of diligence—always keeping to our commitments and responsibilities—is the antidote for procrastination, which is a type of laziness. Procrastination is an insidious fault that can easily become a habit and a trap. For example, we might say, "Perhaps I can get up earlier tomorrow. Today I will just take it easy for another few minutes"—or a half hour or an hour or more. Of course, the next day we do not get up either, but have an excuse. We say, "Today I am really too tired. Tomorrow I will do at least twice as much practice!" But the following day, we find the same excuse. Of course, occasionally we do as we intended.

At another time, we may be involved in some kind of entertainment, a festival or a social gathering. We say, "This is so enjoyable, so exciting! I will attend to my practice tomorrow, but today I think I must do this instead." If we are looking for entertainment, this world has everything to offer. It could go on and on, and we could build up quite an unbreakable pattern. With diligence, we can avoid developing such a pattern.

We need to ask ourselves, "From the time I was born until now, what have I done in the world that was really meaningful? What have I done that benefited others and that benefited me?" In this life, with all the time and energy we have spent over all those years, we may find that only ten percent has been meaningful. I am quite afraid it is not more than that. What does the future hold for us—and how much future is left for us, after all? Here we are, grown-up people. Much of our time has been spent and much of our time is gone. What have we really done? If we review the situation, it is embarrassing, because our only responsibility is to keep our body mechanisms going. Other than that, there is really not much we need to do for ourselves. We have been involved in many affairs and activities. Of all the things we have done, is there anything about which we can say, "This is an achievement"? Is there anything we can be proud of?

At this point, we must tell ourselves it is time to become responsible and realistic. What can we do that is really beneficial, temporarily and ultimately? We think of ourselves as true practitioners of the Dharma, and we have spent time trying to understand the Dharma. We may well conclude that the only important thing is to practice the Dharma. Of course, we must take care of the mundane aspects of our lives and meet our responsibilities. Nevertheless, temporarily and ultimately, it is the practice of the Dharma that makes most sense. We have wasted so much time that we cannot afford to waste any more of the precious, limited time that is left. We cannot afford to indulge in the destructive, seductive, and delusive pattern of procrastination. We must become very determined about this.

No matter what task we are involved in, either spiritual or

mundane, diligence is extremely important if we want to accomplish things and have them go smoothly. A diligent person, who always carries out his or her responsibilities, is generally a very dignified person with a composed and collected appearance. This is not a deception. Such a person is clearheaded. Everything about this person is neat and well organized. He or she always has time for some additional task, because all responsibilities have been met on schedule. The person looks healthy and confident and is always cheerful. Everything runs smoothly; everything has been done.

However, a lazy person who procrastinates has many complaints. Before one job has been finished, another job comes up that needs to be done. There are doubts, worries, and regrets—a whole world of problems and confusion! The person is uncomfortable with himself or herself, and does not get along with others, because he or she is filled with anxieties, and always seems to be at the edge of some crisis in which things could blow up at any moment. A lazy person also looks very dull. Things are very clouded mentally, there is no perspective, and the person seems stuck. No matter what you are involved in, procrastination is a very unsound habit, and diligence is very important.

Procrastination is seductive. When you are sleeping or relaxing in bed, it is sometimes difficult to get up. You can find any number of excuses. But suppose you were completely relaxed and at ease, when suddenly, out of the blue, a poisonous snake fell on top of you! You would not say, "Oh, it looks nice," or "Whatever this snake wants to do to me, let him do it." You would immediately jump up and do something about it! There would really be business to attend to! You could no longer be lazy and put off taking care of yourself.

When you have many excuses not to do your work, ask yourself what guarantee you have of another chance to do what needs to be done. Time lost is lost for good. No matter how much you promise to improve, no matter what good intentions you have for making it up, the time is gone for good. Feeling sorry about the situation will not bring it back. You can never buy back that precious piece of time. You may think, "Well, that piece of time has passed, but I still have a long stretch of time left." No, you do not! What guarantee is there that you will have another piece of time like this one? Wake up and stop the excuses; they never made sense before and do not make sense now. Laziness and procrastination have never worked in a sound and helpful way. It is only sound and helpful to get things moving.

For example, you want to get up at a particular time in the morning. When your alarm clock goes off, you turn on this side and that, yawn and stretch, and begin to wonder whether you should get out of bed or not. Perhaps you could postpone your work until later, but what would other people think? What could you tell others that would not be embarrassing and would still convince them you are getting things done? It is really unnecessary to entertain such ideas. When the alarm goes off, it is much simpler just to get up! Once you get used to it, that is the easiest thing to do. It is completely unnecessary to make it a life-and-death struggle.

In the West, we have a system of doing specific things at specific times, with everything scheduled. In Tibet, unfortunately, there were not any such good rules. Nevertheless, people who meant business wasted no time. They took no two-hour breaks or one-day breaks. They would eat and drink quickly and even go to the bathroom quickly. This may sound unhealthy, but it is simply being diligent. Such people got up early in the morning and studied, read, memorized, and practiced meditation very diligently. They were very punctual with their work, and many became great scholars and meditators. While these students were becoming learned and helpful, others involved in the same kind of practice and study were only beginning to get organized. Their work was very unsatisfactory. As to whether they could be helpful to others, that was still very much up in the air. Thus the practical thing is to meet whatever responsibilities we have, and not to get ideas about leaving them for some other time.

If you practice meditation, it is very sound to develop a habit of setting aside a particular time for it every day, in the evenings, for example. (This assumes that you have some control over the use of your time, that your schedule is not subject to another person's decisions.) Whatever time you set aside, it is important and beneficial to be conscientious about devoting that time to the practice. If you sincerely want to do meditation practice but make no firm commitment to a definite time period, you will have many problems. You may notice that time is going by. You know you have to do some practice, but you really do not want to do it. So you dally around, find other things to do, become nervous, and perhaps end up not doing any practice at all. Even if you finally try to do some kind of practice, it will probably not be solid or meaningful. After all your time and anxiety, you may find your practice was not meaningful at all, so you are upset. In addition, while you are doing this inadequate practice, you may become late for something else. You have no sense of perspective and no order of priority. If this pattern continues, it will be very unsatisfactory. In contrast, if you have a particular time to practice and you make use of it every day, that is very sound. Now if you want to do something else, you can do it happily and joyfully, without feeling embarrassed or guilty and without creating unnecessary confusion for yourself.

The second aspect of diligence is having respect for our capabilities. This counteracts another type of laziness, which is underestimating ourselves unnecessarily. We denigrate ourselves, saying, "Other people can do it, but I cannot." We make the excuse that we are incapable of doing a task. We have a poverty mentality. We cannot do it well enough or completely enough; we are just not the right person; we are not fit to do the job. Others are greater, wiser, more knowledgeable, more talented, and more experienced than we are. We are inadequate and unworthy. Such unwholesome ideas about ourselves have nothing do to with humility. They have to do with underestimating our capabilities and having no respect for our potential.

When we find ourselves involved in such self-denigration,

we must look into the situation more carefully and openly. As practitioners of the Dharma, we hear about buddhas and bodhisattvas, highly awakened beings. We are surrounded by fellow practitioners who are very knowledgeable and accomplished, some of whom have had profound experiences. It should be clear to us that these people were not like this to begin with. They were ordinary beings like us. The buddha nature—the potential to become truly sane and perfect—is possessed by all beings equally. Why do we have unnecessary hang-ups about our abilities? These other people are committing themselves to noble actions because they have understood their potential and they are diligent. The only difference between them and us is that we are not diligent, we have no understanding of our potential. Because we have no diligence and have put no effort into making the practice successful and meaningful, we have no experience or realization. At this point, we must definitely put some effort into our practice. If we remain stuck in this pattern of self-denigration, this poverty mentality, no matter how kind and considerate others are to us, not much can be done about it.

Suppose there are two people who both have their feet and their eyes intact. One person starts walking and reaches a destination a certain distance away. The other person does not walk, has not reached any destination, and has not covered any distance at all. This cannot be blamed on anyone else. It is an unnecessary state of imprisonment. The second person's eyes and feet are intact, so why could he or she not get as far as the first person? One actually had no advantage over the other. In a similar way, we can be as accomplished as even the buddhas and bodhisattvas, or at least as fellow practitioners who are progressing well and have the proper perspective. We do not need to be bound by unnecessary limitations.

You must understand that I am not trying to induce unrealistic optimism or wishful thinking. That is not the nature of Buddhism. I am simply explaining realistic possibilities. Once again, the buddhas and bodhisattvas were not buddhas and bodhisattvas to begin with. As ordinary sentient beings, we are not totally hopeless from the very beginning. It is not that the two can never meet. Our situation is full of promise; our basic potential can be developed. This potential was perfectly developed in the awakened minds of the buddhas and bodhisattvas, and we can develop it in our minds. All the favorable conditions are available in terms of our potential, the path, and the fruition. We cannot ask for more. All we need now is to get moving, to begin taking steps.

This second aspect of diligence is the antidote for laziness and hesitation in the immediate situation. Right now you may be thinking, "No, I cannot do this; there are so many people who are better!" You must make it clear to yourself that this is not the way things are. Even if you cannot do everything, you can do what is needed in the present situation. That is quite realistic. Remind yourself in this way and apply the antidote to challenge the pattern. This kind of diligence is a very important element in the practice of the Dharma.

There are differences between people. Some people are more intelligent than others, and some people understand things more easily than others, but this does not matter if there is diligence. The diligent person is the one who will succeed and accomplish things in both the mundane and the spiritual worlds. You may have heard about how one person was very intelligent but never amounted to much, whereas another person was known not to be very bright—people even laughed about how dull-witted that person was—but suddenly became great because of diligence. He or she was very steady and determined, only going forward, knowing not to backtrack, and became an amazing success. There have been many such instances historically in both the mundane and spiritual realms. These are not just fantasies or fairy tales. They are actual experiences in the lives of people of all kinds.

You might think, "I have some intelligence and ability, but really, I have no diligence at all." This is not true; it is just a way of underestimating and defeating yourself. It is true that some people are more intelligent than others; that is part of the makeup of a person. But it is not true that one person is inherently more diligent than another. Diligence is a matter of clearly understanding what needs to be done and setting out to do those things. Everyone has the same potential to develop diligence. Over the years, you may have become more spoiled than someone else, so it is difficult for you to produce those qualities. This does not mean it is impossible, but only that you think you do not have the potential. If you think you cannot do anything because diligence is somehow not ingrained in you, you are just deceiving yourself.

Questions

Q: How do we distinguish between what is good and bad to do in our daily lives, in relation to the Dharma? How should we divide our time between worldly activities and meditation?

A: Certain things are clear. For example, if you made yourself a slave to gambling, drugs, or alcohol, you would ruin your life from both a spiritual and a mundane point of view. You would destroy your health. People would have negative opinions about you and regard you as a dropout. It is very clear how you would spend your time. If gambling is there, there is life; if not, there is no life. If drugs are there, you live; without drugs, you do not live. You would not fare well in mundane life, let alone in spiritual life. What is the purpose of having been born as a human being who possesses the buddha nature if you have so little respect for yourself and your potential? That kind of situation is totally ridiculous.

There is nothing wrong with the study of science, art, literature, languages, and different aspects of the arts. I am not saying, "Do not touch these; they are not good." It is very good to have some knowledge of one or all of these fields. Whether your involvement in these fields is good or wholesome depends on your attitude and how you use the knowledge. In Buddhism, we talk about five major and five minor outer fields of study—medicine, astrology, and so forth. The Dharma, which includes meditation practice, is the inner field of study in the sense that you benefit from both a temporary and an ultimate point of view. In the outer aspects of study, the question is how well you use this knowledge to take care of life on a mundane level. Using such studies for spiritual benefit depends on your motivation, such as using the knowledge to benefit others.

Here again, diligence is extremely important. Suppose a person is very productive in some mundane field, which could be manual labor or some very complicated scientific or psychological study. When this person is involved in the Dharma, he or she will be able to make sense out of the Dharma, and will definitely appreciate and practice it. Such a person is successful in both fields. If someone is ineffective, timid, and limited in a mundane field and tries to take shelter in the practice of spirituality as a last resort, this person will not be successful. The practice of the Dharma needs equal if not greater diligence than any ordinary work. A person who escapes from one will end up escaping from the other too, and then there will be nowhere to go.

Q: In regard to the alarm clock going off, I have a problem at the other end, going to bed too late. If I get up with the alarm, I feel I have not had enough sleep. Would you comment on that?

A: You should do what is most practical and most healthy. If you have some control over how you use your time, it might be healthier to go to bed a little earlier and then get up earlier. "Early to bed, early to rise," as it is said. If you are subject to someone else's schedule, you must make the best you can of it.

It is very interesting, though, that how much sleep we need really depends on how strongly we are committed to doing things. In the West, we talk about how important it is to get enough sleep, though not everyone sticks to it. To a lesser extent in Tibet, it is also considered healthy to get a moderate amount of sleep. Recently I was in Taiwan. While almost everyone there, young and old, seemed to be engaged in hard work, no one slept more than three and a half hours a night. Everyone was up. People also ate more than you could believe, but at no fixed times. Though only sleeping three and a half hours, people were not yawning and drowsy. Everyone was wide awake. They were quick and up-to-date with everything. Most of the people seemed to engage in some form of physical exercise as soon as they got up and before they went to work. Everyone was alert and vigorous. This happened not just once, but every day, day in and day out. It was like a miracle. There must be some way to make that kind of diligence operate in our lives!

Q: On occasion in our employment, we may be asked to perform certain tasks we are unable to do, no matter how hard we try. How do we deal with the stress that comes about when we are unable to do the required tasks despite such effort?

A: Perhaps you feel it is easy to talk about diligence, but actually doing the work is not so easy. That is quite true. You must understand that in this mundane world there are many limitations. No matter how much effort you put into certain jobs, you may not be able to do them. Nevertheless, there are often alternatives. For example, suppose you have a pickaxe and you want to dig a hole in the ground. If you hit a rock, the pickaxe will not go into the ground. You need to strike a place where there is earth, and then it will go down. If you do not succeed in your work, feeling worried and upset will not make things any better. The best solution is to consider what other options you have.

However, we must also use skillful means. There may be things it would quite clearly not make sense to do, no matter how diligent you are. They would cause so much resentment and upset that they would not be worth any happiness or goodness that might result. Even if you are diligent and capable enough to do such a thing, there is really no point in doing it. There also may be problems that cannot be solved, even if you are diligent and skillful. It would not be intelligent to try to work such a situation out. While it is important to be diligent in both the mundane and spiritual aspects of our work, we must still distinguish between what is workable and beneficial and what is not.

Once at the KTD center, a little girl was playing with me and started hitting me. I said, "Ow! You are so strong!" She got excited and started hitting me more. When I continued to encourage her, she said, "Well, yes, I'm strong, I can even break your house!" I said, "Yes, I think you can! I would like to see it." To my surprise, she banged her head against the wall and started crying. I should have been intelligent enough to know I was dealing with just a little child. But she was so diligent!

THE PERFECTION OF MEDITATION

I will now discuss the fifth perfection, the perfection of meditation. The practices of the six perfections are very much interrelated. Without some appreciation, understanding, and practice of generosity—being open and extending ourselves to others in a beneficial way—it is difficult to develop discipline. Lack of discipline comes from strong neurotic patterns, especially attachment to material things and emotional fixations. To appreciate and practice discipline, we first lessen these patterns through the practice of generosity. To understand and cultivate patience, we must first appreciate and practice discipline. Developing wholesome attitudes and actions gives us some openness toward patience.

When we begin to realize the benefits of patience, this leads to diligence—a sense of joy in what we are doing. If we are experiencing great aggression, restlessness, and frustration, even if we are doing something worthwhile, it is difficult to do it in a meaningful, fulfilling, or joyful way. With patience, exertion becomes a joyful experience, filled with insight. This lays the proper foundation for meditation. To experience tranquility of the mind, we must tame and control the mind, which requires patience and diligence. Because our minds have been distracted for a long time, pursuing the quite different experience of tranquility requires patience, and persisting in the practice requires diligence. When we develop patience and diligence, we are able to do the wholesome practice of meditation, and this brings about growth and enrichment.

With this foundation we engage in the practice of meditation and work toward experiencing the perfection of meditation. The particular term used here is *samten* in Tibetan or *samadhi* in Sanskrit, which literally means "firmness of mind." The mind is not caught up in many kinds of entertainments or overwhelmed by many kinds of distractions. It is not restless, agitated, or confused. Instead, we are able to experience a firm and undistracted state of mind. When the mind is undistracted, there is a calm and clear state of wakefulness, with a quality of firmness and stability.

The practice of meditation has both a mundane aspect and a spiritual aspect that transcends the mundane. In the mundane aspect of meditation, we have a general understanding that as we encounter various situations in our lives, we find tremendous confusion and feel great restlessness and instability. Things are not as reliable or as permanent as we like to assume. Some things break; other things do not function properly. We often find ourselves disappointed. Therefore we begin to practice meditation, which creates a kind of ground, a more firm and wakeful state of mind, so we are not so easily shaken by external circumstances. Things continue to be impermanent and unreliable, yet we can tolerate this. Through the mundane level of meditation practice, we become more composed and centered.

In the spiritual aspect of meditation, we have a deeper insight into the nature of things. We begin to recognize that the confusion and pain, as well as the happiness, that we experience now and in the past and future are not only caused by external circumstances. Things have not simply come into place outwardly. At this point, we realize that we have many negative emotions and confusions—the kleshas—to work out. We understand that we must apply the appropriate antidotes to lessen and finally uproot these unwholesome emotional patterns. We begin to see that we are capable of doing this, that we have the potential and resources, so we actually begin to develop some skillful means.

In addition to recognizing our own confusion and negative emotions, we become more aware of and concerned about the confusion others are involved in, and we become more understanding of them. Now our motivation to engage in the practice of meditation is not only to benefit ourselves, but also to enable us to benefit others and to create a more open and clear situation for them. In this way we develop greater insight. We may even reach the point of liberating ourselves completely from our confusion. That is the spiritual aspect of meditation, which transcends the mundane level.

In the mundane aspect of meditation, our motivation for the practice stems from some disappointment with the ordinary world. We begin to see that all the distractions and entertainments of the world are very deceitful. They cause us to build up many kinds of expectations and lead to many exciting schemes. We treasure these distractions and try to hold onto them, yet we realize we cannot. Thus we begin to see the deceitful, impermanent, changing nature of mundane existence, and we begin to experience some distance from the material world. It is no longer as exciting and entertaining as we had assumed it to be. We become more detached, primarily in a material sense. When we practice meditation, we go to some quiet place, a place of solitude and simplicity, perhaps just under a tree or in some desolate area where we can be alone, with the outer quietness as our companion.

In mundane meditation, the renunciation we experience is not a total or true renunciation. We have a sense of actually being against material things, and we develop an attachment to our experience of calmness and tranquility of the mind. The more we experience a calm state of mind, the more distant we become from material things. The benefit of this type of meditation practice is that we do not find ourselves performing many unwholesome actions or generating many unwholesome attitudes. As a result, for one lifetime or so in the future, we may experience a very tranquil state of birth and existence. However, we have still not become liberated from the kleshas. We have not recognized our neurotic patterns, and since we have made no effort to uproot such patterns, we will once again be subject to cyclic existence. In the spiritual aspect of meditation, the techniques may initially be the same, such as choosing a quieter, more appropriate environment in which to practice. However, there is a difference in the attitude and motivation. Mundane meditation was rather like escaping from outer circumstances. Now we realize that the circumstances are not the problem, but the problem is the negative emotional patterns ingrained in our minds. These egoistic patterns must be uprooted, because continuing to harbor them is destructive to us as well as to others. Because of these patterns, we find ourselves in a constant state of confusion and frustration, without a clear perspective or understanding; hence, whatever we do is harmful to ourselves and to others. For the benefit of others as well as ourselves, we want to work on these patterns. It is for this purpose that we go to a place of solitude or some proper environment to practice, not because we are running away from external circumstances in the mundane world. Instead of seeing outer circumstances as the cause of our confusion and pain, we see our own negative patterns and history of confusion as the cause of our suffering and problems.

We are like a person afflicted with a very contagious disease, who goes to a quieter and simpler place, with few disturbances, because all the complications among which he or she has to live (the dirt and pollution and so forth) are not healthy for such an ill person. Also, since this is a contagious disease, the person would not want to live among other people and allow them to become afflicted by that disease. Thus we try to find a quiet, remote place in which to practice because it is beneficial to others as well as to us.

To apply the meditation practice effectively, we must first understand and recognize the present situation, the real condition of things. In the past, present, and future, our negative patterns have been the cause of confusion and suffering.

As a result of these patterns, we experience constant distractions and continuous chains of thoughts—now aggression, now attachment, now clinging, now grasping. As I said, it is not external circumstances but our own patterns that need to be recognized and worked on before circumstances will cease to cause any difficulty. Recognizing that there are certain areas within us that need to be worked out, we first use this understanding and this technique to become less easily overwhelmed and stimulated by objects of distraction that aggravate the already existing patterns. The initial step is not to intensify our neurotic patterns. There is some possibility that we can understand and accomplish this. Then we can take the further step of lessening the existing neurotic patterns to the point of ultimately uprooting them and experiencing perfect sanity.

The first meditation practice to be introduced is shamata, or sitting meditation practice, which leads to the experience of calmness, mindfulness, and concentration of the mind. If we are able to do sitting meditation practice, there is a great deal of benefit, and the more sincerely we are able to commit ourselves to the practice, the more consistently we will experience the benefit. If we do not practice shamata, that is a defect, because we will not experience the benefit but will continue to have confusion, instability, and problems. As we engage in shamata practice, we begin to realize how important this basic meditation is for a sane and practical life, in both a spiritual and mundane sense. We understand that calmness and clarity of the mind are important in anything we do.

At this initial level, whether the meditation is mundane or spiritual depends entirely on our motivation and our attitude toward the practice. The difference is not caused by culture or personality, but simply by our attitude. For example, we may think that the experience of tranquility of the mind is desirable and exactly what we want. We just cannot stand our problems, and we would love to experience calmness and tranquility of the mind. That attitude and motivation is very mundane. On the other hand, we might be doing the same practice with the attitude that, for our own benefit and the benefit of all beings, our neurotic patterns and confusion are not desirable. We know we must work toward abandoning and uprooting these patterns, and the key to doing this is the practice of meditation. Generating the proper motivation, we resolve to practice meditation. That is a very wholesome attitude.

In addition to the motivation, whether the meditation is mundane or spiritual also depends on the vision behind the practice. In the practice of sitting meditation, for example, with the proper attitude, we understand that we have the potential to experience a perfectly awakened state of mind. Through consistent sitting practice, we begin to experience tranquility and calmness of our mind, but we do not become attached to this experience of tranquility as in the mundane level of meditation. Instead, we use the experience as a kind of stepping stone toward further experience. Once we have taken the first step, we feel some confidence and have a greater, more precise sense of the second step to be taken. As we continue to practice with the proper understanding, the benefit is tremendous—calmness, tranquility of the mind, appreciation of the value of the teachings, devotion to the practices we are engaged in, generosity, diligence, and patience. All these noble qualities become more and more a part of us.

As these qualities become more recognizable and we engage in many wholesome activities, we begin to experience wisdom. With the perfection of meditation, we also experience the perfection of wisdom. We cannot attain the perfection of wisdom without the perfection of meditation. With the proper understanding and vision, doing shamata or sitting practice leads ultimately to the vipasyana experience. This is also called the perfection of wisdom, or the realization of absolute truth, or emptiness. It is given different names because of certain differences in the techniques, but the result is basically the same. It comes from having the proper vision.

Even if we have a very good bow and arrow, if we aim at a target right in front of us, that is as far as the arrow will go. But if we aim at a target off in the distance, because of the good quality of the bow, the arrow will reach the distant target. With limited vision and motivation, our practice becomes quite stagnant, stopping at a tranquil and calm state of mind. Of course, this is better than nothing at all. With greater vision and motivation, even though initially we use the same technique, our practice takes us beyond calmness and tranquility of the mind.

In one case, the experience of tranquility of mind is seen as the fruition of shamata practice. In the other, the shamata practice itself is understood as a vehicle or cause for experiencing vipasyana, which is a clearer vision—the realization of ultimate truth. We supplement shamata meditation with practices for purifying negative patterns through applying various skillful actions and attitudes, and also with practices for accumulating further noble and wholesome qualities. In this way, we follow the path of the awakened ones.

Questions

Q: Does this shift from the mundane to the spiritual happen automatically, or do we say, "Now I will start thinking about spiritual matters"?

A: How and whether the shift happens depends on the situation, such as who your spiritual friend or teacher is. The guidance your spiritual friend is capable of giving you may only be on the mundane level of the practice. You may be taught to concentrate on this, with tremendous emphasis being placed on the virtues of experience at the mundane level. If you work very hard at it and begin to taste a calm and tranquil state of mind, you may believe this is everything you need to experience. Shamata was the goal, and you experienced that goal. With such a spiritual friend, you might remain at that level.

It is also possible that you have met the proper spiritual friend, who has given the proper explanations, and you understand the differences, but because of your limitations, you are not bright or courageous enough to recognize the problems that need to be solved. You are not courageous enough to see the possibility of helping others or of bearing the problems and confusions of others. The instruction and the understanding are available, but you somehow avoid generating the proper attitude, feeling that it is a little too ambitious for you. In that case, it is possible that a gradual shift might take place. On the other hand, when some people are given the instructions, they are able to generate the proper attitude from the very beginning.

Q: Are you equating "mundane" and "hinayana"?

A: No, not at all. The hinayana is referred to as a lesser vehicle, simply because the attitude and motivation are just a little less than those of the mahayana, but hinayana practitioners have a clear vision of the need for complete liberation from confusion. At the mundane level, the only concern is for some experience of tranquility.

Q: Is that not the experience of individual salvation, the fruition of hinayana? I was under the impression that the hinayana practice begins with renunciation of the phenomenal world.

A: No, in the mundane meditation, it is the circumstances, the outer phenomenal world, that are not right. You have almost a hatred for what is going on. Such an attitude is not renunciation. Because some things did not work out for you, out of hatred you go to the wilderness or some quiet place and meditate to obtain isolation and calmness of mind. When you experience a limited calmness of mind, you are content with that. That is the only understanding and possibly the only instruction you have had. In many spiritual movements that is as far as you go.

Hinayana is different. In hinayana, the attitude is that you have many negative patterns to be worked out, and it is not just outside circumstances that cause suffering. Circumstances play a part, but the main problem is internal confusion. Hinayana practitioners recognize their own confusion and understand that it is possible to experience liberation. To experience self-liberation, or arhatship, is to be liberated from the confusion and suffering of samsara.

Arhats are not as fully awakened as buddhas and bodhisattvas, who have the ability to perform beneficial actions, but they are liberated from the suffering of cyclic existence. Someone who has insight only into the mundane level may go for one lifetime to a realm where it is quiet and tranquil, but then they will go back to the same cyclic existence. The mahayana attitude is not only recognizing that your confusion needs to be overcome, but also wanting to overcome it for the benefit and liberation of others as well as yourself.

Q: If we are not supposed to become attached to the quietness of meditation but to aim for the perfection of wisdom or absolute truth, is there a certain experience that makes us feel we have reached this goal?

A: You start with basic shamata meditation. The possible sidetracks, the clarifications you might need, and the obstacles to watch for are explained to you. Obstacles are not caused by the meditation, but may begin to develop through your habitual patterns. You are told how to watch for them, and what kind of antidotes you should apply. In time, things become much much clearer. The recognition of ultimate truth or the perfection of wisdom happens because of your understanding and experience. You are introduced to it gradually, because you would not understand it if you were introduced to it immediately. If you are an advanced meditation practitioner, you will be introduced to the stages of experience you will go through, and the things you will encounter. This gives you a clear understanding, but understanding is not experience. As you work with your practice, you begin to experience the result. This experience becomes compatible with certain understandings you have through your teacher, and you say, "Ah! Yes!" That which was just an understanding for you has now been confirmed by your experience. The understanding helps you confirm the experience, and the experience helps you confirm the understanding.

Q: Did you say we must develop a certain amount of generosity, patience, and so forth before we begin to meditate?

A: In reviewing the six perfections, I said that in order to experience the perfection of meditation, you must have practiced generosity, discipline, patience, and diligence. This is not saying you must have practiced generosity, discipline, and so forth before you begin meditation practice. When you practice sitting meditation or shamata at a beginning level, you try to understand everything together. You practice a little generosity, a little patience, a little meditation, and so forth, in whatever way you can, to develop yourself in a wholesome way. As you continue to meditate and begin to experience its beneficial qualities, you will become more open to the practice of generosity and discipline, the practice of devotion and confidence, and so forth. You do not experience the perfection of meditation without having practiced these qualities.

THE PERFECTION OF WISDOM

We have been exploring the six perfections, the transcendent qualities we need to develop as we travel on the path to enlightenment. The final one is the perfection of wisdom. For our practice of generosity or any of the perfections to be effective, we must first clearly and correctly hear teachings on its nature and significance. Second, we must contemplate what we have heard and develop an understanding of it in which we can be confident. Third, we must put this understanding into practice through meditation, so that it becomes not just an intellectual understanding, but an experiential insight. These three aspects of wisdom—the wisdom of hearing, the wisdom of understanding, and the wisdom of meditation—are required throughout the path.

In general, we can classify wisdom into relative and ultimate wisdom, or mundane wisdom and wisdom that is beyond the mundane. Mundane or relative wisdom is our ordinary knowing ability. We have the ability to know about many different things in the world. We may become a professional in a particular field—science, medicine, art, language, or metaphysics. By investigating different fields of learning, we begin to understand the outer material things around us. We learn to put them together in various ways to bring about various results. This understanding and knowing ability is called relative wisdom because the satisfaction and happiness provided by using it is only temporary. Furthermore, in these mundane areas of learning we become fascinated by the play of outer material things, and we fail to notice more subtle things closer at hand. We are so absorbed in outer phenomena that we constantly miss something. Because of these limitations, we call this relative wisdom.

Most of us are completely involved in the mundane aspect of wisdom. This limits us because we are looking in entirely the wrong direction for the origin of things. With that outlook we can never develop complete knowledge, understanding, or insight. When you see a river, if you want to find out where the water comes from, you will have to go to the source of the river, which is upstream. Suppose instead you search by going down the river. You will not find the source of the water, and in fact, if you follow the river long enough, it will run into an ocean. At that point, not only is the source impossible to find, but you cannot even find the river. There is total confusion. This is much like our involvement in what is happening around us.

In approaching ultimate wisdom, if we try to extend the knowing ability of our minds to encompass the infinite variety of things to be known, a time will never come when we know everything. Instead of trying to capture something limitless, we must have an understanding that is like going to the source of the river. We must turn inward and examine the source of knowledge—the knower, the mind or consciousness that has the ability to know. What is this knower like? Where is the source of this continuous knowing?

To know the nature of the mind is to know the nature of all things. Yet this wisdom—this insight into the knowing ability of the mind—will not come about on its own. It has never come about on its own in the past, and it will never come about on its own in the future. Wisdom does not jump out by chance. To awaken to it, we need the help of spiritual friends, teachers who can give specific instructions on studying and working with the nature of the mind.

First we must hear from these spiritual friends about the way things really are. That is the wisdom of hearing. We are hearing something we have not heard before, something important, practical, and personal. We are hearing something very intimate about ourselves, yet it is something we have not heard before, let alone understood or experienced. The resources for understanding it have always been available, but we have not been able to tap into them. With the help of a spiritual friend, we begin to understand how things are, and thus to develop the wisdom of hearing.

Having heard, we must contemplate what we have heard so we can understand it. Through examining and investigating what we have heard, and then receiving further clarifications, we begin to develop a correct understanding. This is very important, because if we do not understand what we have heard, we will not have a stable ground to work with.

Suppose someone tells you, "If you go in this direction you will find enemies, but if you go in that direction you will find friends. If you go in this direction there are poisons, but if you go in that direction there are medicines." That is what you heard, and as soon as you heard it, you believed it. Now suppose you travel and come to a point where a different person tells you quite the opposite: this way friends, that way enemies; this way medicines, and that way poisons. This puts you in a state of confusion. Which one should you believe? But suppose you make it a point from the very beginning to study why there are poisons at that place. What are the signs and causes? How and why are the enemies, friends, and medicines where they are? You get an explanation of exactly what evidence to look for and what landmarks you will come across. Then you have a clear understanding of the situation that you can be confident about, so if someone tries to convince you otherwise, you will not be confused.

Furthermore, without a correct understanding of what we have heard, we will not be able to put it into practice. If something is based only on hearing, we might hear it today and forget it by tomorrow. We would not remember the meaning and the important guidelines. Even parrots hear and repeat what people say, but they cannot make use of it, because they do not understand what they have heard.

The wisdom of meditation is being able to let the mind rest with the understanding. It is letting the mind get used to whatever clear understanding we have reached, so that it becomes an experience. A true experience, which has come about because we have heard and understood things correctly, is unshakable, whether it is a clear, tranquil state of the mind or a great insight into the nature of things. We have the potential for such insight, and we often experience a spark of something beyond ordinary intelligence, some kind of clear vision. The experience is not continuous, because we are not sufficiently familiar with that state of insight. Our minds are not resting within that state. To make the experience continuous, it is important to develop the wisdom of meditation.

The specific subject we take up in the perfection of wisdom could be shocking to a beginner in the study of Buddhist philosophy and psychology. When we hear it for the first time, it could be shocking if we take things literally. What is said might not make any sense at all, and we could develop mistaken ideas. But if we are patient and intelligent enough to take the matter a little further and examine it carefully, something may open up. We are presented with the statement that the nature of everything we see is insubstantial and without specific identity—the nature of all things is emptiness. If we take this literally, we will say it is contradictory. How can we see something if it is insubstantial and without specific identity? We must examine this further. Though in appearance things seem to exist in a solid and substantial way and have a specific identity, in reality they have only been labeled that way. They are not substantial. Their nature is insubstantial, uncompounded, unborn. The nature of all things is emptiness.

The subjects we explore here are the body, feelings or sensations, the mind or consciousness, and all dharmas, which means everything in the phenomenal world. The nature of these four, which includes everything, is emptiness; they are all insubstantial. We first focus on the body. You have a body, and your friends have bodies. You walk with your body. How could it be insubstantial? How could the nature of this body be emptiness? However, if you open your mind a little further, and examine, from the crown of your head down to the tip of your toes, where do you really find the body? What you call "my body" is only a label. There is no such thing as a body.

There is an accumulation of various parts, combined together in a certain form. This is labeled and clung to as a body, but among all the parts, where is the body? There is flesh, bone, cartilage, and so forth. If we go into greater detail, there are more specific names—head, arms, legs. These can be divided into yet more specific parts—eyes, fingers, toes. All have been labeled with different names. Now where is the head? And for that matter, what is a head? Where are the arms? What in the world is there that is called an arm? We cling very strongly to the belief that there is something definite behind the labels, but when we examine in this way, we cannot find it.

Turning to the second point, feelings, what is it that feels? When there are sensations, pleasant or unpleasant, you may want to say you feel them with your body. You may want to hold onto that idea, but do you really feel with your body? If that were the case, a dead body would also have sensations. You may switch and say it is the mind that feels, but if it is the mind that feels, there is no need for the body. Yet when you feel, there always seems to be a need for the body, even if it is your mind that feels.

If we go into this further, do you really feel, or is the sensation in the object outside you? If it is you that feels, there is no need for the object. If you say the sensation is in the object, how could you feel anything? There is no connection between you and the object. The question is, where is the feeling? In fact, is there really a feeling? A certain circumstance is referred to as a feeling. You become fixated on that circumstance and hold onto it as being there all the time. A feeling is just a circumstance. When certain things meet, something happens at that particular time and at no other time, yet you would like to hold onto the idea that it is always there.

You still want to hold your ground and claim that surely there is a body and there are feelings. Because of your mind, you know there is a body and there are feelings; but where is your mind or consciousness? Not for a moment can you pinpoint it and say, "Here is my mind." Not for a moment can you lay your finger on some particular thing, giving details and descriptions, and say, "This is my consciousness." When there is no mind to know, how can there be something outside to be known? When you cannot even find the one who labels, how can there be something that is labeled?

Still, you may try to go further and say, "Surely there is a mind." It is having a mind that causes you to know many things. You know that something is beautiful and something else is ugly. You know that something is very long and something else is very short, or something is high and something else is low. However, if there were not something you could label as beautiful, something ugly would not exist. If there were not something labeled as long or high, how could there be something short or low? There is interdependence. All things exist interdependently. Nothing exists substantially on its own. No matter how intelligent you are, you can never find even the smallest thing that exists substantially and independently on its own. That is not the nature of things. Even a genius would never be able to find such a thing.

All phenomena exist interdependently. Because of the mind, we have a sense of objects, but how would we know there is a mind without objects? How could the mind exist without objects? On the other hand, without the mind, how would we know there are objects? How could objects exist without the mind? Still, we think things are substantial because of our fixation and clinging. For a long time, we have been repeating a pattern of illusion. If there is an object and a mirror, there is a reflection. There cannot be a reflection without an object and a mirror. Does a reflection exist substantially? Does anything exist substantially? Like the reflection in the mirror, things only come about interdependently, according to circumstances. The appearance is there, but in reality the nature of all things is insubstantial.

You may think this is confusing. At times I seem to be saying, "Yes, there are things." At other times I seem to be saying, "No, there are not." There seems to be a contradiction or paradox. We go through such confusion because we do not want to give up our habitual notion of how things are, the structure we are clinging to out of ignorance. In reality the nature of all things is emptiness. Things are empty of the truth of substantiality. For that matter, things are also empty of faults and limitations.

As an example of how this might be so, when we go to sleep we have dreams and sometimes nightmares. When we are dreaming, everything is very real to us. There is hearing, there is talking, there are feelings, there are emotions. There are objects for the emotions and feelings. Everything is taking place. When we wake up from our sleep, there is neither the doing nor the doer. The people who were doing all those things and experiencing all those things are not there. The things that were being seen, heard, and touched are not there either. Of course, these things never existed in the first place. But while we are dreaming, the things are very real, and we cannot be convinced they are not happening. What causes this confusion? It is the sleep that causes the confusion. When we wake up and are no longer asleep, we see that none of these things took place.

In our present situation, we have feelings that are quite real to us. We have extreme, painful emotions that are real to us. We cannot deny them. This is because we have a long history of accumulated emotional patterns and confusion, the consequences of which are still continuing. This is what we call ignorance. Once we awake from the sleep of ignorance, we will cease to have this experience of confusion. We will look back at the confusion as we now look back at a dream or nightmare. We will shrug our shoulders and say, "Who cares? It was only a dream." We may begin to have an understanding of something that in one sense is new, but in another sense has always been there, beyond time and space.

The actual point of this can only be understood fully through meditation practice, which gives us a deep insight, beyond mere intellectual understanding. We are instructed to let the mind rest in awareness. The more we are able to let the mind rest in awareness, simply letting things be, the more our confusion is clarified. Letting the mind rest in awareness means being neither totally distracted and entertained by various thoughts and external situations, nor simply blank and vacant. It means remaining in a clear state of awareness, as close as possible to a nonreferential state of mind. At this point we are only being introduced to the insubstantial and interdependent nature of things. The more we are able to let our minds become familiar with such things through meditation, the more we will understand and appreciate them.

The realization of the true nature of mind is also known as realizing shunyata or emptiness. Emptiness specifically means empty of delusion and misconception. It means clearing away. It is not just a blank emptiness, being left with nothing to do. There is no need to fear we will be robbed of everything if we attempt to attain wisdom. As an illustration, suppose the sun is behind the clouds. When the clouds drift away, the sun does not go away with them. Realizing emptiness or the true nature of the mind is realizing what has been there all the time. We have not discovered anything new or obtained anything new; we have simply recognized what has been always present. We have recognized the goodness and sanity that have been embedded there from the beginning.

To recognize the nature of the mind is to recognize its richness and dignity, its limitless ability to help ourselves and others. Right now when we talk about extending and expanding ourselves, most of the time it is merely words. When we have experienced the true nature of the mind, this is a reality. You may have heard stories of great meditators who can be in the midst of fire or in the midst of water and it makes no difference. They can wade through anything or play with anything, because they have realized the insubstantial nature of all things. When, out of confusion, we believe everything is fixed and stationary, then for us everything remains fixed and stationary.

This has been a very brief introduction to Buddhist psychology and the perfection of wisdom. At the beginning what has been explained may seem confusing, but if we have the patience and diligence to continue to explore these things, they will make more and more sense.

Questions

Q: I have heard lectures similar to this several times, and I understand all the concepts except insubstantiality. What do I do now? Is there something I can read? Or should I just think about it and meditate? Will meditation at this point help me break through on that concept?

A: It is important not to separate the understanding from the practice. To experience shunyata in meditation, you must first understand the view. If you do not understand the view, your meditation will not necessarily go in the correct direction. Right now we do basic sitting meditation practice, watching the breath, and this begins to bring about a clearer and calmer state of mind with fewer distractions. The view is that the nature of all things is insubstantial, beyond any fixed reference point. Even if you are sincere in the practice, if you do not understand that view or have a sense of it, your meditation may have the quality of there being something fixed and real somewhere. It is as though you mean to go east, but your steps are taking you closer and closer to the west. Thus understanding the view is important.

When you look around and see things, everything has been labeled. I am not telling you not to see things the way you do; that is fine. However, the way you see things now and the way you will see them when you understand the view of emptiness are different. When you experience what you understand, the way you see things will be very different. The appearance of things will not necessarily change, but the way you relate to them will definitely change.

As I said, the nature of all things is insubstantial. You can examine the outward aspect of intelligence. You can say, "Here is the brain with its various parts and with nerves running in various directions." You can find all these physical things, but if you ask who knows this, it is the mind that knows this. If again you ask where the mind is, you are quite speechless. You cannot say there is no mind, because you are constantly knowing and finding things. How could you say there is no mind? On the other hand, how could you say there is a mind? Where is it? What is it that says "There is this" or "There is that"? Since you cannot lay a finger on your mind, how can you lay a finger on anything and say, "There is this"? If things do not hold the truth of what you labeled them to be, what kind of truth do things hold? This should give you some idea of the view.

Q: It is often argued that things in the world must be substantial because there is some object that you see, and I see, and everyone sees, and we all agree that it is there. If it is nonsubstantial, how do we all see it?

A: The point is that things do appear. I am not saying there are no appearances. Things appear and we see them, but the way they appear does not hold the truth of what they are in reality. What you see is fine, and the way you see it is fine. In essence, however, the nature of the thing is not really the way you see it, because if you split that object into various pieces, what we all agreed upon as being there is now not there. The question is, was it not there from the very beginning, or was it not there from just a little while ago?

Something seems to you to be real because of the karmic patterns you have, but it does not hold that reality, because in essence it is insubstantial. Right now you can only understand this intellectually, like trying to figure out a puzzle. Through meditation practice, however, you can understand it experientially. Right now, for example, a big boulder is a big boulder. If you tried to walk through it, you would hurt yourself, because for you it is very solid. But someone who has realized the nonsubstantiality of all things could walk through it, and nothing would go wrong. It appears as a big boulder to that person, just as it does to you, but there is quite a difference between what you hold onto as being the nature of that object and what that person has realized to be its nature.

The Bodhisattva Tara

7 Stages of the Path

Having discussed many aspects of Buddhist practice on both the hinayana and mahayana levels, I will now describe the various stages we go through on the path to buddhahood. We must understand that only our individual effort and enthusiasm can liberate us from suffering. No outer force or energy can remove our kleshas and free us from samsara. When we develop certainty in the Dharma, we must apply it by practicing regularly, with completely sincere devotion and great endurance.

When we have kleshas—the origin of suffering—we are bound to experience suffering. If we are able to remove the kleshas, we can overcome suffering. Knowing and understanding this, we come to the next stage, which is learning to apply the skillful means of the path. The path involves inner practices that can remove all the defilements, and it is essential to participate willingly and openly in these practices. Many people in the past as well as the present have become highly realized and enlightened through practicing the path. This is evidence of the truth of the path. There is no evidence of anyone who practiced the path of the Dharma falling down into the lower realms. Individual effort and enthusiasm are the main keys to accomplishing the goal of the path.

THE FIVE PATHS

There are five different stages of the Buddhist path, which are known as the five paths. The first is the path of accumulation. Once we are facing in the right direction and step on the path that leads toward enlightenment, we are on the path of accumulation. The second stage is the path of unification. In our ordinary lives, we produce countless thoughts and experience vast confusion. When we realize we are confused and begin to move toward a state of nonconfusion, we are on the path of unification. We are uniting our confused state of mind with the nonconfused state of mind. This is like driving down a very narrow street that joins or unites with the main highway.

The third stage is the path of seeing. "Seeing" refers here to an experience; we experience something we have never experienced before. The fourth stage is the path of meditation. In the path of meditation, we continue to develop the quality of what we experienced in the path of seeing. Just as the waxing moon grows from the crescent stage until it becomes the full moon, the experience we had on the path of seeing develops and matures in the path of meditation.

Finally we reach the fifth path, the path of no-learning. There is actually no such thing as a path of no-learning. The term is used to give ordinary beings a hint of the final stage of the path, where all defilements, faults, stains, and confusions of the mind are totally removed and all positive qualities, wisdom and awareness are completely developed. Because there are no more positive qualities or wisdom to develop and no more defilements to purify, the final stage is known as the path of no-learning. In the mahayana, it is called complete enlightenment. In the hinayana, it is called arhatship. In either case, the meaning of the path of no-learning is that there is nothing more for us to accomplish.

The hinayana and mahayana use the same terms for the five paths, and in both cases the fifth stage is the final one. However, because of the difference between hinayana and mahayana, the complete qualities that an individual has developed at that level are different. An elephant has eyes, nose, tusks, legs, ears, and tail—a complete physical body. A mouse also has a complete physical body with eyes, nose, ears, tail, four legs, and so forth. However, these two complete bodies have very different energy, power, and strength. The difference between hinayana and mahayana is like that.

You might wonder why this is so. The practices do not produce the difference between the qualities developed in the hinayana and mahayana; it is the individual's depth of awareness and capacity for understanding that produces the difference. Suppose it is raining outside. If we put out two vessels of different sizes, one very small and the other quite large, both vessels will fill up with water. However, the small container will hold only a very small amount of water compared to the large one, even though the rain fell equally on both. Likewise, the levels reached in the hinayana and mahayana are different because of the individual practitioner's capacity and awareness, not because of his or her particular practice.

THE PATH OF ACCUMULATION

The path of accumulation is divided into three stages: the lesser, medium, and greater paths of accumulation. The lesser path of accumulation involves four examinations. We examine the body, the feelings, the mind, and the objects of the mind. These are the same categories discussed in the last chapter, and they include everything there is. We examine the four categories logically to overcome doubts about their nature.

First we examine our physical body inside and out very carefully, and we come to understand that nothing inside or outside our body is permanent. Everything is bound to change. We also come to understand that there is no such thing as a complete physical body that exists independently or is self-existent. All there is to this physical body is various components, which can be divided into an accumulation of many small particles, even down to atoms. When we realize this, we come to a stage where we can find nothing to be attached to in our body.

By this method we can free ourselves from attachment and especially from clinging to our physical body. In the tradition of the shravakas and pratyekas (i.e., the hinayana), practitioners examine the nature of the body by meditating in cemeteries. In Tibetan cemeteries, the bodies are just covered with stones, so you can almost see them. The practitioners examine the difference between a dead body and their own body, and the only difference they find is a matter of breathing in and out. Other than that there is no difference at all. Just as we are not attached to our skeleton, we can overcome attachment to our physical bodies by meditating in this manner.

Next, we try to free ourselves from clinging to feelings or sensations, by using the same method of careful examination. We see that all our feelings of comfort and pleasure depend on external objects such as wealth, possessions, and so forth. When we examine these feelings and sensations, we come to understand that our feelings can change in an instant. A feeling of pleasure can change into a feeling of pain within a very short time. Here again we find impermanence. In the past, not realizing the impermanence of things, but clinging to the pleasure and comfort of our physical bodies, we have worked extremely hard trying to maintain that pleasure and comfort. This has only resulted in disappointment, pain, and suffering. When we realize that feelings are impermanent, we can free ourself from clinging to them. We can also overcome our attachment to material possessions, wealth, property, and so forth.

Because we take everything as real, solid, and permanent, we are not free from attachment to the body and to possessions. The main way to become detached from the body and possessions is to understand that everything is impermanent. It is the same when we come to the mind, which we can also call the consciousness. In the past, we have held very strongly to the existence of that consciousness, to the feeling of its permanence and solidity. But if we examine very carefully, there is nothing permanent about it at all. We may think that our ideas and thoughts are permanent, but they change every instant. The first thought is the past of the second thought, and the second (present) thought is the past of the third (future) thought. What is permanent here?

The Tibetan word for a very short instant is *kechik*. Within the time it takes to snap our fingers, there are sixty kechiks, so we are speaking of an extremely short period of time. To explain the term *kechik* in another way, suppose we shoot a bullet through sixty layers of paper. To our eyes it seems that the bullet passes through the sixty layers of paper in an instant, but according to Buddhist philosophy, the time it takes to go through each layer is one kechik.

To continue our examination of the impermanence and change of our ideas and thoughts, suppose you are talking. The first word of whatever you say is the past of the second word. It does not really continue, and you cannot bring it back. If you repeat something, it is not the same thing—it is a repetition of what you said. Thus in feelings and consciousness there is change, there is impermanence.

The objects of the consciousness, which means all phenomena, are also impermanent. When you think about what you have done in the past, what you are doing in the present, and what you plan to do in the future, anything you think about is an object of the mind. Since you are able to think about all the objects of your experience in the past, present, and future, there is nothing solid or permanent in these things. Everything changes.

The aim of this meditation on impermanence is to free ourselves from attachment to our physical body, to our sensations or feelings, to the existence of the mind, and to the existence of all the objects of the mind. When we follow this method, we are able to free ourselves from attachment to the existence of the self or the sense of "I." When you examine everything carefully in this manner—your physical body, your consciousness, and your sensations or feelings—you cannot pinpoint anything that is "I." What are you calling "I" here? What is it you are attached to?

The method I have explained of reflecting on the impermanence of everything is used by practitioners of both hinayana and mahayana. In mahayana there is also a more advanced level of realizing the nonexistence of the self and the physical body. After seeing that the body is composed of tiny particles, it is seen that the tiniest particles—the atoms—do not exist on their own.[20]

To give you a better idea about the nonexistence of the self or "I," let me use myself as an example. I declare to you that my body does not exist. If you were to look at me, you would say you could see my body. Not only that, but a rather blunt person would say I have a bald head and a very big stomach. However, all these terms such as body, head, and stomach are just projections of the mind. What we call a body can be divided into parts—two legs, two arms, head, skin, hair, bone. If we take away all the parts, where is the body? The body does not exist. The "body" we are so attached to is simply an idea, a projection of the mind. Likewise, take my head as an example. We say "head," and we believe in the existence of my head. Yet we can divide it into parts—ear, nose, mouth, teeth, hair, skin, bones—and if we take all the parts away, there is no such thing as a head.

We can use the same method for my skin and bones. When we talk about bones, we feel sure they exist because they are so solid. But again we can divide them into parts, and further into smaller and smaller particles, down to atoms. At the mahayana level, the atom itself can be divided into smaller parts, so even an atom does not exist on its own. On the mahayana level, we speak about the emptiness of all things. When we examine, we find that nothing exists on its own, nothing has its own identity, everything is interdependent, everything is an accumulation of something else. Yet because of our confused minds, we have named things and taken them to be real. We have become attached to the existence of things.

When you recognize the nonexistence of the physical body, you also come to understand the nonexistence of feelings or sensations. If you have no physical body, how can you have sensations? When you recognize the nonexistence of sensations, you come to understand the nonexistence of the consciousness itself. You can search for the consciousness, the individual who thinks, "This is right, that is wrong; this is good, that is bad; I did this in the past, I am doing that in the present, I will do another thing in the future." If you search everywhere in your body, you cannot point to a solid or firm individual and say, "This is the one who has been judging good and bad and thinking about past, present, and future." In this way you will come to understand the nonexistence of the mind itself.

Where do you think your consciousness is? Is it real or unreal? Is it inside or outside? In the West, most people would say the consciousness is in the head. If something is real, it should have a form. If it has a form, it should have a color or shape. What shape is your consciousness? What color is your consciousness? You might think that when you look at something red (such as the carpet on the floor) your mind is red, and when you look at something blue your mind is blue. In that case, if you saw a fire, your brain would catch fire and burn! You have been trying to find your mind externally, outside your body. In the practice of mahayana meditation, you must look back at the looker, at the eye, to see the vision itself with the vision, rather than looking with the eye at some external object.

It is very difficult for any of us to answer the question, Does the mind exist or not? You should think about the nature of the consciousness and ask the question again and again, Does the consciousness exist or not? When we examine the mind and look into its nature, we become speechless, almost without thought. The mind is beyond existing and not existing. There is no idea that can relate to the consciousness. Try to maintain that state of speechlessness, not thinking it exists, not thinking it does not exist. That is the vipasyana practice. In the Buddhist view we say that all phenomena and all beings do not exist. We are not saying we do not exist the way we are, but if we examine very carefully through logical reasoning, dividing ourselves into parts, we cannot identify an independent being that exists on its own. Everything is interdependent.

By examining in this manner, we will begin to understand the real meaning of the term *emptiness,* or shunyata, that is used so often in Buddhism. If we simply say that everything is empty, nothing exists, it sounds very odd and crazy. If a person comes to you and simply says, "My body does not exist," it is hard to believe, because you can see that person. However, when the person explains about dividing the body into parts and then into very small particles down to atoms, and how even the atoms themselves do not exist, then through such logical reasoning, you will begin to understand what is meant by emptiness. Of course, here we are simply using words. Although the mind is working, trying to examine things, that is very different from the experience gained through vipasyana meditation.

We must sometimes understand the Buddhist view through logical reasoning. Otherwise, when we meditate with a teacher and the teacher says, "Now we will meditate in the nonconceptual state," it is hard for us to understand what the teacher means. The teacher is referring to the state of speechlessness, the state of being unable to say yes or no, it exists or it does not. That is the nonconceptual state. Of course, we have to understand this state partly through experience in meditation. We can describe it, but words cannot convey its complete meaning. After we have experienced the nonconceptual state once or twice, we can learn to maintain that state regularly. When we are in the nonconceptual state, there are no positive or negative thoughts, so we are not accumulating any positive or negative karma. Since we do not accumulate negative karma, we do not experience suffering. That is following the truth of the path and experiencing the cessation of suffering.

By examining carefully in this way, practicing, and experiencing the result of the meditation, you will come to understand the Dharma. You will also develop confidence, faith, and trust in the teachings of the Dharma and in the existence of enlightened beings.

The key to removing all the kleshas is realizing the nonexistence of the self, or experiencing selflessness. The great master Chandrakirti taught that the origin of all the kleshas is clinging to the existence of the self. When you cling to the existence of the self, you project the existence of others. When there are others, you divide them into three groups. The first group is those you like, and you become attached to them. The second group is those you dislike, and you develop hatred toward them. The third group is those you neither like nor dislike. You are neutral about them, and that is ignorance. By simply holding onto the existence of the self, you have now developed attachment, anger, and ignorance, and out of these, all the other defilements grow. When you realize the nonexistence of the self, there is no being to create projections or to develop any defilements.

To remove your defilements, you do not have to wrestle with them. By simply reflecting on the impermanence and nonexistence of everything, and meditating in that nonconceptual state, you can remove the defilements without having to use any force. That is why meditation practice is so important, and why it is especially important to maintain the nonconceptual state, meditating without thinking of any object.

I have been speaking about the first of the five paths, the path of accumulation. Having covered the four examinations on the lesser path of accumulation, I will now turn to the middle path of accumulation. This stage involves the four ways of perfecting oneself, or the four genuine abandonments. Stating these briefly, we must first purify the negative karma we have accumulated in the past. Second, we must not repeat the faults that led us to accumulate that past negative karma. Third, we must continue the positive actions we have practiced in the past and not allow them to deteriorate. Fourth, we must develop further positive qualities that we have not developed in the past.

On the greater path of accumulation we develop the "four miraculous legs." In the Western world, we might call them the four miraculous wheels. A car has four wheels, and with the help of the four wheels we can drive the car. If the car has lost one of the wheels, we cannot drive it. These four points are so important they are like the four wheels of a car. What are the four wheels of the greater path of accumulation? The first is motivation. If we have a strong determination and motivation, nothing can prevent us from practicing virtuous actions. As a result we accumulate merit, and this leads ultimately to attaining full enlightenment.

The second wheel is diligence. Our motivation gives us interest in the practice of meditation and the practice of virtuous actions. Our interest and joy in that work leads to effortless diligence. The third wheel is mindfulness. Morning, afternoon, and evening, throughout the day and night, we try to be mindful of performing virtuous actions and not engaging in unwholesome actions of the body, speech, and mind. Mindfulness is always keeping that intention in mind, being aware and alert so we can remember to act positively and not negatively.

The fourth wheel on the greater path of accumulation is one-pointedness, and that is slightly harder for us to understand. One-pointedness comes mainly from experience in the meditative state. It is being able to sit with the mind completely focused on an object, without producing any thoughts or conceptions such as reflecting on the past or planning for the future. When we are able to experience such one-pointed concentration, we are quite advanced students.

For practitioners to achieve the goal, it is very important to develop these four miraculous wheels. All of them must be present at the same time; it is not enough to have one and lack others. Looking at them again, the first is motivation to practice virtuous actions, to practice meditation, and so forth. Motivation causes us to heighten our interest. When we have interest, it is impossible not to have enthusiasm. When we have enthusiasm, there is diligence—the second wheel. When we have diligence, we are able to practice with strong longing and determination.

The third wheel is mindfulness. Even if we are motivated to practice and we have the diligence to practice, if we lack mindfulness, we will always forget to practice. We think we are going to practice meditation at nine AM, but we talk with our friends, we distract our minds, and by the time we catch ourselves it is ten-thirty. We really wanted to practice, but we have forgotten! That is why the third wheel is so important, always being mindful that we must be there practicing at a particular time.

The fourth wheel is one-pointedness. This does not apply only to profound meditation or even shamata practice. We should do every virtuous action with one-pointed concentration. For example, we may know how to recite mantras, such as *om mani peme hung*, the six-syllable mantra of Avalokiteshvara, the bodhisattva of compassion. Many people recite the mantra verbally while, at the same time, producing many kinds of neurotic thoughts. Because they lack one-pointedness, many students practice the Dharma year after year but never attain any result. This is not the fault of the practice, and it is not the fault of the Dharma itself. It is because such students have not developed one-pointedness.

In the practice of Buddhism, in performing virtuous actions and developing inner qualities, one-pointedness is very important. Because one-pointedness is so important, many teachers emphasize shamata meditation, which is one of the main keys to developing one-pointedness. The Vidyadhara Chögyam Trungpa Rinpoche had his students practice shamata for years and years and years. Shamata helps the student develop one-pointed concentration, and when we have developed this fourth miraculous wheel, the other three wheels are very easy. One-pointedness is the most difficult to develop because we must remain focused while we are working, walking, talking, sleeping—in everything we do.

If a practitioner develops all these four points and practices virtuous actions, the accomplishment is miraculously fast. This is why we call them the four miraculous wheels, or more traditionally, the four miraculous legs. If we practice virtuous actions or meditation without the four miraculous legs, it is like trying to shoot at a target with an unloaded gun. If we practice virtuous actions with motivation, yet lack the rest of the four points, it is like trying to quench our thirst with an empty cup.

To summarize the three stages of the path of accumulation, in the lesser path of accumulation, the student works to understand the nature of things through logic and reasoning. In the middle path of accumulation, the student works to accumulate positive qualities through virtuous actions of body, speech, and mind. Then in the greater path of accumulation, the student works to develop the four miraculous wheels. Whatever merit is accumulated through virtuous actions on the medium path of accumulation increases through the energy of the four wheels.

It is often said that the path of accumulation is a beginner's practice, but if we are actually practicing on the path of accumulation, we are quite advanced—we are not really beginners.

Questions

Q: I have read about developing detachment, and I was bothered by this. I was afraid this detachment might cool my love and compassion for others, so I stayed away from detachment. I stayed away from the idea that things are not real or people are not real, because I want to love people and love the beauty of this world, and I feared that detachment would make me cruel.

A: You have a slight misunderstanding about the realization of emptiness. Realizing the nonexistence or emptiness of everything does not destroy your love and compassion; it develops your love and compassion. Emptiness is like the sun, and loving-kindness and compassion are like the light of the sun. Where the sun is, there is always light.

When I say we can realize the nonexistence and emptiness of things through logical examination, I am not saying that everything disappears. Everything is still there. Let us take the carpet on the floor as an example. If we break it down into parts, we come to the conclusion that there is no such solid and firm thing as a carpet, but this does not make the carpet disappear. Realizing emptiness does not make sentient beings disappear either. We come to see that everything is impermanent and interdependent. We also see that sentient beings have not understood the impermanence and interdependence of things, and we develop greater loving-kindness and compassion toward these confused beings. Thus understanding emptiness develops our love and compassion further; it does not cool our love and compassion.

There is a slight defect in your question, however. You say you love to enjoy the beauty of the world. That is clearly an attachment that comes from the notion of the existence of "I." It is attachments that create problems for you and keep you mired in samsara.

We must also understand that detachment from the self cannot be experienced through words. We must practice. Through experience after experience after experience, we eventually arrive at complete detachment. When we first hear about detaching ourselves from things, the self, and beings, it bothers us. We cannot believe this is possible or desirable. We ask, "Why should I be detached?" This shows clearly that we have been attached for a long, long time. Right now we have a problem just accepting the word detachment. It is even harder to realize detachment, and the realization has to come through practice.

Q: During shamata practice and even while doing simple physical tasks, I find it possible to remain one-pointed, but at other times my mind often becomes agitated. I wonder if I have been applying the practice incorrectly.

A: With shamata meditation, we do not remove the kleshas; we simply pacify them. While you are maintaining one-pointedness, you may experience peacefulness, but when you no longer maintain one-pointedness, the negative emotions you have pacified by your meditation can arise again. When you become agitated, it shows that you have not removed the negative emotions; they are still there. In the vipasyana experience, you really remove the negative emotions. You are not applying the practice of one-pointedness incorrectly; you are doing perfectly well. You need to apply a vipasyana method. Whenever you experience agitation, look at the nature of the agitation itself.

Any of you can apply this method in daily life. Perhaps you do shamata meditation, but later in your ordinary activities—walking, talking, working—you develop agitation or one of the kleshas such as anger or jealousy. When that happens, apply the vipasyana method of looking at the nature of whatever you are experiencing. Even if you are not experiencing agitation or kleshas, it is always helpful to train in this manner for very short periods. Wherever you are—you need not be sitting—take a moment to look at the nature of the body, the mind, and so on. Even if you are walking, take one second to look back at the nature of the mind in the nonconceptual state.

Q: What is the difference between shamata and samadhi?

A: Buddhism has developed many dharmic terms that have no equivalents in English, just as in the modern world we have many technical terms for which there are no words in Sanskrit or Tibetan. Samadhi and shamata are synonyms, but samadhi is a general or collective name. There are many different divisions, classifications, and stages of samadhi. There is vajra-like samadhi, which is at a very high level.[21] Samadhi can also mean shamata meditation. When you are able to maintain one-pointedness, that is samadhi. You can also practice samadhi on loving-kindness or compassion, which means developing love or compassion and maintaining the mind in that state. The Tibetan term for samadhi is *ting nge dzin. Ting* means profound and *dzin* means to hold, so *ting nge dzin* means to hold the profundity of whatever experience you are having.

THE PATH OF UNIFICATION

We now come to the second stage, the path of unification or linking. In the path of accumulation, we practiced virtuous actions on a worldly level. In the path of unification, we unite these worldly virtuous actions with the activities of superior beings such as arhats. Similarly, whatever experience we have attained on a worldly level in the path of accumulation, we unite with the experience of the path of seeing—an experience we have never had before. The path of unification is the link between the ordinary and superior levels.

There are four stages in the path of unification, which correspond to four signs of development. Strictly speaking, these four signs of development apply to our inner experience. Since worldly terms cannot give the complete meaning of this inner experience, we must use examples to explain the four signs.

The first sign of development in the student's mind is the experience of warmth. This is analogous to the heat produced when we rub two sticks of wood together vigorously, which is a sign that continuing to rub the sticks together will ultimately produce fire. This warmth experienced in the meditation is not actual heat like that from a heater or a fire. The experience is a kind of warming of the qualities that are developing within us, which are called the five powers. Feeling the presence of these qualities is like feeling warmth.

The first power is tremendous devotion. Through devotion we develop the second power, enthusiasm, which was described earlier. With devotion and enthusiasm, we also develop mindfulness, and having developed these three powers, we develop samadhi, the profound meditative state. Through samadhi, we develop wisdom or awareness. These five powers—devotion, enthusiasm, mindfulness, samadhi, and wisdom—are the warmth of the first stage on the path of unification.

The second sign on the path of unification is the peak or the point, which is like the peak or highest point of a mountain. The five powers we developed in the first stage have now been stabilized, and nothing can overcome them. Since our experience is now the highest, this stage is called the peak of our experience. This can be related to the example of rubbing two sticks of wood together. When we first rub the two sticks together very hard, we feel the warmth of the wood. As we continue to rub them together vigorously, we begin to notice a smell of burning and a flicker of flame, and this makes us more certain that if we keep going we will produce fire. Similarly, our certainty and belief in the result of the path have now come to the highest level, so it is known as the peak of our experience.

The third stage of the path of unification is patience or endurance. At this stage the five qualities we developed earlier— devotion, enthusiasm, mindfulness, samadhi, and wisdom— are well stabilized and they are now called the five forces. In addition to the five forces, we develop unchangeable, immovable patience. Patience helps us overcome any obstacles that come our way on the path to enlightenment. We can bear any pain and endure any unfavorable conditions, and thus we can overcome all difficulties, hardships, and problems.

The great yogi Milarepa had to face many hardships to achieve complete enlightenment. Someone who lacked patience and endurance would have given up, but if Milarepa had given up, he never would have achieved supreme realization. It is very important not to give up but to persist and to bear the pain, difficulties, and hardships that come in the path of the Dharma. That is why the third stage of the path of unification is the development of patience.

An individual who possesses patience actually has a greater opportunity to achieve realization. A person with patience and the ability to endure hardship is always happy and content in mind and body, and this gives him or her the strength and the will to practice harder. It is when we are disappointed, when we lack self-confidence, or when we are dissatisfied, that we are unable to practice. If we develop patience, and thus are content and satisfied regardless of the situation, we have a much greater chance to achieve our goal. The great bodhisattvas were able to work tirelessly for the betterment of all sentient beings, even giving their flesh, bones, and bodies to beings without the slightest hesitation. This was because they had developed complete patience.

With that we come to the fourth stage of the path of unification, known as the supreme dharma. At this moment, we determine whether we are ordinary people or superior beings. Suppose we have developed patience, the third sign, and we put ourselves into samadhi, the meditative state. Within a second, we have realized absolute bodhicitta, otherwise known as emptiness or shunyata. Sometimes it is known as *mahamudra*; sometimes it is known as *maha ati*. Whatever name we call it, when we experience that realization, we are no longer ordinary people. Within the matter of a second we have become superior beings. Before we sat down and put ourselves into samadhi, we were ordinary people. Immediately afterward, we have realized emptiness and have become superior beings.

THE PATH OF SEEING

The experience of emptiness or absolute bodhicitta is a completely new experience for us, and thus we have entered into the path of seeing. When we have this experience for just one kechik, 112 confusions and wrong views are eliminated. As ordinary beings, we have vast numbers of confusions. I will not go into detail about what they are, but the mind is cleared of many of them just by seeing.

To illustrate this, suppose I am told about a person named John. I have never seen John before, but ever since I heard about him, I have imagined he had a beard. The moment I see John and notice that he has no beard—even if I have just a glimpse of him—the confusion in my mind of thinking John has a beard is simply eliminated. I do not have to use any other force to eliminate it; I now know John has no beard. Similarly, we overcome 112 confusions by realizing emptiness for one kechik.

We can also call this going beyond the confusion. When a plane is moving on the ground, the pilot has to be extremely cautious and look in all directions, to see whether the plane is headed the right way and whether there is any traffic on the right or left. However, when the plane is above the clouds, the pilot can fly with ease because he or she knows that nothing will be in the way. In the same way, when we realize absolute bodhicitta on the path of seeing, we go beyond a great amount of confusion.

THE PATH OF MEDITATION

We now come to the path of meditation. Continuing the analogy of the plane, if the path of seeing is like taking off, then the path of meditation is like flying above the clouds. It is the same plane, yet taking off from the ground and flying above the clouds are slightly different. There is likewise a slight difference between the path of seeing and the path of meditation. In the path of meditation, we develop the experience of shunyata or absolute bodhicitta that was attained on the path of seeing.

Individuals who have reached the path of meditation are known as authentic teachers, the extraordinary Sangha, or exalted beings. You may be familiar with the refuge prayer which says, "I take refuge in the Buddha, I take refuge in the Dharma, I take refuge in the exalted Sangha." It is the exalted, supreme Sangha—the extraordinary Sangha—in which we take refuge, not the ordinary Sangha. Beings who have reached the level of the paths of seeing and meditation have the capacity to lead and benefit others, and that is why they are called the extraordinary Sangha.

At this stage of realization, an individual has a great capacity to benefit sentient beings through various skillful means, through wisdom, and by manifesting in different forms. The ability to benefit others has developed completely, because the individual who has reached this level is not stained by any faults or mistakes. In the practice of the mahayana, our teachers continually emphasize that we must develop the altruistic attitude, we must think of benefiting all sentient beings with the result of every practice we do. Right now, we are training our minds, becoming familiar with the aspiration to help others, so that when we reach the path of meditation, helping others will be spontaneous and effortless.

As I said, the path of seeing and the path of meditation are only slightly different, like a plane taking off and a plane flying above the clouds. In the path of seeing, we realize shunyata, and in the path of meditation, we develop that realization, experiencing it more regularly and constantly. There are ten bhumis or levels on the path of meditation. We describe an individual on the path of meditation as stainless and faultless; however, while he or she has removed the gross kleshas, there are still subtle habitual patterns that exist in such an individual from the first to the sixth bhumis. How can someone be described as stainless when there are still some habitual patterns? To make it clear, I will give you an example—a Tibetan example.

Suppose we have made a fire on the ground in this room. Let us take the fire itself, and the wood we are burning, as an example of the kleshas. Suppose we put out that fire and remove the wood and ashes completely. After one or two days there is no mark of the fire on the ground, but when we come into the room, we can still smell something from the fire. That smell is like the habitual patterns that remain. The gross kleshas have been removed and, because of that, the person is known as stainless. Yet some subtle habitual patterns remain, like the smell of what we burned two days ago, to show that he or she is not a completely enlightened being.

From the first bhumi to the sixth bhumi,[22] the individual develops what is known as the seven branches of enlightenment. The first branch of enlightenment is a perfect memory, such a strong memory that there is no chance for us to forget anything, even if someone tries to make us forget. We remember not only what is happening now, but what we have to do later and what we did earlier, very clearly and precisely.

The second branch is the wisdom of seeing all phenomena as they are. When we see things as they are instead of the way they appear to be, we have no confusion about whether they are right or wrong. The third branch of enlightenment is diligence, and especially diligence in working ceaselessly to benefit sentient beings. The fourth branch is developing not only diligence, but also perfect joy in working for beings. Laziness never overcomes us; we can work twenty-four hours a day to benefit all sentient beings, because of the strength that comes from joy.

The fifth branch of enlightenment is blissfulness and peacefulness of mind and body, as well as mental clarity. Having developed peacefulness, clarity, and blissfulness, there is nothing that can disturb or agitate our minds, and thus we can work continuously to benefit sentient beings. The sixth branch is samadhi, the profound meditative state, in which nothing can distract our minds. No matter what we are doing—walking, sitting, sleeping, or talking—we are able to maintain the state of samadhi.

The seventh branch of enlightenment is the perfect state of equanimity. We work to benefit all sentient beings equally, without any discrimination. When we try to benefit others, sometimes people accept our help and sometimes they reject it. Sometimes they react badly, and sometimes they thank us. We do not discriminate between beings who are good to us and those who are trying to harm us. Having developed a perfect state of equanimity, we can always work spontaneously to benefit sentient beings, whether they praise us or blame us. When we have fully developed these seven branches of enlightenment, we have fully developed compassion as well. Since we have profound, sincere compassion, nothing can hinder us in benefiting sentient beings.

When we have reached the level of the path of seeing and the path of meditation, we do not have to depend on a spiritual master. In the paths of accumulation and unification, the need to rely on a *guru* is greatly emphasized. The student is told how important it is to have faith and trust in the guru. At that level our own awareness and wisdom cannot lead us on the right path, so we must depend on someone else to guide us.

On the first of the ten bhumis, we develop many qualities, such as being able to emanate in a hundred different forms to benefit sentient beings. At the same time, within the matter of a kechik, we are able to listen directly to teachings from a hundred enlightened beings. These are the qualities of the first bhumi. On the second bhumi, we are able to emanate in a thousand forms to benefit sentient beings, and within a kechik, we are able to receive teachings from a thousand enlightened beings. Likewise, on the third bhumi it is ten thousand, and so forth. That is how we develop as we go through the ten stages. Because we can receive teachings and instructions directly from enlightened beings, we no longer need the physical form of a guru.

When people do not understand the qualities of the bhumis, they find it hard to believe Shakyamuni Buddha's prediction that the buddha activity of His Holiness Karmapa would pervade a billion worlds. However, when we know about the qualities of the bhumis, it is not so hard to believe. Enlightened beings can manifest in a billion different forms in a billion different worlds. They are present in many different worlds, benefiting the beings in each one. That explains why the Buddha said the Karmapa's buddha activity would pervade a billion worlds. In the modern world, our capacity to accept such things is very limited. Sometimes we hear that a lama or realized teacher has taken rebirth in three different incarnations, said to be the body, speech, and mind incarnations of that one teacher. This is very difficult for us to believe, not because we do not believe in the Dharma, but because we do not know the power and capacity of highly realized beings.

From the first to the sixth bhumis, we completely remove the karmic defilements of attachment, aggression, greed, ignorance, jealousy, and pride. Then, beginning with the seventh bhumi, we remove the wisdom defilements. As we progress from the seventh bhumi onward, we develop eight superior qualities of enlightenment[23] that remove the wisdom defilements. The first and second superior qualities can be applied for our own benefit. The first is perfect unobscured view, which means that our view becomes so clear that we have no doubt at all. The second is perfect clear thought, which is seeing the ultimate nature of things without any error.

The third superior quality is perfect unobscured speech, and this is applied to benefit others. At our worldly level, we try to explain things to people with words, assuming they will understand the words. However, it is often very hard to make people understand through words, especially if they speak a different language. If we have perfect unobscured speech, each individual listening to us hears the teaching in his or her own language, and understands the words as soon as we utter them.

The fourth superior quality is perfect unobscured action. There is never any sign of a mistake in the actions an individual at this level performs to benefit other beings. That person's behavior and ways of dealing with people—indeed all that person's activities—are perfect, correct, and effective. No one can point to any mistake such an exalted person has made, so it is called perfect action.

The fifth superior quality is perfect unobscured livelihood. An individual at this level of realization does not have to depend on food and water as we do, but is able to live on the food of meditation. Such a person does not have to live on meat, rice, barley, and so forth, which could eventually obscure the mind.[24] When we are eating or selling meat, we are always accumulating negative karma. Beings at this stage have gone beyond the need of food, but we call it perfect livelihood just to understand at what level they are.

The sixth superior quality is perfect unobscured effort. Every effort that beings at this level make is directed solely toward benefiting sentient beings. They do not waste a single moment of their time in activities that benefit themselves alone and do not benefit others. That is why it is known as perfect unobscured effort.

The seventh superior quality is perfect unobscured memory. Within the matter of a kechik, an individual at this level can reflect back to a thousand births he or she took in the past, remembering them as if they were happening in the present. That is called perfect unobscured memory. Shakyamuni Buddha was able to describe the births he had in the past, such as those that involved the five men and 80,000 gods who were present when he first turned the wheel of Dharma. That is evidence that at this stage we are able to remember all the past births we have taken.

Finally, the eighth superior quality is perfect unobscured samadhi, the profound meditative state. When an individual at this stage enters into that state of perfect unobscured samadhi, he or she can enter into a thousand forms of samadhi within one kechik.

I have now explained about the qualities we develop from the first path, the path of accumulation, through the fourth path, the path of meditation. I have yet to speak about the fifth path, which is the fruition, the actual complete result. From the first path through the fourth path, we develop thirty-seven qualities. In explaining these, I first spoke about the four ways of examining, and next about the four ways of perfecting oneself. Then I described the four miraculous legs, which makes twelve qualities. The five powers and the five forces make ten more qualities. Next I talked about the seven branches of enlightenment, and finally the eight supreme qualities of enlightened beings. If we add these together, they total thirty-seven. From the path of accumulation through the path of meditation, we develop these thirty-seven perfect qualities of the bodhisattva, and thus we perfect the Buddhadharma. Beyond this, on the fifth path, is complete enlightenment.

As was explained, at the stage of the path of seeing, we remove 112 confusions and delusions. From there onward we continue to develop, and by the end of the path of meditation we have removed 414 more confusions. As a result of removing these 526 confusions, we become an enlightened being, a buddha—*sangye* in Tibetan. As explained earlier, the first syllable, *sang*, means removed completely. What we have removed is all of the 526 confusions and delusions. The second syllable, *gye*, means developed, or blossomed, and this refers to all the good qualities we have developed. I will discuss the complete blossoming of the qualities later. Again, *sangye* is the blossoming of all the positive qualities, after removing all the confusions and delusions.

Why have we gone into such detail about the stages of removing the confusions and developing the qualities? At the beginning, it was very hard to believe the story of how the Buddha took birth from the right side of his mother and how flowers blossomed as his feet touched the ground. When we do not know the qualities of an enlightened being, it is hard to believe such a story. Now that we know all the qualities of a perfect enlightened being, we can see that the miracles the Buddha performed at his birth were very, very small.

It is fascinating to hear about the capacities of bodhisattvas and the qualities of enlightened beings. Sometimes we fail to realize that all these qualities are present within us. If we understand that all the qualities of enlightened beings are within us, we can work to understand and experience them for ourselves, rather than simply appreciating them in someone else, whom we think of as a superior being. That superior being could be us. If we know the right way to practice—what to give up and what to adopt—we can develop these qualities without needing to relate them to anyone else. It is important to remove the confusion of thinking of ourselves as inferior beings and some others as superior beings. That confusion is removed when we know that we all have the capacity to develop these qualities if we practice diligently. Each of us has the opportunity to realize and accomplish this.

THE PATH OF NO-LEARNING

The fifth path is the path of no-learning. A complete explanation of this path would take a long time, but for now I will explain it very briefly and as clearly as possible. The path of no-learning is on the eleventh bhumi, known as the bhumi of the total elimination of obscurations. This corresponds to *sang*, the first syllable in *sangye*, the word for buddha. I will now discuss further the second syllable *gye*, the development of the qualities.

In addition to the thirty-seven qualities we described before, a buddha experiences three *kayas* or three bodies. The experience of the *dharmakaya*, or wisdom body, is the buddha's own realization of ultimate wisdom. After that, in order to benefit limitless beings, a buddha manifests the *sambhogakaya* or body of bliss, and the *nirmanakaya* or emanation body. Both of these kayas are only manifested to benefit others; the dharmakaya is realized for oneself. Sambhogakaya beings benefit and teach all the bodhisattvas from the first bhumi to the tenth bhumi. Ordinary beings are unable to receive teachings from the sambhogakaya buddhas, so the nirmanakaya buddhas are manifested in order to benefit ordinary, unrealized beings like us.

The historical Buddha Shakyamuni is the fourth buddha who has come to the earth to give teachings. According to prediction, there will be a thousand buddhas who come to turn the wheel of Dharma in this kalpa, all in the form of nirmanakaya beings. Out of the thousand buddhas, four have come already, which means 996 are yet to come. These nirmanakaya buddhas come to the earth to benefit sentient beings, and since they are emanations of enlightened beings, they take miraculous birth. I have talked about Shakyamuni Buddha taking birth from the right side of his mother, and flowers blossoming wherever his feet touched the ground. These are the miraculous powers of an enlightened being who comes in the form of a nirmanakaya buddha to benefit sentient beings.

Enlightened beings in the nirmanakaya form have three kinds of qualities. First, there are 112 qualities of their physical appearance. When sentient beings look upon the buddhas, much of their confusion, pain, and illness is removed simply by the physical appearance of the buddhas. The moment we see the buddhas, we do not want to blink our eyes. We want to stare at them because they are so magnificent and pure.

Second, there are sixty-four qualities of the speech of nirmanakaya beings. For example, by simply uttering one sentence, the buddhas answer whatever question is on the mind of any individual who is listening, and they fulfill everyone's needs. When a buddha speaks, everyone understands in his or her own language. Regardless of whether the listeners are far or near, they hear the voice of the buddha equally well.

Third, the nirmanakaya beings have developed two qualities of the mind: knowing everything as it is and knowing everything as it manifests. Knowing everything as it is means a buddha can see not only his or her own previous births, but those of other beings. They also know what will happen to them in the future. Knowing everything as it manifests means the buddhas know the needs and requirements of all sentient beings, without having to talk to them. Knowing what sentient beings need enables a buddha to be more helpful and effective.

This is only a tiny portion of the qualities of the nirmanakaya beings: the qualities of the body, the qualities of the speech, and the qualities of the mind. There are so many qualities that we do not have time to talk about them all, and even if we did, it would be hard to understand and believe them. Therefore, I have just touched on them to complete the explanation of the five paths.

These many qualities are none other than the tathagatagarbha, or buddha nature, that we all possess. The complete experience of that buddha nature gives rise to all these qualities. It may seem hard to believe that so much can come from so little, but consider an example. A flower has a tiny seed, which we can plant in the ground and cultivate. When the plant grows, it produces many colorful, fragrant flowers that have many qualities the tiny seed did not have. What is the origin of the colorful, fragrant, beautiful flowers? Without that tiny simple seed, the colorful flowers would never have appeared. Likewise, the buddha nature seems very simple, but the qualities seem complex. These qualities have developed from the tathagatagarbha. They were there all the time; we have just removed the obscurations that covered them.

I do not expect you to believe everything I have said. You must develop belief from your own side. However, the Dharma is very profound. Even if we do not practice, we are able to accumulate much merit simply by listening to the Dharma. If we also develop belief in the Dharma, the merit accumulated is beyond measure. Those of you who are practitioners must always aspire to develop the qualities I have talked about and to benefit beings.

In the practice itself, you will undergo many experiences, some of them wonderful and pleasant, and some unbearable and unpleasant. Sometimes you will experience the warmth, sometimes the notion of emptiness, sometimes the clarity. Whatever you experience, it is important not to cling to the experience but to know that this pleasant or unpleasant experience will change. If you have a pleasant experience, watch the experience and do not cling to it. Likewise, if you have an unpleasant experience, do not be frightened by it or try to push it away, but watch it as well. In the practice of meditation and in the achievement of these qualities, you will have to overcome many pleasant and unpleasant experiences; therefore, do not hesitate and do not doubt. Part of the process of development is overcoming all the obstacles and hindrances in the meditative path.

Questions

Q: How does bodhicitta fit into the five paths?

A: Bodhicitta has several aspects. Aspiration bodhicitta is wishing to remove the suffering and pain of all sentient beings, to give them happiness and joy, and to establish them in the state of unchangeable happiness. This is simply an aspiration. We are not practicing it; we have just developed the idea of wanting to give happiness and remove suffering. Perseverance bodhicitta is more advanced. We take the bodhisattva vow, either from our guru or by ourselves before superior beings we have visualized. We vow that from today onward we will practice with body, speech, and mind to benefit sentient beings and to establish all beings in the state of unchangeable happiness. From then on, whatever practice we do (such as meditation) becomes perseverance bodhicitta. Aspiration bodhicitta and perseverance bodhicitta are both relative bodhicitta.

We develop bodhicitta as we travel the five paths. From the lesser path of accumulation until the highest path of unification, we develop and practice relative bodhicitta, including aspiration and perseverance bodhicitta. Then from the path of seeing until the tenth bhumi, we develop absolute bodhicitta, or profound wisdom. When we attain the complete realization of a buddha, we have completely developed absolute bodhicitta.

Q: You spoke about having a glimpse of nonduality on entering the path of seeing. Is that irreversible? Is there no falling back?

A: Yes, it is not possible to fall back at that stage. At the moment you attain the experience of shunyata in the path of seeing, you have removed 112 confusions. Since you have taken off much of your burden, you cannot be pulled back. Even when you experience the four miraculous wheels in the greater path of accumulation, you can never fall back. Using our example of the car, a car can go in reverse, but here you cannot. However, when you reach the level of the four miraculous wheels, you might experience many misfortunes, because all of the past negative karma you have accumulated ripens at that point.

Q: How does the vipasyana practice fit into the path?

A: The vipasyana experience is the same as absolute bodhicitta or shunyata. It starts on the path of seeing. However, the practice of vipasyana is not the vipasyana experience. The vipasyana experience is the fruition of the vipasyana practice. It is like building a house. It is always called a house, yet at the beginning, when you just wanted to build it, the house did not exist at all. At the end, when you have finished building it, the house exists for everyone to see. The same word is used in both cases.

Earlier we examined the physical body to see the nonexistence of the self, and then examined all phenomena to see the nonexistence of phenomena. At the last moment we asked, "Does the self exist or not? Do the phenomena exist or not?" and we reached a gap where we could not say yes or no. That gap is the vipasyana practice. When through that practice we have achieved vipasyana realization, we know the nonexistence of everything. In the practice we are uncertain. We can neither be totally sure things exist nor totally sure things do not exist. We are between yes and no. When we realize vipasyana, we know for sure.

There is also a more direct method that we may be taught. The direct method is not examining at all, but just putting ourselves into a nonconceptual state. Without examining the world, outer phenomena, or the physical body or self, we sit down and meditate on nothingness at the very beginning. The disadvantage of such a practice is that sometimes we tend to develop doubts when we are meditating in this way. Sometimes we think, "What am I doing by meditating on nothing? Am I doing it right? How can I be sure nothing exists?" This kind of doubt can prevent our development. Otherwise, this method is more direct.

Whether we use the analytic method of examining through logic, or the direct method of meditation, we reach the same point.

Q: In the story of the Buddha, I was surprised when you said that before he discovered vipasyana, the Indian tradition did not go beyond shamata. I have understood that shamata practice is the foundation on which vipasyana arises. Why did they get stuck? Was the technique different from what we are using now?

A: It is very good that this question came up, because it is true that shamata practice can lead to the experience of vipasyana, provided that the student knows the correct method. In other forms of meditation, shamata gives an experience of peacefulness and clarity, and those who do not know the right method become attached to the peacefulness. They take the peacefulness as solid and final, and they do not look beyond it to further experience. In our style of meditation, when we experience peacefulness in shamata, we do not become attached to it. By understanding the insubstantiality of the peacefulness, we are led to experience the vipasyana state.

Q: You used the words peacefulness and clarity to describe the shamata state. Would you be willing to describe in words what the vipasyana state feels like, as contrasted with shamata?

A: The experience of the vipasyana state is beyond words, beyond expression. It is called the realization of emptiness. There are no worldly terms we can use to describe emptiness. Everything we are using now is materialistic, even the words. How could we find a nonmaterialistic word? It is like trying to tell a man who has been blind from birth about red, white, and blue colors. Although the blind man can hear, he has no idea of the meaning of red, white, and blue because colors cannot be expressed in words. They have to be seen. If a skilled physician cures this man's blindness, he then knows what red, white, and blue mean.

Another example is a woman who has never in her life experienced summer and never even knew that summer exists. This woman lives in a cold, snowy, frozen world. Suppose you tell her that in our world there is summer when the flowers grow, all the earth turns green, and butterflies fly. You could tell this woman many things about this beautiful world, but she would find them hard to believe, because she sees only white everywhere. To make her believe, you have to take her to a place where there is summer.

8 The Three Vehicles

There are three levels of practice in Buddhism—three Dharma paths. These are traditionally known as the three vehicles or yanas. In the preceding chapters I have discussed many practices and teachings of the first two: hinayana, the path of self-discipline, and mahayana, the path of the bodhisattva. In this chapter I will review and summarize these teachings, and in addition, give an introduction to the third vehicle, vajrayana, the path of profound methods. In Tibetan Buddhism, these three vehicles are integrated and viewed as a progression, each building on the one before.

HINAYANA

I will first explain the importance of the hinayana level of practice and give some insight into the differences between the hinayana and mahayana. Although the mahayana is more profound than the hinayana, we cannot enter into the mahayana stage of the path without first being prepared through the practices of the hinayana stage.

The teachings at the hinayana level are the four noble truths, which were presented by Shakyamuni Buddha when he first turned the wheel of the Dharma at Sarnath near Varanasi at the age of thirty-five. These teachings were attended by such beings as Brahma and Indra, as well as five human beings and 80,000 beings from the god realm, who were the Buddha's first disciples. At that time, the Buddha explained the four noble truths three times. At the end of the third explanation, the five human beings attained the state of arhat, the highest level of realization attainable from the practice of hinayana. The 80,000 gods attained the path of seeing on the mahayana level.

The four noble truths are suffering, the cause of suffering, the cessation of suffering, and the path that leads to the cessation of suffering. The Buddha taught that the truth of suffering must be known. We must recognize that beings in cyclic existence constantly experience suffering. Knowing about suffering, we must understand the cause of suffering. Only then can we abandon the cause of suffering and thereby eliminate suffering. When we do not understand suffering and its cause, and have no idea how to eliminate it, the experience of suffering constantly holds truth.

The cause of suffering is karmic patterns. In former lifetimes, we have performed many kinds of negative actions based on kleshas such as greed, hatred, and ignorance. As a result, the upheaval of these negative emotional patterns is repeated within this lifetime. Having accumulated such karmic patterns in the past, we experience suffering now. Adding to the accumulation of such patterns at present causes suffering in the future. This continual repetition is the truth of the cause of suffering. That is what we must abandon.

In order to liberate ourselves from suffering, we must apply the truth of the path. The path serves as an antidote for the cause of suffering. When we follow the path, we eliminate the cause of suffering and attain the truth of the cessation of suffering.

The truth of the path can be described in terms of view, meditation, and action. First we must understand the view, which is that the cause of our suffering and confusion is ignorance. Because of ignorance, we develop the idea of self or ego, the idea that we have some kind of fixed, substantial identity. By developing ego, we create the realm of duality. Clinging to the notion of "I" or ego, we regard all objects and beings we find to be attractive and pleasing as being in our territory, and we develop attachment and clinging toward them. We regard all objects and beings we find to be unpleasant and unattractive as not being in our personal territory, and toward them we develop aggression and hatred. In this way dualistic clinging develops from the sense of "I", and everything is governed by this plan of the ego.

If we examine things carefully, however, we cannot find anything that we can identify as "I." If we investigate external objects, we cannot find "I" in any of them. We can look instead at the body, but here again we cannot find "I." From the tip of our toes to the crown of our head, we cannot find "I" in the body. If we investigate further and divide the body, we find fingers, legs, and head; we find flesh, blood, and bone, but we cannot find "I." Next we might try to say the mind is "I," but when we examine the mind, we find only a chain of thoughts. There is nothing fixed in the mind. The mind has no color, shape, form, or specific location. We cannot lay a finger on anything and say, "This is 'I.' "

Besides that, often without thinking about it, we say, "This is my mind" or "This is my body." When I say "my mind," the mind cannot be "I." When I say "my body," the body cannot be "I." At this point we can clearly say that "I" is neither the body nor the mind! This is not just a matter of logical reasoning. In reality there is no such thing as "I" or self; there is no substantially existing essence. That is the basic view of the hinayana path.

We can gain an understanding of the view, but that is not the same as realizing the view. Simply understanding the view does not help us, because we are still driven by our habitual patterns. Our egoistic clinging and grasping continue even though we understand that the view says something quite different. We must begin to practice the path, and the first step is to understand and recognize the transitory nature of the phenomenal world. Samsara is impermanent; things are constantly changing. Nothing is certain or reliable about samsaric existence.

Samsara is understood to be very deceitful. Hinayana practitioners, living in the mundane world in a town or city, see everything as garbage. People are like skeletons walking around, and nothing is worth having. There is a sense of disappointment in and rejection of the world. This is somewhat narrow from the point of view of the greater vehicle, but at this stage it is very precise. Everything in the outer world and everything in the body is seen as totally meaningless. Normally we cling tremendously to our bodies. In the hinayana approach, we begin to examine each and every organ of the body, and we find flesh, blood, bones, mucus, and feces. There is nothing desirable or worth holding onto here.

When we understand the body and the outer world in this way, we are driven to renounce them and escape from samsara. We long to be liberated and to experience the happiness and peace of arhatship. Thus we go into a remote, quiet place such as a cave, forest, or monastery, and practice meditation. The basic practice is shamata or sitting meditation, aimed toward calming the mind. This leads to a lessening of distracting thoughts and upheavals of the kleshas. In this way we diminish and eventually eliminate such neurotic patterns.

In the practice of discipline at this level, there is a great emphasis on moral conduct. There are what are known as the seven families of pratimoksha discipline, which are various levels of moral precepts. Sometimes these are classified as four families of pratimoksha discipline. The first two families are the precepts followed by laypeople. These are the *upasaka* and *upasika* precepts, for male and female lay practitioners respectively. The next two families are the precepts for the *getsulpa* and *getsulma*, the lesser ordination of monks and nuns. Next are the *gelopma* precepts. When a nun who has taken the lesser ordination wishes to take the higher ordination, she first practices these eight special precepts for a period of time. The final two families are the precepts for the higher ordination of monks and nuns, *gelongpa* and *gelongma,* or in Sanskrit, *bhikshu* and *bhikshuni.*

In summary, there are the lay precepts, the lesser monk or nun precepts, the special nun precepts that come before higher ordination, and the higher monk and nun precepts. This makes four families, or seven if the male and female are counted separately. Ultimately it is the precepts of the highest monk and nun ordination that should be followed in terms of outer discipline at the hinayana level. For people who cannot follow such a large number of precepts immediately, the pratimoksha is like a staircase. Practitioners can work up to the ultimate level of precepts by gradual stages, starting from the lay vows, going next to the lesser ordination, and finally to the highest ordination. For the various levels, there are four, ten, and seventeen precepts, or more elaborately five, thirty-six, and 253 or 340.

At this stage, there is a tremendous emphasis on outer physical discipline and moral conduct. It is as if we are wearing a very special outfit and cannot stand to get it dirty. We see the indulgences of samsara as dirt or garbage, and want no part of them. We put our minds under a very strict restraint, as if we are working under a powerful and demanding leader in whose presence we cannot afford to make any mistakes. Or we see samsara as a burning, blazing fire, and we must avoid burning ourselves. It is very important to watch the mind, to have an attitude of renunciation at all times, and to avoid indulging in the entertainments of samsara. This is emphasized very precisely.

With this understanding of the view and the discipline, I will now review the stages of practice or the five paths from the hinayana perspective. The first is the path of accumulation, and this begins once we have developed an understanding of the view and the importance of following the disciplines. The second stage is the path of unification or linking, in which we are beginning to switch from the pattern of egoistic clinging to having a glimpse of egolessness. This is not the actual realization and there is no certainty to it, but it is a link to the next stage, the path of seeing.

The path of seeing is like the breaking of dawn. It is the first moment of establishing the experience of egolessness, which is something we have not experienced before. At this point, it is no longer just an intellectual understanding. Next is the path of meditation, which is a further expansion of and training in the experience of egolessness. Finally, there is the path of no-learning, which is the fruition of the path. For those strictly involved in the hinayana path, the fruition is the attainment of arhatship, the realization of egolessness or the selflessness of self.

By following the five stages of the path, the practitioner develops the qualities of confidence, diligence, mindfulness, samadhi, and finally wisdom, which is the realization of selflessness. To elaborate on the five paths, the path of accumulation has three stages, the path of unification has four, the path of seeing has one, the path of meditation has eight stages, and the path of no-learning has one stage.

The time it takes to attain arhatship depends on the diligence and perseverance of the student. It can be attained within one lifetime, or in three or five or as long as seven lifetimes. An arhat is individually liberated from suffering. The Tibetan term for arhat is *drachompa*. *Dra* means "enemy" and *chompa* means "to conquer." The enemy here is the karmic patterns and emotional upheavals that are the cause of suffering. Thus *drachompa* means one who has conquered the enemy of the neurotic patterns.

An arhat is liberated from the sufferings of samsara, yet from the point of view of the ultimate awakened state of mind, which is complete buddhahood, this is a sidetrack. It is as though we are driving somewhere, and we go off on a side road and find ourselves at a house, which is at a dead end. Since we do not know how to get back to the main road, we seek the hospitality of the family, asking if we may spend the night with them. Arhatship is a kind of resting place in which to rest from the sufferings of samsara, yet if we are ultimately to attain buddhahood, we have to give up our rest and work further.

One class of hinayana practitioners who become arhats is the shravakas. The Tibetan term for shravaka is *nyen tö. Nyen* means "to listen" and *tö* means "to hear," so shravakas are those who learn by listening to and hearing the teachings. The second class of beings who tread on the hinayana path are the pratyekabuddhas. The view, the practice, and the path of the pratyekabuddhas are exactly the same as for the shravakas. The only difference is that they have more wisdom than the shravakas. Having listened to and heard the teachings during one lifetime, in the next lifetime they can work on their own, without needing a spiritual friend. They are intelligent enough and their wisdom has developed enough so they can work on their own.

Pratyekabuddhas have the insight, for example, to look at a skeleton or a bone as a question. Why is there a bone? There is a bone because of death. Death is because of birth. Birth is because of karmic patterns. They have insight into what is known as the twelve links of interdependent origination, or the twelve *nidanas*.[25] Like the shravakas, they attain arhatship through following the path, but because they have realized these twelve links, their understanding is greater. The Tibetan term for pratyekabuddha is *rang gyal. Rang* means "self" and *gyal* means "victorious." At the last stage, the pratyekabuddhas are able to attain the state of arhat on their own, without the help of a spiritual friend, so they are the self-victorious ones.

I have very briefly given some background for understanding the hinayana aspect of the Buddhist teachings and practices. In order to practice the mahayana and vajrayana stages of the path, we must first practice at the hinayana level. We must follow at least one of the seven families of pratimoksha discipline before we can practice the mahayana path and undertake the bodhisattva vow. In the same way, before we can receive the transmissions into the vajrayana methods, we must follow one of the families of disciplines at the hinayana level and also live up to the bodhisattva vow. Only then does it make sense to receive the vajrayana empowerments.

Questions

Q: Must one always practice the hinayana before going on to the other vehicles?

A: Basically we are involved with all three vehicles. The unique quality of Tibetan Buddhism is the integration of the three yanas. Sometimes they are given sequentially, and sometimes aspects of all three are given at the same time. For example, the practice of Avalokiteshvara combines all three (hinayana, mahayana, and vajrayana), beginning with refuge, which is the first level of commitment on the hinayana path.

Q: Would you explain the different numbers of precepts?

A: You may recall that there are four root lay precepts (not killing, not stealing, not lying, not indulging in sexual misconduct) and one branch precept (not taking intoxicants), making five. If the ordinary monk and nun precepts are given in detail, there are thirty-six. Ten of these are root precepts and the rest are branch precepts. Similarly, in the advanced or full monk precepts, there are 253 (for nuns it is 340), out of which seventeen are root precepts and the rest are branch precepts.

Whatever set of precepts we take, the most important are the root precepts. If we somehow violate a branch precept— and there are also different degrees of violation—it is much easier to repair than a root precept. We benefit from following the branch precepts for whatever time we are able to live up to them. If a situation arises when we happen to break certain branch precepts, they can be repaired. They are like the branches of a tree. If the trunk is strong and well-rooted, and plenty of moisture and fertilizer has been provided, even if the winter damages the branches, the changing of the season can rejuvenate them, and more branches will grow.

Q: What brings the arhat back to the main road, so to speak?

A: Such a person remains in the state of arhatship for a long, long time. It is a state of absorption, like a very deep slumber. If we fall into a deep slumber after being very tired, when we wake up it seems as though we have been asleep only a moment. To the arhat, the state of absorption seems to last a moment, but it actually lasts many eons. Because the arhat does not experience the pains and diseases of samsara, it is the cessation of suffering, but it is only a resting place.

The arhats' deep state of absorption occurs because of their longing to experience self-liberation and let go of suffering. After many eons, that longing gradually fades away, and the arhats experience rays emanating from the Buddha. If we are in a deep slumber, and the sun shines right into our eyes, we wake up. The rays emanate from the Buddha because of the goodness of the liberation the arhats have attained. As the Buddha makes it clear to them that they have not reached buddhahood but are just experiencing a state of rest, they gradually come back to the main road and work toward buddhahood. Thus it takes a very long time for arhats to come to a point where they can benefit other beings, though individually they are liberated from the suffering of samsara.

Q: Is the primary limitation of the arhat level of realization that arhats cannot benefit other beings?

A: There are actually quite a number of limitations. It is because of these limitations that arhats cannot benefit other beings. Arhats have not developed any skillful means. They have experienced partial purification of their negative patterns but no accumulation of beneficial qualities. Their gross habitual patterns have been purified, yet subtle patterns of ignorance remain, so they have less wisdom and awareness than bodhisattvas.

Q: How do we work with egolessness, and how does that lead to the development of faith?

A: For a beginner in any level of practice, it is difficult. Although the truth of the teaching has existed all along, this is all rather new to us, and we have to disengage ourselves from heavy layers of habitual tendencies. Before we can realize egolessness, we must develop a confident understanding about its nature. We must train our minds in this understanding until we have no more doubts, until it is just a matter of realization. Then it becomes a little easier to work with our neurotic patterns. We also find it hard to adjust to meditation practices and disciplines that are new to us. These practices are not as entertaining and attractive as the games our neurotic patterns begin to play. So diligence is very important—reminding ourselves again and again to persevere, through the understanding we have established.

Once we have a glimpse of selflessness, it is not so difficult, because we begin to experience many things at once. It might take us a long time, but when we begin to have a glimpse, on the path of unification, we have a tremendous experience of joy. Even if we wanted to procrastinate or be lazy, we would not be able to, because we have developed certainty and experience fewer and fewer distractions. When things happen that could distract us, our experience of the joy of the meditative state makes all these things unimportant. Our sleep begins to become very light, we feel very healthy and uplifted, and we do not need to eat so much or rely on external things. It is like rubbing two sticks of wood together to make fire. At first we have to work hard. When the sticks start to get warm, we are encouraged but are still not sure of any result. However, when smoke begins to rise, we go ahead at full speed with confidence.

Q: Can you say that it is admirable for the followers of the hinayana to refrain from harming other people, but the limitation is that this is done with the understanding that by harming others they would really be hurting themselves?

A: Yes, it is precisely that way. The hinayana practitioner follows the discipline of not harming others and of not laying the cause for harm to others. The motivation is the fear that this will get him or her into trouble. You might say there is compassion, but the compassion is not fully directed toward helping others. It is as if someone is beating your friend, but you are a coward. You are concerned that your friend is in trouble, and you really want to help, but you are afraid to go and help.

Q: Is the practice essentially the same for shravakas and pratyekabuddhas?

A: Yes, the path and the practice are the same. There is simply a greater development of wisdom in the pratyekabuddhas. From the point of view of twofold selflessness, shravakas realize the selflessness of self. Pratyekabuddhas do not really realize the selflessness of the *dharmas* or phenomena as do the bodhisattvas, yet they have the wisdom to understand that the dharmas are interdependent.

MAHAYANA

I have briefly explained the hinayana view and practices, and the realization attained on that path. The teachings given by the Buddha on the hinayana level of practice, the vinaya teachings, are collected in thirteen volumes, each containing from one thousand to two thousand pages.

I will now give a brief explanation on the mahayana level of the teachings, which were given by the Buddha in a place called Rajagriha, or *Chakra Pungpa Re* in Tibetan. These teachings were requested mainly by the eight greatest bodhisattvas, including Manjushri, Maitreya, and Avalokiteshvara, who had experienced the highest bodhisattva stages. Others who requested the teachings included numerous nagas and beings from the different god realms. The mahayana teachings were attended by not just five human beings and 80,000 gods, but by countless beings.

These teachings concern the view and practices of the mahayana path, the path of the bodhisattvas. The teachings on conduct include certain aspects of the pratimoksha disciplines or moral precepts. When we are on the hinayana path, and we follow the precepts with the hinayana view, they are hinayana precepts for self-liberation. When we are on the bodhisattva path, however, even though we follow the same precepts, they become the precepts of the bodhisattva. When a king possesses an object, it is a king's object. When his minister possesses the same object, it is a minister's object, and when an ordinary person possesses it, it is an ordinary person's object. Likewise, what matters is who possesses the precepts at this point.

There are two families of beings who follow the mahayana path: lay practitioners, and bhikshu and bhikshuni practitioners, or householders and those who have renounced the life of a householder. From the point of view of moral conduct, we might say that the bhikshus and bhikshunis are higher, since they keep more precepts than the lay practitioners. However, the level of performance on the bodhisattva path depends on the individual, not on how many precepts are followed. What is most important is generating the correct motivation, insight, and wisdom. The precepts can help us follow the bodhisattva path, if we have the proper understanding and perspective.

There are seven ways in which mahayana practitioners are superior to hinayana practitioners. The first is a greater development of the wisdom of hearing and understanding the teachings. The shravakas and pratyekabuddhas only work with the thirteen volumes of teachings that give the vision and insight into self-liberation. The followers of the mahayana also study the seventeen volumes of teachings on the prajnaparamita, the development of transcendental wisdom, and the thirty-three volumes of teachings on the stages of the bodhisattva path—fifty volumes altogether. Because they have heard and reflected on a greater body of teachings, the followers of the mahayana have a greater vision and insight into what level of realization is attainable.

Second, the bodhisattvas' practice is greater. Shravakas and pratyekabuddhas practice for their own liberation, while bodhisattvas practice to benefit all other sentient beings, both temporarily and ultimately. The temporary benefit is helping beings at a mundane level, and the ultimate benefit is leading them to buddhahood, the completely awakened state of mind.

Because the practice is done for the benefit of all other beings as well as themselves, it is greater than the practice of the hinayana.

The third superior quality of the bodhisattvas is having greater transcendental wisdom or jnana. The hinayana view is understanding the selflessness of self, and the level of fruition does not go beyond that experience. This is taking only one object away, leaving everything else behind. The mahayana view is understanding twofold selflessness, the selflessness of self and the selflessness of dharmas or phenomena. It is understanding that the nature of the phenomenal world is like a dream or a magician's trick—illusory and insubstantial. By realizing twofold selflessness, the bodhisattva realizes the essential nature of beings and the phenomenal world completely, rather than having only a partial insight.

Fourth, bodhisattvas have greater diligence than shravakas and pratyekabuddhas. Although hinayana practitioners are very diligent, they work only for their own liberation. As a result, within one or up to seven lifetimes, they experience a state of rest. Bodhisattvas commit themselves to work for the liberation of all beings without exception, no matter what courage, determination, and diligence it may require. They vow to continue to work for the liberation of all beings, regardless of how many lifetimes or even eons it may take.

The fifth way in which bodhisattvas are superior is that they display greater skillful means in their work. From the moment they begin to generate bodhicitta—the enlightened mind—until perfect awakening, they are able to work for the benefit of beings with body, speech, and mind. They benefit others day and night, using whatever means are required to meet the needs of beings, and providing whatever remedies are necessary. Because of the merit they accumulate by working for the benefit of others, bodhisattvas automatically attain the higher stages of realization. Bodhisattvas thus have greater skillful means than shravakas and pratyekabuddhas, who are able to work only for their own liberation.

Sixth, bodhisattvas achieve a greater result. Shravakas and

pratyekabuddhas attain arhatship or self-liberation. They are liberated into a state of tranquil absorption, and remain in that state for eons before they can begin to work for the benefit of beings. As a result of treading on the mahayana path, bodhisattvas ultimately attain the perfect awakened state of buddhahood. As bodhisattvas, they have been working for the benefit of beings. When they attain the state of buddhahood, they continue to work for the benefit of beings but in greater and more encompassing ways.

When a buddha utters the words of the teachings, neither distance nor language presents an obstacle to their being heard by those who are uplifted enough. If we have the opportunity to listen to the words of a buddha, no matter how far away we are, we hear the teachings as clearly as those who are right in front. Also, everyone understands the buddha's words in his or her own language. In the same way, if we have the auspicious opportunity to see a buddha, we will see the radiant, brilliant, and majestic appearance of the buddha equally clearly whether we are near at hand or far away. A buddha has such all-encompassing wisdom that, whatever may be the temperaments, mental capacities and neurotic patterns of beings, the buddha has insight into each one individually.

The seventh and final superior quality is the greatness of the buddha activities. It has never been known that a buddha stopped working for the benefit of beings. A buddha always continues to work for the benefit of beings—directly or indirectly, immediately or at a certain future time, depending on the appropriateness of the situation or the readiness of the beings. A buddha benefits beings of many universes and of all times. This buddha activity goes beyond our limited understanding.

The way of the bodhisattvas is certainly greater and more profound than that of the shravakas and pratyekabuddhas. The root of this greatness is bodhicitta, the practice of loving-kindness and compassion, *maitri* and *karuna*, with the view of understanding twofold selflessness. The nature of the bodhisattva's loving-kindness is to see all beings equally. A mother would surely want her only beloved child to experience all good things. To a bodhisattva, all beings are like a mother's only beloved child. Bodhisattvas want to do everything they can for the benefit and happiness of all beings, without discrimination. Their loving-kindness extends equally to their children and their enemies.

Also, since they truly experience love for all beings, they automatically generate compassion for all beings. If we dig a furrow, water will run into it automatically. If the bodhisattvas' wish for all beings to experience happiness and harmony is sincere, they will naturally want all the suffering of beings to be eliminated. Beings cannot experience happiness, or ultimately attain liberation, unless their suffering is removed. Compassion is the sincere longing and aspiration for the suffering of all beings to be uprooted and eliminated. There is compassion at the hinayana level, to the extent of not wanting to harm others. At the mahayana level, in addition to not wanting to harm others, there is the wish to remove their suffering.

How can we reach this attitude of wanting all beings equally to experience happiness and have their suffering eliminated? There is a simple way. If we look at the world, it is clear that all beings without exception desire happiness and well-being, and do not desire suffering. There is not one being who wishes for more suffering and less happiness and well-being. All species of beings in all circumstances of time and space share this wish to gain happiness and avoid suffering, whether they are rich or poor, popular or totally unknown, powerful or powerless, huge beings or tiny creatures such as insects.

There is continual struggle, busyness, and restlessness in the world. This is because everyone wants to experience happiness and eliminate suffering. Yet since they are totally caught up in ignorance and confusion, when beings participate in the world, their actions work against their own wish to experience happiness and eliminate suffering. The great wisdom and vision of bodhisattvas leads them to understand that, since all beings equally desire happiness, they cannot afford to discriminate. They develop a tremendous longing for all beings, equally and without exception, to experience happiness, peace, and harmony, and for their suffering to be eliminated.

What is the difference between sentient beings and bodhisattvas? Ordinary beings wish to experience happiness, well-being and harmony, but they work toward happiness in a completely selfish, egoistic way. They look for personal feedback and entertainment at all times. The bodhisattvas' wisdom, on the other hand, is working for the temporary and ultimate benefit of all beings.

With this understanding, we begin to generate loving-kindness and compassion toward all beings without exception. If we regard ourselves as practitioners on the mahayana path, we must recognize and attend to this responsibility. If we have such an understanding and motivation, and actually commit ourselves to work for the benefit of all beings, we are bodhisattvas. Otherwise there is no point in being called a bodhisattva, just as it is pointless to be called a sun when we cannot emit the sun's rays. As bodhisattvas, we must produce something unique: the courage to want to benefit all beings, the courage to commit ourselves to this responsibility. If that happens, it does not matter whether or not we are called bodhisattvas. Our work will speak for itself.

We may have the idea that it is impossible to have equal love and compassion for all beings. How can our minds be big enough to encompass all beings? It seems to be simply too much for us. Or we may feel that it is easy and sensible to have love and compassion for friends and relatives, but that it makes no sense to generate loving-kindness and compassion toward an enemy or someone we do not even know. However, if we consider the situation with some intelligence and openness, we will see that it is simply a matter of training our minds, not of giving away material things to people. Still we might say that we could never change our minds, that something about the mind is very established and fixed—but the moment we say that, we realize it is not true. The mind has limitless power and adaptability. If anything can be changed, it is the mind.

For example, suppose you feel that a certain person is your enemy. You have so much hatred and anger toward this person that you feel you can never, never forgive or forget what happened between you. As long as you live, you will always have hatred toward this person. But suppose the person comes to you unexpectedly and says, "I would like to explain to you about what happened. It was all my fault. I acknowledge that and I apologize for my mistake." Immediately everything is fine between you. Just because of some words that passed between the two of you, you are now friends. Or suppose someone right now at this moment is your friend. You say to yourself, "I will never, never give up this friend." But it does not take much. If this person just frowns at you, that is enough to change your mind.

You might hear on the news that our country has developed a friendly relationship with a certain nation. When you hear this, you develop a sense of openness toward the whole country and the people of that country. Although you have not met a single person from that country, you feel excited and happy when you hear that something good is happening to them. You do not know what they are like, what they do, or what their attitudes are. You like them simply because of this news you heard. On the other hand, suppose you hear that our country has had problems with another nation. When you hear the name of that country, you have a sense of resentment. You reject those people, and criticize them in any way possible, although you have no basis for your criticism whatsoever. Again, you have not met anyone from that country or even talked to one of them. They may be extremely friendly, yet you dislike them.

The mind can thus be changed quite easily, in ways that have no purpose or benefit. Clearly then, the mind can be trained to develop bodhicitta—to have a sincere wish for the happiness of all beings and the elimination of their suffering—and that is purposeful and meaningful. By practicing the enlightened mind in this way and training ourselves to develop this jewel of mind, we benefit others and ourselves by working toward the experience of perfect buddhahood. We do not only aspire to work for the benefit of beings. When we progress to treading on the bodhisattva stages and attaining buddhahood, we will work continuously—without a break—for the benefit and liberation of beings. What greater purpose can we commit ourselves to? By all means, we must do this. First we must have the correct understanding of the situation, and then there is definitely something we can work with.

Because we are caught up in dualistic clinging, we might have the idea that it makes sense to generate loving-kindness and compassion for the poor and the helpless, but not for those who are rich and powerful, who are well-off from a mundane point of view. Because of some auspicious moment of positive action in a former lifetime, such people are experiencing temporary comfort and well-being for a short span of time. Even so, they are still entangled in samsara and could very well experience suffering in the future. We can surely generate compassion and loving-kindness toward them, also.

Again, you might say you can generate loving-kindness for humans and higher animals but not for insects. You are, however, in a position to help yourself, and still you have many problems, pains, and confusions. These tiny insects wander aimlessly, having no strength, wisdom, or skill to protect themselves. Sometimes they are burned by the sun; sometimes they are blown away by the wind. They do not know where the next meal will come from, or where the next shelter will be. They are totally helpless. If you cannot have compassion and loving-kindness toward such helpless beings, what do you think compassion is? Try to put yourself in such a being's place. How would it feel? We should generate loving-kindness and compassion toward all beings, no matter who they are, where they are, or what their species is.

With this foundation, we make a commitment to work for the benefit of beings by all means and under all circumstances, whether desirable or undesirable to us personally. This heartfelt commitment is the bodhisattva vow. After we lay the foundation, which is bodhicitta or enlightened mind, we build on it stage by stage, by applying different levels of skillful means and practices. The stages are explained quite clearly in many of the sutras concerning the bodhisattva's path, and especially in *The Jewel Ornament of Liberation.*[26] They have been described briefly in the previous chapter.

Practitioners on the vajrayana level are called yogis and yoginis or tantrikas. After they have generated the enlightened mind of loving-kindness and compassion and taken the bodhisattva vow, tantrikas use the skillful means of the vajrayana path as a way to expedite the journey to enlightenment. We are not yogis or yoginis if we do not have limitless compassion and loving-kindness toward others. If we call ourselves tantrikas without generating the enlightened attitude and taking the bodhisattva vow, it is almost like calling ourselves sorcerers. The skillful methods of the vajrayana path make sense only if we integrate them with the bodhisattva motivation.

Questions

Q: How is loving-kindness and compassion related to a spiritual friend who continually rejects and disappoints a student? I suppose this is for the student's benefit, but I am not sure how.

A: The relationship depends both on the spiritual friend and on you. A spiritual friend can be several things. It can be just someone who has an intellectual understanding of the teachings but no realization whatsoever, and who has many limitations and flaws. A spiritual friend can also be a highly realized being, who has not only understanding but experience in various aspects of the teachings. This would be a bodhisattva spiritual friend.

Then there is your side of the relationship. Do you have sincerity and devotion? Are you inspired by the example of the spiritual friend? Do you approach the spiritual friend for inspiration, encouragement, and guidance out of a tremendous longing to benefit all beings? Or is it just a temporary infatuation because a big smile or an attractive gesture was extended toward you? Perhaps you want to be connected with the spiritual friend because of this attention that was given you, and you want further entertainment and feedback. Perhaps you want to learn something from this person that would help you develop more credentials and more spiritual powers. If that is your intention, the spiritual friend is not to be blamed.

If you are rejected, the teacher could be at fault because he or she is not a true spiritual friend, or you could be at fault because of limitations in your motivation and sincerity. There is another possibility, though not a very frequent one. A teacher may know that it would be more beneficial for you to work with a different spiritual friend. For example, Milarepa's relationship with a great Nyingma teacher ended, not because there was any deficiency in the spiritual friend, but because the teacher realized that Milarepa's karmic connection was with Marpa. If that were the situation, you would be made well aware of it. On the other hand, if you have devotion, sincerity, and (most importantly) a longing to benefit beings, and you are rejected by a spiritual friend to whom you go for inspiration and guidance, that is not a true spiritual friend.

Q: Were the four limitless contemplations taught by the Buddha, or were they a later development?

A: The Buddha himself taught the contemplations on limitless love, limitless compassion, limitless joy, and limitless equanimity. Because these are very profound thoughts to work with, great scholars and practitioners have since made many commentaries on them. The four limitless contemplations are a simple explanation of the nature of Buddhism, yet they are vast and deep.

VAJRAYANA

Having covered the hinayana and mahayana paths, I will now give a brief explanation of the vajrayana or tantrayana, which is also called the fruition vehicle or the secret mantrayana. All of these names have essentially the same meaning.

As we go through the preliminary stages of taking refuge

(which lays the foundation for Buddhist practice in general) and following one or more levels of moral precepts (pratimoksha), we gradually develop an understanding of the bodhisattva path. This understanding leads us to generate the aspiration and perseverance aspects of bodhicitta, take the bodhisattva vow, and live up to the bodhisattva commitments. This preparation is the ground for engaging in the vajrayana or tantrayana.

The teachings on the vajrayana or secret mantrayana were given by Shakyamuni Buddha toward the end of his life. When he was eighty years old, the Buddha went with a group of disciples to Mount Malaya, where he gave the vajrayana teachings. The teachings were attended by many dakas and dakinis, who are quite highly realized beings, and an assembly of bodhisattvas. Among those present, the most prominent was Vajrapani, the bodhisattva of power, who is also called Sangway Dakpo, which means "holder of the secret teachings." The vajrayana teachings were given mainly at the request of Vajrapani, who promised he would protect and preserve these teachings as well as master and expound them.

As mentioned above, the vajrayana path has different names. The name *fruition yana* is given first because it is the outcome of the practice of the hinayana and mahayana paths. Practicing these two vehicles enables us to appreciate and be open to this profound level of the teachings. Second, the name *fruition yana* is given because the practice involves visualizing deities and reciting mantras, which is working with the very forms and profound qualities of enlightened beings that are the fruition of the path. We can thus experience the meaning of the teachings in a very direct and immediate way.

This path is also known as the secret mantrayana. The word *mantra* is used to emphasize the tremendous effectiveness of the practices.[27] If we sincerely commit ourselves to work with these methods, it is possible to realize buddhahood within one lifetime. It may also take three, seven, or sixteen lifetimes, depending on our diligence and capacity. The word *secret* is used because this level of teaching is self-secret. Without profound wisdom and positive karma, we can neither understand nor respond appropriately to such a teaching. It requires a certain advancement in our spiritual practice and a great amount of diligence, intelligence, devotion, and courage. Since a beginner may not have such courage and openness, it remains quite secret to him or her.

This level of teaching is secret, not because there is some kind of partiality or exclusiveness, but because a given practitioner may not have sufficient openness and intelligence to receive it. For example, because human beings have language, we can communicate with each other more completely than animals. Because we have greater intelligence, we can understand and learn from each other more effectively than animals. We have not somehow hidden our language and intelligence from the animals, but no matter how much we might want to communicate our concepts to them, they are unable to comprehend them. Just as our concepts are incomprehensible to the animals, the vajrayana is self-secret to some people.

Furthermore, if a person cannot handle the vajrayana teachings and profound methods, it is possible that instead of bringing greater enrichment and understanding, they could bring about greater confusion. It might be necessary not to expound the vajrayana to such a person, so in this sense, also, it is secret.

The vajrayana path is more profound than the other two yanas, first because of the richness, directness, and sharpness of the methods. Without immediately having to abandon our neurotic patterns, we can apply these direct methods to transform our existing emotional patterns. A very profound psychology is involved, and through these rich and direct methods, we are elevated to a highly uplifted psychological state.

Second, this Dharma is more profound because of the easiness of the methods. If we can truly connect with these teachings and apply the methods, we can experience the perfect awakened state of mind, the primordial state of mind, the state of Vajradhara,[28] within one lifetime. Because the methods can enable us to realize the ultimate state of enlightenment so quickly, this Dharma is more profound than the other two yanas.

Third, this Dharma is more profound because of the greatness of the practitioner of the vajrayana. To understand and appreciate the teachings and apply them correctly, the student must possess great courage as well as wisdom and intelligence. In addition, the student must have devotion and confidence—devotion to the goodness and saneness of the methods, and confidence in himself or herself and the workability of the practice. A student who has courage, intelligence, devotion, and confidence and who knows no turning back is undoubtedly the appropriate vessel for receiving this level of teaching.

In our relationship to this level of teaching, the wisdom of listening to the teachings and the wisdom of reflecting on the teachings—whatever painstaking means we must apply to understand and appreciate them—are similar to what is required on the levels of the first two yanas. Once we have been prepared through hearing and understanding the teachings, the transmission of the teachings takes place through empowerment or initiation.

The transmission of an empowerment takes place on different levels, depending on the preparedness or ripeness of the student. For example, the Buddha once gave an empowerment into the vajrayana teachings to the great Dharma King Indrabuddhi in India. The Buddha knew that the king was quite a highly realized being and an advanced practitioner, and so were his consort the queen, his ministers, and many of his subjects. His domain, one of many small kingdoms in India at that time, was a very dharmic environment. When the Buddha asked the king what kind of empowerment he wished to have, the king requested an empowerment in which he could attain realization without having to renounce his kingship, his queen, his ministers, or his kingdom. Because the king was mentally prepared and the situation was ripe, the Buddha gave him what is known as the empowerment of meaning, in which the transmission and the realization happen simultaneously. Had the king not been prepared, had his psychological state not been uplifted enough to receive it, such an empowerment could not have been transmitted. As the empowerment was being transmitted, the king and many of the people there experienced the awakened state of mind in different forms.

This empowerment of meaning is also known as liberation at hearing, or liberation at the time of transmission. For such people, it is simply a matter of a powerful coincidence. At any moment they are ready for a complete breakthrough, like a spark that is ready to burst into flame. When the empowerment is given, what was ready to be recognized is recognized. The five poisons, or the five emotional patterns that are ingrained in beings, are immediately recognized as the five Buddhas or five wisdom bodies.[29] The mind is uplifted to such a state of openness and transcendence of limitations that this inner aspect of the realization is attained. Also, in the same highly uplifted state of mind, the outer aspect of the realization is attained. The nature of the phenomenal world, or the five elements, is recognized and experienced as the five mother Buddhas.[30] In this way, such people realize the true essence and nature of inner and outer phenomena.

For people who do not attain realization in this way, the same empowerment is known as the empowerment of upaya or skillful means. After receiving the unbroken transmission of the empowerment into a particular practice, they are instructed in how to work with the practice. Each empowerment is related to a particular deity or embodiment of enlightened mind. The practice connected with the deity is known as a sadhana. The sadhana involves working with the mandala of the particular deity, visualizing the deity and reciting mantras. The practices are related to various aspects of our psychological makeup, from both the neurotic and enlightened points of view. The different sadhanas are directed toward transforming different aspects of our negative patterns. By working with such profound skillful means, the most open, diligent, and intelligent students are able to attain the awakened state of mind in one lifetime.

The self-secretness of the teachings is evidenced by the outrageous manner in which the empowerment of meaning can come about. It can happen in ways you would never expect, completely transcending traditions and conventional barriers. You may have heard of the great mahasiddha Naropa, one of the forefathers of the Kagyu lineage. When Naropa was following his guru Tilopa, in appearance Tilopa put him through many kinds of trials. He made Naropa do many unpleasant jobs and undergo many nasty experiences. Once Tilopa said to Naropa, "If you were really determined to learn about the teachings, you would obey my order to jump off this cliff without any hesitation." Naropa jumped off the high cliff and fell to the ground, and all his bones and joints were broken into many pieces. Tilopa went down to Naropa and asked, "Are you experiencing any pain?" Naropa replied, "The pain is killing me." (This is how Naropa got his name, since in Tibetan, *na* means pain and *ro* means killing.) Then Tilopa touched Naropa's body, and all his broken bones joined together and were healed.

Naropa underwent many other painful experiences. From our point of view, this was outrageous, but Naropa had no problem dealing with it. He was working on the purification and transformation of various subtle patterns, and developing great openness. At one point, Tilopa suddenly slapped Naropa on the head with his sandal, and that was it! That was the body empowerment of meaning, simultaneously transmitted and realized. It was self-secret; it was outrageous. For ordinary people like us, just looking at the situation would evoke resentment. But through this, Naropa experienced a state of realization equal to that of his teacher, Tilopa.

There was another case in which an empowerment happened in an unusual way. The fifth Karmapa, whose name was Deshin Shekpa, was once traveling to a place in Tibet near Lhasa called Tambakna, with a retinue of monks, disciples, and attendants. As they approached Tambakna, they came to an area where many animals were being slaughtered, and there was blood everywhere. Some of the monks ran from the sight, overcome with pity and fear, their hair standing on end. It was so intolerable that some of the monks covered their heads with their robes. But the fifth Karmapa walked right into the midst

of the slaughtering area. Seeing this great teacher and bodhisattva walk into such a violent and destructive place, all of the
monks became very concerned. It was a disgrace for him to
go into such an unhealthy environment. However, he walked
with a kind of decisiveness, and they could not stop him.

A woman who appeared to be in charge of the slaughterers
was sharpening a knife on a great slab of stone. The Karmapa
went straight up to the woman and made three prostrations
to her. That disturbed the monks even more—this was totally
outrageous and indefensible. As the Karmapa made the three
prostrations, the woman spat on the knife she was sharpening
and put it on his head. She then spat on the slab of rock and
sharpened the knife once more, then put the knife on his head
again and said, "Ya." Again this was totally outrageous to the
monks who witnessed it. Because they were ordinary people
whose confused minds were full of neurotic patterns, they saw
her as the head of the slaughterers. But the Karmapa, in his
uplifted state of mind, recognized her as Vajrayogini, a profound deity of meditation, in full presence.

There are traditionally three vajra empowerments: those of
the body, speech, and mind. When the woman touched the
Karmapa with the knife, it was the body empowerment. When
she spat on the slab, she imparted the speech empowerment,
and when she put the knife on his head again while uttering
the sound "ya," it was the mind empowerment. This then
was the transmission of the body, speech, and mind empowerments. This is self-secret, and how in the world can we relate
to it? It has to do with wisdom, with devotion, and with an
uplifted state of mind.

Personally, I am well aware of the self-secretness of the vajrayana teachings, because I have received hundreds and
hundreds of empowerments and none seems to have made any
dent. The same old numbness just continues. If you want to
talk about signs, the heavy vase they put on my head has made
me more and more bald, so perhaps that is a sign.

When the empowerment of meaning is transmitted, it is not
as if something is poured in. It is rather that, because of a

person's openness, wisdom, and uplifted state, when the empowerment is transmitted, there is simultaneous liberation. If you are blindfolded but your eyes are intact, as soon as the blindfold is taken away, you can see. The breakthrough could happen at any moment, and the person is prepared for it, so there is simply an acknowledgment. It is a matter of a moment, a point in time, like the first moment a flower blossoms. What is important here is the preparation. In Buddhist practice, there is a tremendous emphasis on purification of negative qualities and accumulation of positive qualities or merit. These practices gradually uplift us to a state where we can recognize the profundity of the teachings.

What we receive is the empowerment of skillful means. This is also known as the blessing empowerment, because it connects us with the sacredness of the method and the sacredness that is actually our nature from the vajrayana point of view. There is a meeting of the two, and when we work with that, there is a gradual warming. The blessing empowerment transmits the authorization to do the sadhana of a certain deity. From the vajrayana point of view, the deity of the sadhana is also the fruition. Therefore, when the method is presented to us, the fruition is in some sense also presented to us. We are provided with all the prerequisites and with the inspiration that comes from the profound method. We are now able to practice that method and identify ourselves with the sanity of the practice, which involves a kind of mirror-image state of uplifted mind. This is why it is extremely important to receive the blessing empowerment, even though the immediate simultaneous realization does not happen.

Perhaps you have not received the blessing empowerment for a given practice. Being a literate person, you might happen to take up a book that describes vajrayana empowerments and practices. These days, such material is easily available. (Unfortunately, some people have made it available for, quite frankly, unhealthy purposes.) You might try to work with such a book even though you have not received the authorization and have no idea of whether you are prepared to work with that practice. If you approach the vajrayana practice in such a way, at best there will be no benefit. At worst, it will backfire, just as holding your breath long enough (out of stupidity) might cause you to burst. Since you have no understanding and no sincere commitment, it could increase your confusion and put you further off the track.

Furthermore, if at some future point you have the opportunity to go through the proper progression of practicing the different yanas and receiving the empowerment before doing the deity practice, it will not work for you, or it will not work as effectively or directly as it should. In some sense, you have shown disrespect for your potential, and in terms of the need for proper preparation, you have disrespected the practice itself. You have really violated the vajrayana teachings, so the practice will not work as it should. For these reasons it is essential to receive the empowerment before doing any vajrayana practice.

Those who have practiced the teachings and experienced realization are known as open yogis or hidden yogis. Open yogis have practiced the hinayana, mahayana, and vajrayana stages, following the different levels of discipline, and have experienced realization of the nature of the mind. In that state of realization—which transcends blame, credentials, limitations, and boundaries—they manifest in the form of herukas (wrathful deities), with quite outrageous appearance and behavior. Such open yogis present the teachings in quite unexpected and unconventional ways.

Hidden yogis are those who have also practiced the hinayana, mahayana, and vajrayana paths. Having become realized, they completely master all levels of the teachings. Yet they manifest as bodhisattvas, as ordinary persons, or as bhikshus and bhikshunis, outwardly following the hinayana as well as mahayana disciplines, and in such forms they present the teachings. Hidden yogis do not manifest in outrageous open ways; they are not really unconventional.

I would like to emphasize that the vajrayana path is not a legend, not a tale about something that happened long ago in the past and is no longer continuing. The teachings and the methods are all preserved. They do continue, and vajrayana is still as available, as fresh, as direct, and as profound as ever. There are many highly realized beings who are in the best position to give transmission into this profound tradition. We ourselves must come up with the courage, the openness, and the commitment to be students of vajrayana.

The commitments of vajrayana are known as samaya vows. Among the many aspects of the samaya vows are the commitment to the practice and the commitment to the teacher or the guru. For example, if we are students of vajrayana, it is a violation of samaya to criticize our teacher, thinking that we are more realized, that the guru made a mistake, or that we could have said or done something better than he or she did. We are really in no position to judge the situation at all. With samaya, the sense of involvement and openness is so total that were a situation to arise—it would not come to this, but just taking an extreme case—where we had to choose between giving up our commitment to the practice and the guru or giving up our lives, we would give up our lives.

There was a very great teacher in Tibet named Khenpo Gangshar, who was very highly realized. A year before the communists took over Tibet, Khenpo Gangshar announced that he would give some profound teachings on the vajrayana. He said that time was very short and there was only a year in which to work things out before dramatic, drastic changes would take place. People had no idea what he meant. He said that he would not hesitate at this point to expound the vajrayana teachings in the open, to anyone who saw the need for it and came to receive the teachings with devotion. He was willing to grant the teachings to everyone, from monks and nuns with many vows who had practiced for years to simple lay practitioners. He would even give the teachings to not very diligent practitioners with a limited history of practice, as long as they saw the importance and need for it at that time.

He said that he was doing this work for the benefit of beings, even though he might have to experience the lowest of psychological states, called *vajranaroka* or the vajra hell, for bringing the vajrayana teachings out into the open. He cared little about what would happen to him, because of the importance of this transmission both for those who would be able to leave Tibet and for those who would not. Although these people might have to go through physical torture and torment, the stability and sanity of their minds could continue because of these teachings. That was his purpose in giving them.

That transmission also happened in quite an outrageous way. Khenpo Gangshar appeared in the form of a vajra heruka, a wrathful deity. There was a commanding decisiveness and directness in his appearance and behavior, instead of his usual soft, gentle, and calm manner. There was a sense of toughness and straightforwardness in the transmission, and many things happened. Some people became totally devoted—very unexpected people, who had not done much practice. Others developed tremendous wrong views, because they were very disturbed by the unconventional appearance of this teacher who had always looked and behaved like a monk, with robes and so forth. Many people were disoriented and could not get back to any kind of workable perspective. Unfortunately, many people became quite turned off.

One of Khenpo Gangshar's main disciples, Chime Gonpo, could not accept his teacher appearing in that form. Chime Gonpo said that unless some meaningful experience happened, he could not continue to be Khenpo Gangshar's student. When he said that, the great master waved a *purbu* (ritual dagger) toward the monk's face and said, "Tell me now what happened." It made a cut between Chime Gonpo's eyes, which looked as though it happened by accident, and a little blood came out. When Chime Gonpo saw a drop of blood come down like a teardrop, the whole situation was transformed, and he suddenly had no questions and no doubts.

Many other highly realized people were there also. This happened in Eastern Tibet in a place called Soma, which is where the Venerable Trungpa Rinpoche came from, and he was one of the people receiving that empowerment. Later Khenpo

Gangshar came to Trangu Monastery, where I was living, and gave this direct and most profound empowerment to hundreds of monks, along with many teachings. In a very short time—just a few days—many of the monks changed totally. Their usual arrogance, uptightness, and uneasiness were transformed, and the whole situation loosened up. There was a tremendous sense of openness and, at the same time, a tremendous sense of dignity. There developed what is known as the experience of sacred outlook. I was fortunate to be there at that time, but again it did not produce any change in me, though I could not blame the teachings for that. I heard and saw and witnessed everything, but since I was totally steeped in neurotic patterns, it did not make any difference.

To summarize, the unique quality of the presentation of the Buddhist teachings in the Tibetan tradition is the integration of the three yanas. Fortunately, these three yanas have been preserved both in words and in essence, just as they were presented originally. They are imparted to any students who can receive them, in Tibet as well as here. The integration of the three yanas combines the pratimoksha or self-discipline of the hinayana path with the enlightened attitude of loving-kindness and compassion of the bodhisattva path, and into that incorporates the profound methods of the vajrayana. What is most important is how we can make a connection with the teachings and how we can best practice, appreciate, and realize the teachings. This must be done with understanding, intelligence, and confidence, with courage, determination, and diligence.

In whatever way the teachings are presented to us, the three stages are preserved, and there are still great bodhisattvas who can fully transmit these teachings. There will be no benefit, however, if we have no openness or commitment. The teachings are available, we can put them into practice, and many profound results can come through these teachings.

Questions

Q: In regard to the unique integration of the three yanas in Tibetan Buddhism, the Buddha originally gave the teachings on the three yanas separately in India, and then each of them became established. Later when Buddhism came to Tibet at the time of teachers like Atisha, it was a critical period in which Buddhism was being driven out of India by the incoming Muslims (as I understand it), and the teachings had to be transferred to another culture. Is it possible that this unique integration of the three yanas occurred because the three stages were all brought over at once?

A: Not exactly. Certainly the teachings on the path of the shravakas and pratyekabuddhas were given separately. A certain group of people had only the capacity to understand the hinayana level of the teachings. You may have read in *The Jewel Ornament of Liberation*[26] about the different families of beings: the cut-off family, the uncertain family, the shravaka family, the pratyeka family, and the bodhisattva family. The people I am talking about were strictly of a hinayana family. They were exposed to the mahayana and vajrayana teachings, but they could not comprehend them. They had at that point only the capacity to practice the hinayana. Those people who practiced the mahayana teachings—the bodhisattva path—were definitely exposed to the other two paths, the hinayana and vajrayana. Of course, the practitioners of vajrayana also practiced both the hinayana and mahayana.

You may have heard of the eighty-four great mahasiddhas of India. They, of course, first followed the hinayana disciplines and took the bodhisattva vow as lesser or fully ordained monks or lay practitioners, and then worked with the vajrayana teachings. After they had experienced the full realization of the teachings, they appeared as if nothing needed to be guarded, because there were no limitations, credentials, or barriers. The mahasiddhas appeared in the form of herukas or yogis, acting in outrageous ways, because nothing could now interfere with or destroy their state of realization, no matter how and where they manifested. Some came as householders in many kinds of outrageous occupations. In reality, they were always benefiting beings and connecting beings to themselves so they could directly or indirectly help them experience ultimate liberation. People whose vision did not go beyond the strictly hinayana view strongly criticized their behavior and made many accusations. Such people said there was no such thing as vajrayana teachings in Buddhism, that vajrayana was just something these crazy people had made up. They said the mahasiddhas could not keep up with being monks, so they had to marry. Or the mahasiddhas were crazy and went out into the wilderness and then came back with all these outrageous appearances. It would be too embarrassing to admit they had to give up their vows and disciplines, so they invented vajrayana. That was what people with limited vision said at that time.

What was brought to Tibet was the integration of the hinayana, mahayana, and vajrayana. When it was brought, the hinayana was not taught separately. The Tibetan people are basically of the mahayana family because of their close connection with the bodhisattva Avalokiteshvara. It is said that the Tibetan people originated from an emanation of Avalokiteshvara, who appeared in that land as a result of aspirations he had previously made. Because of this history, the Tibetan people were open to the mahayana and vajrayana, and thus there was no need for the hinayana teachings to be given separately, and no need for the unhealthy view that one is part of Buddhism but not the others.

Q: When the fifth Karmapa decided to walk out and prostrate himself before the butcheress, was he teaching something to his monks, or was he working with one of his neurotic patterns?

A: That is hard to say precisely, but it would seem that such a bodhisattva would not really have to work out any neurotic patterns. It may be more like a message, not only to the monks but to people in general, that we should not make assumptions, that the vajrayana teachings and the play of crazy wisdom could take place in any way and in any form. We should be cautious about criticizing something that does not conform to our patterns and our idea of what is proper or improper. We should not be self-righteous. He was showing the different ways in which great realized beings can manifest. Unfortunately, it is often very difficult to distinguish a crazy person from an enlightened yogi.

Q: As I understand it, the great thing about the vajrayana is the skillful use of emotions. The story of Naropa sounds almost like a Zen story. In all his trials, I wonder why the slap of the sandal worked, when being dashed into pieces and various other things did not work. Could it be that he finally felt anger, rather than simply pain?

A: No, it was not because he felt anger. If there were anger, nothing would have penetrated, and nothing would have happened. The transformation of emotional patterns does not mean that we need to experience the upheaval of some emotion, and that presenting the method at that time would liberate us and make us realize the essence of that emotion. The trials and hardships Naropa went through were in some sense not hardships at all. They were stages of purification of subtle patterns. That is essentially what was happening.

Naropa's experience was constant devotion and a continual sense of commitment, which is the vajrayana samaya principle. The samaya principle is not like the hinayana precepts or the bodhisattva vow. It is very fragile, and can be at the same time powerfully advantageous and powerfully destructive. It is a very delicate situation, in that if we have the slightest wrong view or inhibition at this point, let alone having anger, it could block our experience of realization. We must have constant openness and tolerance, no matter how the guru manifests or what stages of practice we are made to go through. Such experiences may not seem very comfortable or easy, but they may be the most valuable thing for us. Tilopa's slapping Naropa with the sandal was the culmination of the purification. It was what might be called an auspicious coincidence.

Notes

1. According to tradition, Shakyamuni Buddha was the fourth Buddha of this eon (see p.231).
2. This was simply being very truthful. In the normal sense, if someone says, "I am the superior one," it sounds egotistical, but here there is no ego involved. It is just being honest and telling the truth. If we asked what is the most clear, powerful light in the whole world, it is the sun; there is nothing brighter than the sun. To say the sun is brightest is not egotistical. (Khenpo Karthar Rinpoche)
3. The order has changed here. Rinpoche explained that the usual order of the four noble truths (suffering, cause of suffering, cessation, and path) is from the point of view of cause and effect. First we present the result and then we go into the cause. But from the point of view of practice, the path comes before the cessation.
4. The cremation was held in December 1981, at Rumtek Monastery in Sikkim, the main seat of His Holiness Karmapa. Similar rainbows were seen at the cremation of the Vidyadhara Chögyam Trungpa in Vermont in 1987. Actually these phenomena are halos.
5. In Tibetan, there are two words for uncle. The father's brother is called *aku*, and the mother's brother is called *ashan*.
6. In Tibetan Buddhism, there are four major lineages: Nyingma, Kagyu, Sakya, and Gelug. Khenpo Karthar Rinpoche belongs to the Kagyu lineage.

7. This refers to His Holiness the Gyalwa Karmapa.

8. The specific prayers and detailed commitments would depend on the individual teacher. Note that the offerings and gestures of respect are not made to an idol, but to the awakened mind and the sources of refuge.

9. This refers to the three bodies of a buddha or the three kayas (see p.231).

10. These one-day vows are more strict than the ordinary lay vows.

11. The Tibetan term means "holding as one's own." If someone else takes your spouse, do you get angry or not? The reason you get angry is that you think this person belongs to you. (Khenpo Karthar Rinpoche)

12. In the case of a person who is terminally ill, the Buddhist teachings do not say that extraordinary and artificial measures must be used for keeping the person alive.

13. It is important to receive individual instruction from a qualified meditation instructor if you wish to practice meditation.

14. Transference of consciousness is a practice in which, at death, either the dying person or a lama directs the consciousness toward the attainment of an enlightened state of mind or a better rebirth.

15. An analytical form of vipasyana practice is described in chapter seven (see p.213).

16. Chakravartins are wheel-turning kings of Buddhist legend. A golden wheel appears when they are crowned, which "turns" and marks out a vast region to be ruled by the king.

17. Brahma is the highest god, and Nagaraja is the king of the nagas, who are powerful serpent-like beings.

18. Bodhisattvas give away everything they have any sense of possession or ownership of. This includes the members of their family, such as spouses and children. If a bodhisattva wishes to give away his wife, he says to her, "I would like to offer you." If she should shed one tear, he would not do it, but if she sees the benefit and wants to go along with his desire, then it is absolutely fine. This extends to friends as well. A bodhisattva says to a friend, "There would be great benefit if I offer you for this purpose," and if the friend says, "That is fine with me," the bodhisattva can do it. However if the friend says, "No, I really do not want to be offered," it cannot be done. The friends themselves are sentient

beings, and the bodhisattva is interested in their benefit as well. (Khenpo Karthar Rinpoche)

19. The 253 refers to the monk's precepts, which are discussed in chapter eight. For nuns there are 340 precepts.

20. The argument is given that an atom is supposed to be indivisible, but either it has no extension at all, in which case it cannot make up a finite object, or it must have parts. If it is to be part of an object, it must have sides that touch other atoms. Traditionally it must have six sides, so it must have parts. Our modern atoms are made up of smaller particles, each of which interacts with other particles, so they are not self-existent.

21. Vajra-like samadhi is the point at which the very final obstacles to complete enlightenment are cleansed or cleared away, so this is the samadhi preceding the attainment of complete enlightenment. This is not something that is practiced by the bodhisattvas on the bhumis. (Khenpo Karthar Rinpoche)

22. The practices of the six perfections are also connected with the first six bhumis.

23. Also called the noble eightfold path. In some traditions the Buddhist path as a whole is described as the noble eightfold path.

24. Such beings are not harmed by eating coarse food, but they have the choice of living on the food of meditation.

25. These are ignorance, mental formations, consciousness, name and form, the six senses, contact, sensation, craving, grasping, becoming, birth, and old age and death.

26. *The Jewel Ornament of Liberation*, by Gampopa, translated by Herbert V. Guenther (Boulder: Prajna Press, 1981).

27. The Tibetan term for secret mantrayana is *sang ngak*. *Ngak* means mantra, but with *sang* (secret) it also means profound and highly respected, so *sang ngak* means secret and profound. (Ven. Bardor Tulku Rinpoche, KTD, Woodstock)

28. Vajradhara is the primordial Buddha, the ultimate aspect of enlightened mind, the dharmakaya.

29. The five Buddhas are Vairochana, Akshobhya, Ratnasambhava, Amitabha, and Amoghasiddhi, the enlightened aspects of ignorance, hatred, pride, greed, and jealousy.

30. The five elements are space, water, earth, fire, and air, and their enlightened aspects are Buddhas Akashadhatish, Lochana, Mamaki, Pandaravarani, and Samayatara.

The Buddha Vajradhara

Glossary

Absolute bodhicitta: The ultimate nature of mind and phenomena; emptiness.

Animal realm: The third of the six realms of existence, related to the defilement of ignorance and the suffering of fear and stupidity.

Arhat or **arhati:** (Tib. *drachompa* or *drachomma*) One who has conquered the enemy of negative emotions and so is liberated from suffering. The fruition of the hinayana vehicle.

Avalokiteshvara: (Tib. *Chenrezik*) The bodhisattva of compassion.

Bardo: An interval or gap; in particular, the intermediate state between death and rebirth.

Bhikshu or **bhikshuni:** (Tib. *gelongpa* or *gelongma*) Fully ordained monk or nun.

Bhumis, ten: Stages on the bodhisattva path.

Bodhicitta or **relative bodhicitta:** The enlightened attitude. The altruistic attitude of loving-kindness and compassion toward all beings; the aspiration to attain enlightenment for the benefit of all beings. This is sometimes called aspiration bodhicitta, to distinguish it from perseverance bodhicitta, which is the bodhisattva activities. There is also absolute bodhicitta (*q.v.*).

Bodhisattva: The mahayana practitioner who works for the benefit and enlightenment of all sentient beings.

Bodhisattva vow: The vow to attain enlightenment for the benefit of all beings and to bring all sentient beings to enlightenment.

Brahmin: A Hindu priest or a member of the priestly caste.

Buddha: (Tib. *sangye*) An enlightened or awakened being, someone who has completely fulfilled his or her potential to experience absolute wisdom.

Buddha nature: The potential to attain enlightenment which all beings possess. Also called the seed of enlightenment or tathagatagarbha.

Daka or **dakini:** A highly realized practitioner of the vajrayana.

Dedication of merit: After we have practiced virtuous actions, if the merit is dedicated to the benefit and enlightenment of all beings, rather than being kept to ourselves, the result becomes indestructible.

Deity: A buddha or bodhisattva visualized in vajrayana meditation, to help the practitioner develop the enlightened qualities they embody.

Demigod or **jealous god realm:** One of the higher realms, related to the defilement of jealousy and the suffering of quarreling and fighting.

Deva: (Tib. *lha*) A being of the god realm.

Dharma: (Tib. *chö*) Teachings of the Buddha. Also, dharmas are elements of existence.

Dharmakaya: The wisdom body of a buddha; the ultimate enlightened mind.

Duhkha: Suffering; the unsatisfactory nature of ordinary existence.

Egolessness: The lack of a substantial and permanent self or ego. The realization of egolessness frees us from suffering.

Eight superior qualities or **eightfold noble path:** Perfect view, thought, speech, action, livelihood, effort, memory, and meditation. Qualities developed by a bodhisattva on the path of meditation from the seventh to the tenth bhumi.

Empowerment: A ceremony in which a lama transmits to students the inner meaning of the vajrayana or the authorization to do a particular vajrayana practice after further instruction. The level depends on the preparedness of the student.

Emptiness: The lack of self-existence in things. The true nature of mind and phenomena.

Enlightenment: Complete awakening of the mind; buddhahood.

Five forces: Same as five powers, but indestructible. Qualities developed on the patience stage of the path of unification.

Five paths: A description of the stages of the Buddhist path to enlightenment: (1) Path of accumulation: Acquiring merit and wisdom for the journey. Classified into lesser, middle, and greater paths of accumulation. (2) Path of unification or linking: Provides the link between the ordinary and the superior practitioner. Classified into heat, peak, patience, and supreme dharma stages. (3) Path of seeing: The instant of seeing the true nature of the mind. (4) Path of meditation: Developing the insight gained in the path of seeing. Includes the ten bhumis. (5) Path of no-learning: The fruition of the Buddhist path.

Five powers: Faith, enthusiasm, mindfulness, samadhi, and wisdom. Qualities developed on the heat and peak stages of the path of unification.

Four genuine abandonments: Abandoning unvirtuous actions we have been engaged in, not adopting any further unvirtuous actions, increasing virtuous actions we have been engaged in, and adopting further virtuous actions. Qualities developed on the middle path of accumulation.

Four immeasurables: The wish that all beings may experience immeasurable happiness, freedom from suffering, joy, and equanimity.

Four investigations: Body, feelings, thoughts, all phenomena. The four are investigated to see that they lack a substantial self, on the lesser path of accumulation.

Four miraculous legs: Motivation, diligence, mindfulness, and one-pointedness. Qualities developed on the higher path of accumulation.

Four noble truths: The truths of suffering, the origin of suffering, the cessation of suffering, and the path. The first teaching of the Buddha.

Gelug lineage: One of the four lineages of Tibetan Buddhism, especially known for scholarship.

God realm: The highest of the realms of samsara, related to the defilement of pride and the suffering of change and falling.

Guru: *see* Lama.

Hell realm: The lowest of the six realms, related to the defilement of aggression and the suffering of heat and cold.

Heruka: A wrathful deity.

Hinayana: The small or self-liberation vehicle of the Buddhist path, concerned with developing discipline, freeing ourselves from attachment, and realizing egolessness. If practiced alone, the hinayana is somewhat narrow and limited, but it is not to be scorned, because it is a necessary foundation for the mahayana and vajrayana.

Human realm: Related to the defilement of attachment and the suffering of birth, sickness, old age, and death, the human realm comes about from a mixture of positive and negative karma. It is a favorable place of birth because there is a mixture of happiness and sorrow and the opportunity to practice the Dharma.

Hungry ghost realm: A lower realm related to the defilement of greed and the suffering of hunger and thirst.

Interdependent origination: An important concept in Buddhist philosophy, which can be understood at several levels. The first is the law of cause and effect—from this, that arises; this being not so, that ceases. The four noble truths are an example of this. A more detailed understanding is the twelve links (*see* note 25), which are an interdependent sequence of causes and effects that keep us bound to samsara. At yet another level, it is an expression of emptiness, because everything arises dependent upon something else, so nothing exists on its own.

Jnana: (Tib. *yeshe*) Primordial wisdom.

Jnanasattva: The wisdom aspect of a deity of meditation.

Kadampa lineage: A lineage based on teachings of the eleventh-century master Atisha, which emphasize *tong len* practice (*q.v.*). The lineage is no longer a separate school; its teachings have been incorporated into the other lineages of Tibetan Buddhism.

Kagyu lineage: The lineage of Tibetan Buddhism to which Khenpo Karthar belongs. The lineage of the Karmapas.

Kalpa: An eon; a vast period of time.

Karma: The law of cause and effect—the positive or negative actions we performed in the past have led to present happiness or suffering, and the positive or negative actions we perform now will lead to future states of happiness or suffering.

Karuna: Compassion.

Kechik: A very short instant of time, described as one sixtieth of a finger-snap.

Khenpo: An abbot; the chief instructor or spiritual master of a monastery. Also, a lama of great learning.

Klesha: Defilement, neurotic emotional pattern. The main kleshas that keep us in samsara are greed, hatred, ignorance, attachment, pride, and jealousy.

Lama: (Skt. *guru*) A spiritual guide or master. A realized teacher who has undergone extensive training in retreat.

Lay precepts: The five moral precepts (refraining from killing, stealing, lying, sexual misconduct, and taking intoxicants) are not commandments imposed upon Buddhists, but one or more are taken on as practices of discipline.

Maha ati: (Tib. *dzog chen*) Great Perfection. Realization of mind as taught by the Nyingma lineage.

Mahamudra: (Tib. *chag gya chen po*) Great Seal of Emptiness. Realization of mind as taught by the Kagyu lineage.

Mahasiddha: A highly realized yogi or yogini of the tantric path. The eighty-four mahasiddhas were a group of renowned masters in India, including Tilopa and Naropa.

Mahayana: The great vehicle of the Buddhist path. The vehicle of the bodhisattvas, concerned with developing loving-kindness and compassion toward limitless sentient beings, and realizing the emptiness and interdependence of the self and all phenomena.

Maitri: Loving-kindness.

Mandala: The sacred environment of a deity.

Mantra: Sacred syllables; the essence of the speech of the enlightened ones.

Mantrayana: A name for the vajrayana.

Merit: Positive qualities and habits developed by performing virtuous actions, which are the seeds for future happiness.

Nirmanakaya: (Tib. *tulku*) The emanation body of a buddha. The form of a buddha that can be seen and experienced by ordinary beings.

Nirvana: Liberation from samsara.

Nyingma: The oldest lineage of Tibetan Buddhism.

Paramitas: *see* Six Perfections.

Poisons: The three poisons are greed, hatred and ignorance, the most fundamental kleshas. Adding jealousy and pride makes five poisons, and adding attachment makes six poisons which correspond to the six realms of existence.

Prajnaparamita: The scriptures on the perfection of wisdom, which are important mahayana sutras.

Pratimoksha (Tib. *sosor tarpa*) Buddhist practices of personal discipline and conduct aimed at enlightenment.

Pratyekabuddha (Tib. *rang gyal*) A hinayana practitioner who has reached individual liberation without the need for a teacher and without the altruistic aspiration to benefit all beings. A type of arhat or arhati.

Preta realm: The hungry ghost realm.

Purbu: A ritual dagger.

Rebirth: According to Buddhism, this life is but a link in a chain of past and future experiences, conditioned by positive and negative karma. Highly realized bodhisattvas take birth in samsara not out of necessity, but through the force of their compassion and their wish to benefit beings.

Refuge: Accepting the Buddha, Dharma, and Sangha (*q.v.*) as guides on the path.

Rinpoche: Precious one; a name given to a lama who is recognized as the incarnation of a past teacher, or to an outstanding teacher.

Sacred outlook: In vajrayana, seeing the world as a sacred realm and all beings as enlightened.

Sadhana: A structured meditation practice in the vajrayana with a liturgy, including visualizations, prayers, mantras, and silent meditation.

Sakya lineage: One of the four main lineages of Tibetan Buddhism.

Samadhi: (Tib. *ting nge dzin; samten*) A general term for meditative absorption. *Ting nge dzin* literally means holding the profound nature, and *samten* means concentration.

Samaya vows: The vajrayana commitments to the lama and to the practices.

Samayasattva: The visualized form of a deity of meditation.

Sambhogakaya: The bliss body of a buddha; the way a buddha appears to highly realized bodhisattvas.

Samsara: (Tib. *khorwa*) The cycle of conditioned existence based on ignorance and characterized by suffering.

Sangha: (Tib. *gendun*) The Buddhist community. At different levels, sangha can mean the community of practitioners, the community of ordained monks and nuns, or the assembly of highly realized bodhisattvas on the bhumis.

Sattva position: Meditation posture with one leg in front of the other, in the manner of the bodhisattvas.

Seven branches of enlightenment: perfect memory, wisdom, diligence, joy, blissfulness, samadhi, and equanimity. Qualities developed on the first six bhumis of the path of meditation.

Seven dharmas of Vairochana: The seven aspects of the meditation posture.

Shakyamuni Buddha: The historical Buddha.

Shamata: (Tib. *shinay*) Tranquility meditation; calm abiding.

Shravaka: (Tib. *nyen tö*) Hearer; hinayana practitioner who learns by listening to the teachings.

Shunyata: *see* Emptiness.

Six perfections or six paramitas: The main practices of the mahayana path: generosity, discipline, patience, effort, meditation, and wisdom.

Six realms: Hell, hungry ghost, animal, human, demigod, and god realms (*q.v.*); various possible experiences of cyclic existence. Can be thought of as psychological states, but Buddhist teachers insist that other realms are as real to those who experience them as our realm is to us.

Sojong: Vows taken for one day during periods of intensive practice.

Stupa: A Buddhist monument or reliquary containing relics of enlightened beings, symbolic of the enlightened mind.

Sutra: A discourse of the Buddha.

Tantra or tantrayana: Vajrayana.

Tantrikas: Practitioners of the vajrayana.

Thanka: A traditional Tibetan form of sacred painting, generally depicting deities or mandalas used in meditation.

Thirty-seven qualities of the bodhisattva: The qualities developed on the five paths. They fall into seven groups (*q.v.*): The four contemplations, the four genuine abandonments, the four miraculous legs, the five powers, the five forces, the seven branches of enlightenment, and the eight superior qualities.

Three bodies of a buddha: Dharmakaya, sambhogakaya, nirmanakaya (*q.v.*).

Three jewels: The Buddha, Dharma, and Sangha; the three sources of refuge.

Three vehicles or **three yanas:** (Tib. *theg sum*) Hinayana, mahayana, and vajrayana; three approaches to the Buddhist path, which are integrated in the teachings of Tibetan Buddhism.

Tong len: The practice of sending and receiving: we imagine that we are giving our happiness and good qualities to all beings, and taking their suffering onto ourselves.

Turn the wheel of Dharma: A traditional expression for the Buddha's teaching activities.

Upasaka or **upasika:** (Tib. *genyenpa* or *genyenma*) Ordained lay practitioner of the Dharma.

Upaya: Skillful means to liberate beings.

Vairochana: (Tib. *nam nang*) One of the five Buddhas (*see* note 29).

Vajra: Scepter symbolizing indestructibility.

Vajra hell: (Skt. *vajranaroka*) The lowest of hells, reserved for those who break the vajrayana samaya vows.

Vajra posture: The traditional meditation posture as seen in statues of the Buddha.

Vajrayana: The third vehicle of the Buddhist path, in which profound methods are used to attain enlightenment swiftly.

Vajrapani: (Tib. *sangway dakpo*) The bodhisattva of power.

Vipasyana: (Tib. *lhak tong*) Profound meditative insight; literally: "greater or higher seeing." Often explained as "panoramic awareness." Also, meditative practice aimed at developing such insight.

Wind energies, five: The subtle energies that circulate and control various functions of the body. They correspond to the five elements. (1) All-pervading wind energy (water) relates to circulation and muscle movement. (2) Wind energy of metabolism (fire) relates to digestion. (3) Upward-moving wind energy (air) relates to speech. (4) Downward-moving wind energy (earth) relates to excretion. (5) Life wind energy (space) relates to breathing and consciousness.

Yana: A "vehicle" or approach to the Buddhist path. *See* Three Vehicles.

Yogi or **yogini:** A practitioner of the vajrayana.